T0301613

The Making of China's Exchange Rate
Policy

For Kirsten and Huizhen

The Making of China's Exchange Rate Policy

From Plan to WTO Entry

by

Leong H. Liew

Department of International Business and Asian Studies, Griffith Business School and Griffith Asia Institute, Griffith University, Australia

Harry X. Wu

School of Accounting and Finance, Hong Kong Polytechnic University, Hong Kong

Edward Elgar
Cheltenham, UK • Northampton, MA, USA

© Leong H. Liew and Harry X. Wu 2007

All rights reserved. No part of this publication may be reproduced, stored in a retrieval system or transmitted in any form or by any means, electronic, mechanical or photocopying, recording, or otherwise without the prior permission of the publisher.

Published by
Edward Elgar Publishing Limited
Glensanda House
Montpellier Parade
Cheltenham
Glos GL50 1UA
UK

Edward Elgar Publishing, Inc.
William Pratt House
9 Dewey Court
Northampton
Massachusetts 01060
USA

A catalogue record for this book is available from the British Library

Library of Congress Cataloguing in Publication Data

Liew, Leong H.
    The making of China's exchange rate policy : from plan to WTO entry / by Leong H. Liew, Harry X. Wu.
        p. cm.
    Includes bibliographical references and index.
    1. Foreign exchange rates–China. 2. Monetary policy–China. I. Wu, Harry X. II. Title.
    HG3873.C45L54 2007
    332.4'5620951–dc22

                                                                    2006037182

ISBN 978 1 84376 008 5

Printed and bound in Great Britain by MPG Books Ltd, Bodmin, Cornwall

Contents

Preface

It is really critical that people know China is acting within the recognized rules of the international economy and there is an understanding of the responsibility that comes with rapid economic growth. (Condoleeza Rice, quoted in McGregor 2005)

The US in order to defend its position as the world's hegemon (*bazhu*) must contain the rise of any potential competitor and attack is the best form of defence (*xian fa zhi ren*). The demand of the US for renminbi revaluation is an important tactic in this strategy. (SCD 2004, p. 13)

... it remains in China's interest to move gradually to greater exchange rate flexibility. (IMF 2004c, p. 37)

Renminbi appreciation is ... needed to help reduce China's current surplus and increase China's contribution to global demand growth. (Setser 2006, p. 4)

Many scholars, policymakers and even lay people no longer consider the exchange rate merely as an instrument that monetary authorities use to achieve specific national economic objectives. That is why exchange rate policies have become a talking point not only among economic policymakers but also among people in the wider policymaking network. Post-Mao China's phenomenal economic growth, with huge increases in foreign trade and investment, has made the nation a powerhouse in the global economy. Many observers see judicious management of exchange rate policy as instrumental in China's rise to the status of an economic power and China's currency, the renminbi, has from time to time become a leading news item in print and electronic media around the world.

This book therefore seeks to enhance understanding of exchange rate policymaking in China and grows out of our long term observation of China's economic reform. We have observed how the Chinese authorities have largely gone their own way in transforming the national economy from a planned to a market economy, adopting a 'Beijing Consensus' instead of a 'Washington Consensus' for their reform agenda. In reform of its foreign exchange system, China has come up against international criticism, especially from the US, that its exchange rate policy is narrowly mercantilist and that the Chinese authorities should act responsibly on exchange rate policy now that market reform has brought unprecedented economic growth. Many Chinese citizens interpret the pressure that the US applied on China to discontinue the renminbi–US dollar peg and revalue the renminbi as an attempt by the US to contain China in its ascent to 'great power' status. Other observers of the renminbi, however, see that China has much to gain from a more flexible exchange rate.

Whatever the merit of the various views on China's exchange rate policy, it is clear that this policy has become a talking point among not only policymakers but also the general public. Exchange rate policy is manifestly a potent mix of politics as well as economics. Yet political analysis barely surfaces in the voluminous amount of scholarly research conducted on the renminbi. Where politics are discussed it is usually in the narrow context of Sino–US relations and the perceived competition between these two nations over their relative standing in the post-Cold War world. The role of Chinese domestic politics in exchange rate policymaking seldom appears on the radar screen. Moreover, with attention on economics, discussion of currency policy is often couched in absolute terms rather than in terms of trade-offs that have a political price, ignoring how the practice of economics, like that of politics, is the art of the possible.

On 21 July 2005 Chinese authorities ended the nation's 11-year practice of pegging the value of the renminbi to the US dollar. The end of the peg had been widely anticipated ever since China's current account surplus and capital flows combined to produce in 2003 an increase in China's foreign reserve of 8 per cent of GDP. This is only the latest among several milestones in the relatively short history of the renminbi.

China's post-1949 history is a treasure for students of policymaking. For a quarter of a century Mao Zedong oscillated between utopianism and pragmatism, with politics or economics in command, before Deng Xiaoping and his cohort in 1978 clearly placed 'making money' (*zhuan qian*) ahead of 'making revolution' (*gao geming*). As we make clear in this book, politics in policymaking did not die with Mao. The death of Mao and ascension of 'Deng's line' did not end but only changed the substance and form of political contests over policies.

In fact, our book reveals that there is more politicking among policy actors over exchange rate policy in the post-Mao period than there was under Mao. More freedom in the post-Mao political arena has allowed more players, more space and more ideas to contest. Monetary and exchange rate policies were subservient to the plan under Mao, and the position of the State Planning Commission as the supreme economic ministry was unchallenged. However, policies become contestable with economic reform as the economy and policymaking become more complex and institutionalized. Forces of the market and of globalization push to loosen political control but simultaneously impose new constraints on policymakers. The former create more opportunities at least within the party and state bureaucracy for contests over exchange rate policy; both further complicate economic policymaking because the market and globalization create choice.

This book, then, is an inquiry into the economics and politics of exchange rate policymaking in the People's Republic of China (PRC) – from the creation of the renminbi as the national currency in November 1948 to the end of the renminbi–US dollar peg in July 2005. It examines key factors that shape and determine PRC's exchange rate policies from the birth of the People's Republic and early years of socialist construction and central planning with their varying degrees of centralization and disengagement from the global economy. We then move our analytical lens across the post-Mao years of economic reform and hesitant re-engagement with the global economy, until China finally gained membership of the World Trade Organization in 2001 and in 2006 is confidently embracing globalization on its own terms. Here we do not seek to explain what exchange rate policies we believe should have been implemented, but to explain why specific exchange rate policies were adopted.

Chapter 5 in this book is a revised and expanded version of an article in the *Journal of Contemporary China*. We have made some revisions for this chapter, based upon further research. Such are the great challenges of research on contemporary China, not least because much of the workings of party and state are still opaque, and a project on contemporary China in one sense never ends because of the continuing imperative to reassess old positions in the face of new research findings.

Throughout our project we received help from many quarters. We have benefited from our discussions with many people, including Chen Ping, Chen Zhenyi, Ge Zhengyi, Guo Wei, Hua Min, Willy Wo-Lap Lam, Liu Hongzhong, Lu Jun, Niu Hong, Peng Zhige, Tsang Shu-ki, Wang Jun, Xu Zhong, Yang Fan and Zhang Jilin. Liu Xian tracked down many useful references and Nicholas N. Wu, Esther Y.P. Shea and Fu Lei assisted in data collection and processing.

Maureen Todhunter provided invaluable editorial assistance and Robyn White dedicated many hours preparing the manuscript for publication.

Finally, we wish to acknowledge the Australian Research Council for funding our research that made this book possible.

1. Why does the rest of the world, especially the US, care about the renminbi? The rebirth of China and rise of the renminbi

The overvaluation of the dollar against the world's currencies has been a major contributing factor in the worsening of the US trade deficit over the last several years. Of particular concern is the undervaluation of the yuan [renminbi] against the dollar. (USCC 2004, p. 37)

Exchange rates are a major economic variable that regulates trade and capital flows across countries in an increasingly deregulated global economy, and the value of China's exchange rate, because of the country's enormous trade and capital flows, has caught the attention of global commodity and financial markets and policymakers. Economic policymakers in China's major trading partners are concerned with how the value of the renminbi (RMB) will affect their ability to generate domestic economic growth and employment while controlling inflation and managing their countries' balance of payments. But exchange rates are not all about economics. In this chapter we show that global interest in the value of the renminbi extends beyond its immediate impact on international economics to include its potential ramifications on international relations and national security. Subsequent chapters in this book will concentrate on examining the factors that determine China's exchange rate policy.

During the Asian financial crisis (1997–2000), national governments and central bankers in Europe, Japan and the US feared that China would devalue the renminbi. They feared renminbi devaluation would destabilize the economies of China's neighbours, which collectively constitute a major market for European, Japanese and US exports. In 2004 the concerns of European and Japanese governments over the renminbi exchange rate were more direct. Many financial analysts saw the renminbi linking the fates of the economies of the euro zone and Japan with the US economy. In 2003–04 exports were the major source of growth in the euro zone and the falling value of the US dollar relative to euro threatened this source of growth. Economic growth in the third quarter of 2004 in France and Germany was only 0.1 per cent, so there was concern that the fall in the value of the US dollar could push France and Germany into recession. Japan was also vulnerable, given uncertainty that its economy was finally back on a growth path after more than a decade of economic decline, and similarly did not welcome a falling US dollar.

Despite previous depreciations, the US dollar continued to depreciate against the euro and yen in 2004 because of lingering concern in currency markets about US current account deficits, which the US government attributed largely to the renminbi–US dollar peg that prevented the renminbi from appreciating against the US dollar. In December 2003, seven of 11 currency analysts surveyed by Bloomberg News predicted that China would revalue the renminbi by the end of 2004 (Bloomberg 2003). When the predicted revaluation did not happen, France, Germany and other countries in the euro area as well as Japan increasingly saw the renminbi–US dollar peg as a serious obstacle to the macroeconomic management of their economies because the peg forced the euro–US dollar and yen–US dollar rates to bear the major brunt of exchange rate adjustments to correct the imbalances in the US current account. From early 2002 to the end of 2004, the value of the US dollar fell by about 35 per cent against the euro (*The Economist* 2004c, p. 63) and about 23 per cent against the yen.[1] The US dollar would have fallen more against the yen had the Bank of Japan not intervened massively in 2003 and early 2004 (Roach 2004). In the first nine months of 2003 alone, Japanese authorities spent well in excess of US$80 billion to stem the rise in the value of the yen (Roach 2003) and in the first quarter of 2004, Japan's Ministry of Finance sold a record US$130 billion of yen (*The Economist* 2004b, p. 81). When the ministry stopped intervening in foreign exchange markets after this major sale, world attention was switched to the renminbi.

Influential US economists like Goldstein (2004) and Roubini and Setser (2004) believe that reducing US fiscal deficits and expanding the domestic demand of US trading partners are insufficient responses to global payments imbalances and have called for revaluation of the renminbi and currencies of other countries with current account surpluses against the US dollar; expenditure-switching policies, they believe, must support expenditure-changing policies. Goldstein (2004, p. 2) has pointedly accused China of '"manipulating" its currency, contrary to IMF rules'.

Although the value of the renminbi is of special interest to China's major trading partners, it is the US that is most vocal about China's exchange rate policy. The Sino–US relationship is one of the most significant country-to-country relationships that have a bearing on post-Cold War global peace and security, and Sino–US disagreement over exchange rate policy has been a major source of tension in this relationship. The remainder of this chapter will therefore concentrate on examining why the renminbi is of particular interest to US policymakers.[2]

That the renminbi has become a focus of attention among US policymakers is undisputed. This is clearly expressed in the quotation at the beginning of this chapter. But the quotation hides more than it reveals. What the quotation does not reveal is that US concerns about the renminbi extend far beyond whether its value in relation to other major currencies is the major cause of US massive trade deficits and inappropriate for the maintenance of global macroeconomic stability. The quotation is from the 2004 *Report to Congress* of the US–China Economic and Security Review Commission, which has the mandate 'to monitor, investigate, and report to Congress on the national security implications of the bilateral trade and economic relationship between the United States and the People's Republic of China [PRC]' (USCC 2004, p. iii). That the US Congress has established a commission to report to it on the strategic implications of Sino–US economic relations is indicative of the suspicions that the US has about China. These suspicions have provoked debates in policymaking circles in the US about whether to engage or to contain China. Debates in US policymaking circles over China and the value of the renminbi have precedents in debates during the 1980s over Japan's economy and the value of the yen, when the US perceived the strengthening of Japan's economy as a threat. The concern in the US then was the rapid rise of the Japanese economy and perceived invincibility of the 'Japanese model' of a state-led economy, paralleling the perceived decline in US economic prowess. Books on the 'Japan model', like those by Johnson (1982) and Tyson (1992), were must-reads on reading lists of leading schools of business and political science, and governments of newly industrializing countries like Malaysia began to look to Japan as an economic model for their nation. The then Malaysian prime minister, Mahathir, openly advocated a 'Look East policy' for his country.

But the bursting of Japan's bubble economy in the late 1980s ended the adulation and adoption of the Japanese model. In the new millennium the concern of US policymakers has shifted away from Japan and the yen to China and the renminbi. The break-up of the Soviet Union, following soon after the end of the Japanese 'economic miracle', left the US as the world's sole superpower. The People's Republic of China (PRC), although no longer regarded by many observers and policymakers as 'communist' in any shape or form, continues to be regarded as the remaining major ideological competitor of the US. China's eclipse of Japan as a major economic power in the new millennium, following its two decades and longer of rapid economic growth alongside economic stagnation in Japan from the end of the 1980s, poses policy challenges for US policymakers. Interest in the rapidly growing Chinese economy, with its vast economic potential, has overtaken interest in

Japan's economy. A 2004 report by a UK think-tank with close links to the British government labelled China's post-Mao approach to economic management as the 'Beijing Consensus' in contrast to what it considers to be the 'widely-discredited' neo-liberal 'Washington Consensus' approach to economic management (Ramo 2004). In the world of business, William Pesek Jr went so far as to cast China as 'the economic equivalent of sex – it sells. If you want headlines and investors calling for prospectuses stick the word "China" in the name of your company or product' (Pesek Jr 2004).

THE REBIRTH OF CHINA

The shift in attention of US policymakers from Japan and the yen to China and the renminbi has been brought about by what Richard Nixon's secretary of state, Henry Kissinger, refers to as the 'rebirth of China'. In one sense, China has been reborn many times. Over the centuries, stories of the rise and fall of Chinese dynasties point to circularity as individual dynasties were established, prospered, inevitably declined and were finally destroyed and replaced. The life of the Chinese nation has long reached into the world beyond. From about 200 BC onwards China had participated actively in international networks of trade and commerce that stretched 'from Syria in the west to Japan in the east and from Korea in the north to Indonesia in the south and, by the sixteenth century, included Europe and the New World' (Waley-Cohen 1999, p. 5). Until at least 1750, China stood at the centre of the world economy (Frank 1998) and was the world's principal manufacturing power before the European industrial revolution and colonialism intervened (Golub 2004, p. 8). After 1750 China fell into a 'long sleep' and there has long been speculation and concern in some quarters that the sleeping giant would awake.[3] Napoleon Bonaparte is reported to have remarked: 'Let China sleep. For when China awakes it will shake the world'. China's 'awakening' or 'rebirth' began in 1978 with the Chinese Communist Party's (CCP's) replacement of Maoist policies and its re-engagement with the global economy, and continued with its subsequent spectacular economic rise, after many years of economic autarky under Mao and, before that, foreign invasion and civil war.

In 2004 Henry Kissinger argued forcefully in the current affairs magazine *Newsweek* that the latest 'rebirth of China' is of great historical significance. China's 'rebirth', according to Kissinger, 'raises massive global economic challenges that cannot be ignored' and marks 'a shift in the center of gravity of world affairs from the Atlantic to the Pacific' (Kissinger 2004, p. 30). China's 'rebirth' has seen its national economy grow at an annual rate averaging 9.7 per cent between 1978 and 1998 (Lardy 2002, p. 12) and at an annual rate averaging 7.7 per cent between 1998 and 2002 (NBS 2003, p. 27). After 2002 China's growth rates did not fall according to the law of diminishing returns. Instead, growth rates increased to an average of 10 per cent (NBS 2006).[4] These spectacular economic growth rates have propelled the size of China's economy in the world's rankings to number two after the US, according to purchasing power calculations. On the basis of purchasing power parity valuation of gross domestic product (GDP), China's GDP in 2003 was 12.6 per cent of world GDP compared to 21.1 per cent for the US and 7 per cent for Japan. China's share of world GDP was only marginally smaller than that of the euro area, with 15.9 per cent, but more than double that of the other rising Asian power, India, with 5.7 per cent (IMF 2004c, p. 191). In 2004, China and India increased their shares of world GDP. China's and India's shares of GDP rose to 13.2 per cent and 5.9 per cent, respectively, while shares of the US, Japan and the euro area fell to 20.9 per cent, 6.9 per cent and 15.3 per cent, respectively (IMF 2005a, p. 193).

The editor of the influential journal *Foreign Affairs*, James Hoge Jr, echoed the views of Kissinger in the journal's July–August 2004 issue where he claimed that China and India are Asian powers on the rise, and Asia's growing economic clout is inducing a major transfer of power from West to East. According to Hoge Jr, China will replace Japan as the power centre in Asia and the West must be prepared to face this challenge because major shifts of power between states and regions are infrequent and seldom peaceful. Kissinger and Hoge Jr are not alone in linking influence in world affairs to economic power. Paul Kennedy made this link in his influential 1987 book, *The Rise and Fall of the Great Powers*. But Kennedy also argued that a powerful nation like the US was at risk of 'imperial overstretch' – overspending on military research and development (R&D) and underspending on productive civilian R&D – thereby weakening its economy, its military power and ultimately its influence on world affairs. Kennedy's book was published at the height of Japan's and Germany's post-World War II economic prosperity and influence in the world – just before the burst of Japan's bubble economy and enormous costs of German reunification ended the widely held perceptions of the invincibility of both national economic systems. Kennedy's book triggered lively debates in academic and policymaking circles as to whether Japan and Germany, concentrating on civilian investment, would one day overtake the US economically and politically. Interest in the book waned, however, as the US economy entered a long period of steady and uninterrupted growth under President Bill Clinton and as the economies of both Germany and Japan faltered. By the end of Clinton's eight-year administration in 2000, talk of the dangers of the US overstretching had been overtaken by concerns about the US 'lack of guts' to stretch – to devote 'a larger percentage of its vast resources to making the world safe for capitalism and democracy' (Ferguson 2002, p. 416).

However, the landscape shifted dramatically under the presidency of George W. Bush. In 2004, when the Bush administration was re-elected for a second term, the US appeared unassailable militarily, but it soon became obvious that the US was becoming bogged down in Iraq and would not be able to extricate itself easily. Compounding US problems in Iraq are its not-unrelated mounting fiscal and current account deficits, which pose a serious future threat to its economy and have caught the attention of global financial markets. Growing recognition of vulnerabilities in the US economy and widespread perceptions of the 'rise of China' lend support to the views of a sizable and influential group of US scholars and policymakers of the 'realist school' who believe that China as a rising power will want to extend its global influence and challenge US power. Realists, whose rise in influence parallels the rise in China's economic strength, believe the increasing size of China's post-Mao policy set it has at its disposal – provided by its rapid economic growth – has advanced China's capabilities relative to the US and allows it to expand the arenas where it can challenge US power (Friedberg 2000; Johnston 2003, pp. 5–6). Some realists are also sometimes labelled 'dragon slayers' – a popular term in US foreign policy circles – who believe China's challenge to the US's dominance must be contained. The 'dragon slayers' under George Bush have overshadowed the 'panda huggers' – another popular term in US foreign policy circles – who formed a majority in the Clinton administration that believed China can be a stabilizing force in the world and therefore should be engaged rather than contained. The 'dragon slayers' tend more than the 'panda huggers' to see a causal link between China's rise and the value of its exchange rate.

GLOBALIZATION AND CHINA'S REBIRTH AND RISE

Since the 1990s China has resumed its role as a huge global trader, which it had forsaken under Mao. Foreign trade and investment are crucial drivers of post-Mao China's spectacular economic growth. Before the CCP made its decision in 1978 to embrace economic reform at the historic third plenum of the Eleventh Party Congress, China's engagement with the global economy was minor. But once the nation opened its doors to foreign trade and investment, its international engagement took off. It deepened significantly in the 1990s and culminated in China's entry to the World Trade Organization (WTO) in 2001. From 1979 to 2003 China's foreign trade grew at an average annual rate of 15 per cent, compared with an average annual expansion in world trade of 7 per cent over this period (Prasad and Rumbaugh 2004, p. 1).

According to official Chinese statistics, in 1978 the share of foreign trade in China's GDP was 9.8 per cent; in 1992 when Deng Xiaoping kick started economic reform with his 'southern tour' after reform was stalled by divisions in the CCP, the share of foreign trade had jumped to 35.3 per cent; but just 11 years later the share had soared to 58 per cent (NBS 1999, pp. 6, 60; NBS 2004, pp. 65, 714). China's shares of world merchandise imports and world exports more than doubled from 2.7 per cent and 2.8 per cent respectively in 1994 to 5.9 per cent and 6.5 per cent in 2004 (IMF 2004a; WTO 2005a, p. 21). In 2004, China's merchandise imports increased by 36 per cent and merchandise exports by 35 per cent from the previous year and China ranked third in the world after the US and Germany in the value of merchandise imports (US$561.4 billion) and exports (US$593.4 billion) (WTO 2005a, p. 21). Two years before, China was ranked sixth in world imports after the US, Germany, the UK, Japan and France, and fifth in world exports after the US, Germany, Japan and France (WTO 2003). China's ranking in world trade is expected to rise further. In September 2005, the OECD *Economic Survey of China* predicted that China would become the world's largest exporter by 2010.[5]

Expansion of China's foreign trade and national economy has seen its impact on the global economy increase significantly. China's large share of world trade indicates the high degree of economic inter-dependence between China and the rest of the world, which has made China a vital engine of world economic growth. A slowdown in China's economy, just as for a slowdown in the US economy, would have worldwide repercussions. China is an important node in international production networks (UNCTAD 2005b, p. 137). China's exports of finished products to the US and the EU depend on its imports of parts and components largely from the rest of East Asia, and while China runs a surplus in its trade with the US and the EU, it runs a deficit in its trade with East Asia (NBS 2004, p. 719). Purchasing power parity calculations show that between 2001 and 2003 China accounted for about 24 per cent of growth in world GDP (Prasad and Rumbaugh 2004, p. 1). In 2003 exports to China accounted for 32 per cent of Japan's annual export growth, 36 per cent for Korea, 68 per cent for Taiwan, 28 per cent for Germany and 21 per cent for the US. Incredibly, Japan's exports to China accounted for about 30 per cent of Japan's GDP growth in the second half of 2003. In 2003 China consumed about 20 per cent of most of the world's commodities, compared to 4 per cent in 1985, and accounted for 11 per cent of the world's nickel sales and 44 per cent of the growth in world nickel demand (Roach 2004).

Foreign direct investment (FDI), especially since 1992, has played a major role in the growth in China's foreign trade. The share of China's exports attributed to foreign-invested enterprises has been increasing every year since

1986, from 1.9 per cent in 1986 to 57 per cent in 2004 (Morrison and Labonte 2005, p. 15). China's large domestic market, abundant low-cost labour and WTO membership make China an especially attractive location for the production of goods for the domestic market and exports, and are the magnets attracting FDI flows into China. Between 1995 and 2000, China received 40 per cent of all FDI flows into Asia (CSRC 2002, Chapter 5). In 2003 China received $US53.5 billion of FDI, which was more than the US received (US$29.8 billion), and became in that year the largest recipient of FDI after Luxembourg (US$87.6 billion) in the world (UNCTAD 2004, pp. 367–71).[6] Many countries in Asia, such as the members of ASEAN, are more concerned by China's competitive power in attracting FDI than in its volume of foreign trade. In the early 1990s, ASEAN received 30 per cent of FDI inflows into developing Asia, while China received 18 per cent. By 2000 the share for ASEAN had fallen sharply to only 10 per cent while China's share jumped to 30 per cent (Yang 2003, p. 13). In 2003 China's share of FDI into developing Asia increased further to 53 per cent (UNCTAD 2004, pp. 367–70).

China is a fierce competitor for FDI flows not just because of its plentiful cheap unskilled labour but also because of its abundant relatively cheap semi-skilled and skilled labour, which are particularly attractive for manufacturing investments. Major Japanese corporations, such as NEC and Toshiba, are among the electronics giants that have relocated production facilities from Taiwan to mainland China to take advantage of the easily available low-cost skilled labour, as well as the mainland's huge domestic market (Reuters 2002b, 2002c).

THE RENMINBI AND THE RISE OF CHINA

The value of the renminbi has become a great concern to the European Union (EU) and even more so to the US, following post-Mao reform and the unmistakable rise of China as a significant global manufacturing centre after its admission into the WTO. China's entry into the WTO introduces significant competitive challenges to existing major global centres of production because China is a low-cost producer (Rumbaugh and Blancher 2004). Firms in the US and elsewhere are wary of cost competition from China. A 2004 *Business Week* special report on China claimed that 'the China price' are the 'three scariest words in US industry'. The repeated message is 'cut your price at least 30 per cent or lose your customers' (Engardio et al. 2004). Even some poor and middle-income countries are wary of competition from China. Countries like Bangladesh, Sri Lanka, Indonesia, Morocco, Tunisia and Turkey are concerned that they will be unable to compete successfully against China in textiles, their major exports, after the multi-fibre agreement ended at the close of 2004 (*The Economist* 2004a, p. 77). Fear that China is a trade competitor extends even to Mexico's special economic zones (*Maquiladora* system), which have lost investments and jobs to China (Rosen 2003). Chinese goods are providing stiff competition to Mexico's producers even in Mexico's domestic market. A *Washington Post* article reported that cheaper Chinese goods were driving Mexican goods from the Mexican market, quoting a Mexican worker worried about the threat that imported cheap Chinese blankets pose to her job: 'Maybe next time, I'll be the one who gets fired; China is going to make Mexico go broke' (Jordan 2003).

The US regards the value of the renminbi as an important policy issue because it sees its large current account deficits and China's accumulation of significant foreign reserves and increasing economic clout impacting on its national security (USCC 2004, 2005). China ranked first among the group of countries with which the US had run up balance of trade deficits. In 2003 the US ran a trade deficit of US$124 billion with China, which was 23.2 per cent of the total US trade deficit of US$535.5 billion. One year later the US trade deficit with China increased to US$162 billion and the increase in $38 billion from the year before accounted for about one-third of the total increase in the US trade deficit of US$119 billion during that year. The 2005 US trade deficit with China increased to US$201.6 billion, which was almost two and a half times the US trade deficit with Japan – the country that ranked second – and represented 25.8 per cent of the total US trade deficit of US$781.6 billion (Table 1.1; USCB 2006).[7]

Table 1.1 US balance of trade deficit by country (2005)

	Balance (US$ billion)	Share of total (%)
Total (census basis)	−781.6	100.0
China	−201.6	25.8
Canada	−76.4	9.8
Japan	−82.7	10.6
Germany	−50.7	6.5
Mexico	−50.1	6.4
Venezuela	−27.6	3.5
Nigeria	−22.6	2.9
Malaysia	−23.3	3.0
Saudi Arabia	−20.4	2.6
Ireland	−19.3	2.5
Rest of the world	−207.0	26.5

Source: USCB (2006).

US Deindustrialization

A reason why the US views its large overall balance of goods trade deficit as
a security issue is because of the widely held perception in the US that
continuous US trade deficits reflect ongoing US deindustrialization, which
has US firms relocating production to China and elsewhere.[8] Much of the
so-called deindustrialization in the US is simply an outcome of economic
development, where the structure of the economy shifts over time from
concentration in agriculture, to manufacturing and later to services. It is also
a result of globalization and changing international division of labour, where
production of simple-technology goods is transferred to low-cost countries.[9]
Yet it has inflamed negative emotions in the US because it impacts on the
livelihood of poorly educated and low-skilled Americans. [10] Many
policymakers in the US hold China largely responsible for the perceived US
deindustrialization, blaming what they call China's 'unfair trade practices'.
These are said to include, as highlighted by the quotation at the beginning of
this chapter, the undervaluation of the renminbi.

**The US, a Rising International Debtor, and China, a Rising
International Creditor**

Concern in the US over its mounting trade deficit reaches well beyond the
perceived threat of deindustrialization from its large deficit in goods trade.
The US is well aware that its large trade deficit ultimately contributes to
current account deficit, which weakens its net investment position. The
nation's net international investment position (NIIP) has deteriorated *pari
passu* with its growing current account deficit.[11] Until 1989, the US was a net
creditor to the rest of the world, but the US NIIP has deteriorated, gradually
in the early 1990s but rapidly in the late 1990s, and in the 2000s the US
became the world's biggest debtor nation. At the end of 2003 the amount that
the US owed to the rest of the world, as measured by its negative NIIP, was
US$2.65 trillion, compared to the US$360 billion it owed at the end of 1997
(Roubini and Setser 2004, p. 2). Roubini and Setser estimated that at the end
of 2004, the US NIIP was negative US$3.3 trillion. *The Economist* (2004b,
p. 65), in a special issue on the future of the US dollar, points out that in 1913
Britain was at the height of its empire and the world's largest creditor, but it
became a net debtor 40 years later, allowing the US dollar to usurp the role of
the pound sterling as the world's reserve currency. The transformation in
Britain's position from the world's biggest creditor to a net debtor nation is
rich in historical lessons. There are different interpretations of the precise
relationship between the downward shift in Britain's international investment
position and Britain's loss of empire status, but holding the title as the

world's biggest debtor over time can only weaken the soft power of the US and undermine its status as the world's sole superpower.

According to official US statistical data, in the first half of 2004 the US current account deficit was US$594 billion (adjusted annual rate and on national income and product account basis) or 5.1 per cent of GDP. On a balance of payments basis the deficit was US$627 billion. FDI inflows into the US have fallen significantly since the collapse of the dotcom boom in 2000 and US outward FDI significantly exceeds inward FDI. Foreign interest in US equities has also cooled (Roubini and Setser 2004, p. 18). As a result, purchases of US dollar assets by foreign central banks have become a major source of finance for the US current account deficit, which in the first half of 2004 amounted to US$403 billion (OPA 2004b; Roubini and Setser 2004, p. 18). For several reasons, [12] estimates prepared by the US statistical authorities are likely to underestimate foreign central banks' holdings of US dollar assets compared to estimates prepared by the Bank of International Settlements (BIS). For example, US official data do not count as foreign official holdings those holdings where the first foreign holder is not a foreign central bank, even though the first foreign holder could be holding the US dollar asset for the foreign central bank. US statistical authorities valued foreign central banks' holdings of US dollar assets at the end of 2003 at US$1.34 trillion compared to a BIS valuation of US$2.1 trillion (Higgins and Klitgaard 2004, p. 8). But by whichever set of statistics we consider it, the US current account deficit is rapidly increasing the external debt of the US and reinforcing its position as the world's number one debtor, while deepening its dependence on foreign central banks' purchases of US dollar assets. More worryingly for US policymakers, central banks in Asia were the largest purchasers of US dollar assets, financing 71 per cent of the US 2003 current account deficit, with the largest purchasers likely to be the central banks of Japan and China (Higgins and Klitgaard 2004, p. 6).

China is building up its stock of foreign exchange reserves with large inflows of foreign capital and current account surpluses. Between 1994 and 2003, China's foreign exchange reserves increased from US$51.6 billion to US$403.3 billion. [13] At the end of 2003, China had 275.3 billion SDRs (Special Drawing Rights) of international reserves or 12.8 per cent of the total of 2.2 trillion SDRs of international reserves held by all IMF member countries (IMF 2004a). The composition of China's foreign exchange reserves is not known. However, in 2003, 63.8 per cent of official holdings of foreign exchange of all IMF member countries were US dollar holdings and 19.7 per cent were euro holdings. In the same year, 59.3 per cent of official holdings of foreign exchange of IMF-member developing countries were US dollar holdings and 18.9 per cent were euro holdings

(IMF 2004b, pp. 103–4). If 60 per cent of China's holdings of foreign exchange reserves were in US dollars and 20 per cent in euros, this means China held 13.5 per cent of all the US dollars and 14.6 per cent of all the euros held as official holdings of foreign exchange in the world at that time.[14]

Prasad and Wei (2005, p. 26) estimated that as of December 2004, China held US\$194 billion of outstanding US Treasury securities recorded against foreign holders, compared to US\$712 billion for Japan and US\$164 billion for the UK. According to Prasad and Wei's assessment, the amount of US Treasury securities held by China at that time accounted for 30 per cent of China's foreign exchange reserves. But if US agency debt is included, the 30 per cent estimate becomes 52 per cent. Table 1.2 shows estimates by the US Treasury of the distribution among different countries of US federal debt held by foreigners in 2000, 2005 and 2006. They show that in September 2005 and January 2006, China held US\$250–260 billion or about 12 per cent of US federal debt, compared to Japan, which held US\$670–690 billion or about 30–33 per cent. Thus Japan's holdings of US federal debt in December 2004 were 3.7 times that of China's, but fell to 2.5 times in January 2006.[15] China's holdings are increasing but still well below those held by Japan. Nevertheless, any decision by the monetary authorities in China to switch their holdings of foreign exchange reserves from US dollar-denominated instruments into euros or yen, or vice versa, will have an impact on exchange rates and interest rates of these currencies, and will be a concern to the monetary authorities responsible for these currencies.

Table 1.2 Foreign holders of US federal debt

	US\$ billions (as of January 2006)	% share
Japan	668.3	30.5
Mainland China	262.6	12.0
United Kingdom	244.8	11.2
Caribbean banking centres	97.9	4.5
Taiwan	71.6	3.3
Germany	65.2	3.0
Korea	68.3	3.1
OPEC	77.6	3.5
Canada	54.9	2.5
Hong Kong	48.3	2.2
Total top 10 countries	1659.5	75.9
Remaining countries	528.1	24.1
Total	2187.6	100.0

Table 1.2 (continued)

	US$ billions (as of January 2005)	% share
Japan	687.2	33.3
Mainland China	252.2	12.2
United Kingdom	183.0	8.9
Caribbean banking centres	100.8	4.9
Taiwan	71.8	3.5
Germany	63.5	3.1
Korea	60.6	2.9
OPEC	54.4	2.6
Canada	47.7	2.3
Hong Kong	48.1	2.3
Total top 10 countries	1569.3	76.0
Remaining countries	494.3	24.0
Total	2063.6	100.0
	US$ billions (as of January 2000)	% share
Japan	317.7	31.3
Mainland China	60.3	5.9
United Kingdom	50.2	4.9
Germany	49.0	4.8
OPEC	47.7	4.7
Taiwan	33.4	3.3
Hong Kong	38.6	3.8
Caribbean banking centres	37.4	3.7
Korea	29.6	2.9
Belgium–Luxembourg	29.6	2.9
Total top 10 countries	693.5	68.3
Remaining countries	321.7	31.7
Total	1015.20	100.0

Source: USDT (2006).

Neo-con Aaron Friedberg (2000), in a controversial and widely discussed article, suggested that China could use the US dollar-denominated assets at its disposal as an economic weapon against the US, dumping the assets to raise US interest rates, or trigger a run on the US dollar or even a stock market crash. He suggested that because China's economy could suffer as well as the US economy if such an economic weapon were used, using this weapon would have the same effect as using nuclear weapons: mutual devastation. But mutual devastation, he argues, is no guarantee that this weapon will not be used.

Globalization and China's Acquisition of Technology

Economic growth and accumulation of foreign exchange influence China's ability to access and develop technological know-how. While the US government may consider the leverage that China has over US dollar interest rates and equity prices to be an important national security issue for the US, this issue pales into insignificance against US concerns over the perceived contribution of China's currency policy to China's impressive economic growth and accumulation of foreign exchange, and therefore its ability to acquire foreign defence and defence-related technology. The US Department of Defence (DOD) pointed out in its 2004 report to the US Congress that rapid economic growth has enabled China to devote more resources to its military, enhancing its military capabilities with significant purchases of defence and defence-related technology from France, Germany, Israel, Italy and Russia. According to that DOD report, official Chinese statistics indicate real double-digit annual percentage increases in China's defence budget between 1990 and 2002 and an almost 10 per cent real increase in 2003 (USDOD 2004). Hence, quantity and quality of defence purchases are increased, enabling China's rise as a military power.

Economic growth and foreign exchange earnings have also provided China with the means to fund basic scientific research and purchase foreign assets to lift its general level of industrial technology and management know-how. China's technology is also benefiting from FDI in its more advanced industries. R&D activities are increasingly global and China was ranked number one ahead of the US, India and Japan in an UNCTAD survey of the world's largest R&D spending transnational corporations (TNCs) on the most attractive prospective R&D locations for 2005–09 (UNCTAD 2005a, pp. 151–2). China's technical know-how as a producer and user of information technology (IT) is improving rapidly, so much so that the China Semiconductor Industry Association estimated that by 2010 China will become the world's second-largest semiconductor market (Reuters 2002a). Another example from the IT industry that provides ammunition to those in the US convinced of the 'China threat' is US imports of computer equipment. As can be seen from Table 1.3, China is rapidly replacing other major foreign suppliers of computer equipment to the US. Between 2000 and 2004 US imports of computer equipment from China increased by 255 per cent, while imports from Japan and Taiwan fell by 53 and 51 per cent respectively. Over the same period China's share among foreign suppliers increased from 12 to

40 per cent at the expense of all other major suppliers. In the broad category of advanced technology products (ATP), China's trade with the US was balanced in 1998, with about US$6 billion in exports and imports. But by 2004 China's ATP exports to the US had increased to US$46 billion, while its ATP imports from the US had increased to only US$9 billion (Preeg 2005, p. 7).

Table 1.3   Shares of major foreign suppliers* of US computer equipment imports and change in $ values (%)

	2000	2001	2002	2003	2004	2000–04 change
China	12.1	13.9	19.3	29.2	39.9	255.4
Malaysia	7.2	8.5	11.4	12.5	11.8	77.6
Mexico	10.1	14.4	12.7	10.9	10.0	7.2
Singapore	12.7	12.0	11.4	10.8	8.9	−24.1
Japan	19.6	16.1	13.0	9.8	8.5	−53.0
Taiwan	12.1	11.9	11.4	8.4	5.5	−50.6
Other	26.3	23.2	20.9	18.3	15.3	−37.2
Total	100.0	100.0	100.0	100.0	100.0	7.9

Note: * Ranked according to top six suppliers in 2004.

Source: Calculations using data in Morrison and Labonte (2005, p. 17).

In 2005 China was behind the US and Japan as the world's third-ranking spender on research and development, but there is a huge national collective effort in China to lift its scientific performance. National and sub-national governments in China are providing generous funding to laboratories and are luring scientists with Chinese backgrounds in the West with attractive salaries (Tomlinson and Adam 2005, p. 5). As an illustration of China's rapid advancement in scientific research, a report by the Department of Trade and Industry in the UK describes stem cell research in China as 'at, or approaching, the forefront of international stem cell research' (cited in Tomlinson and Adam 2005, p. 5). The rapid development of China's advanced technology is also highlighted in a 2005 'Report of the Task Force on the Future of American Innovation' that had Lucent and Microsoft as members, which concluded: 'China has been investing heavily in nanotechnology and already leads the US in some areas … and is making rapid progress in biotechnology' (cited in Preeg 2005, p. 8).

In a deal that was reported widely in the international media, in December 2004 China's Lenovo agreed to pay IBM US$1.75 billion for its personal computer business, which will make Lenovo China's fifth-largest corporation, with US$12.5 billion sales in 2003. Under the deal IBM agreed to allow Lenovo to use the IBM brand for five years and IBM took a 18.9 per cent stake in Lenovo (Lohr 2004). As explained by Lohr, IBM's objective in the deal was to cement its strategic relationship with Lenovo to forge closer links with China. For Lenovo, the deal provides access to US technology and management expertise. IBM already operated a research laboratory that employed 150 Chinese scientists and a software development laboratory that employed 500 engineers working on projects related to Linux, an operating system that competes with Microsoft.

'Mercantilist' Behaviour and Energy Security

There is obviously a direct relationship between China's current account surplus and its accumulation of massive foreign reserves, but many US policymakers also draw the connection between China's accumulation of foreign reserves and its purchase of foreign assets overseas. Lenovo's purchase of IBM's computer business is just one of many Chinese overseas strategic acquisitions of major corporations. Most of China's foreign acquisitions have attracted no or little international attention, but the attempt by the 70 per cent state-owned China National Offshore Oil Corporation[16] (CNOOC) (*Zhongguo haiyang shiyou zonggongsi*) in June 2005 to make a US$18.5 billion takeover bid for UNOCAL Corporation[17] raised eyebrows in Washington. Many US policymakers viewed this bid as a serious threat to the US's national security. UNOCAL has extensive oil interests in Central Asia and the CNOOC bid for UNOCAL, if successful, was seen as threatening the US's energy security. With China's economic growth fuelling global demand for energy and raising world energy prices, these US policymakers considered the CNOOC bid to be a greater threat to US security than Lenovo's purchase of IBM's computer business. Chairperson of the US House of Representatives Armed Services Committee, Duncan Hunter, told a July 2005 hearing of his committee that 'China's purchase of UNOCAL would dramatically increase its leverage over these countries, and therefore its leverage over US interests in [Central Asia]'. The only witness before the committee who did not object to the bid was Jerry Taylor, director of natural resource studies at the neo-liberal CATO Institute, who pointed out that UNOCAL produced only 0.23 per cent of the world's oil output and China's control of this small output would not give China an 'oil weapon'. All other witnesses and lawmakers at the hearing, however, did not share his view. The Armed Services Committee hearing promised to be only the first among many other official congressional hearings – the House Energy and Commerce Committee, for example, had scheduled a hearing into the deal a few days later for 19 July (Eckert 2005). In the face of strong congressional and public opposition, CNOOC withdrew its bid on 2 August and UNOCAL's management ultimately accepted a lower buyout offer of US$17.1 billion from Chevron Oil. A month after CNOOC's bid failed, deputy secretary of state Robert B. Zoellick in his speech to the National Committee on US–China Relations drew a link between the US administration's constant criticism of what it perceived to be China's unfair trade practices and CNOOC's bid for UNOCAL when he said China's mercantilist efforts to '"lock up" energy supplies are "not a sensible path to achieving energy security"' (Kessler 2005, A16).

The CNOOC–UNOCAL episode was just one of many deals that China has attempted to arrange to secure its energy supplies. In addition to competition from the US, China's efforts at energy security face competition from other large import-dependent energy users in Asia, notably India and Japan. The *Yomiuri Shimbun* (2005), Japan's and the world's largest newspaper, highlighted Japan's anxiety over the impact of China's increasing clout in the world economy on Japan's future energy security when it ran a series of articles on 'Planning National Strategies: Resources and Energy' that examined Japan's resource security in the light of rising tensions in China–Japan relations, pointing out that many Japanese specialists are calling China a 'resource-gorging country'. But the US appears to be the only country that has linked China's exchange rate policy with China's strategy to achieve energy security. According to US critics, an undervalued renminbi has allowed China to accumulate the vast foreign exchange reserves that China uses to purchase energy and other assets abroad. There will be more IBM and UNOCAL-type episodes in the future that will continue to keep the spotlight on the perceived link between the value of the renminbi and China's accumulation of foreign reserves, and the development of China's long-term capabilities to challenge US power and influence.

DISSENTING VOICES

There are, however, sceptics among policymakers and analysts about the existence of this link. The sceptics can be divided broadly into two camps. Members in the first camp, while they may believe that China is mercantilist in its conduct of international trade, doubt the sustainability of China's impressive economic growth in the long term and are unconvinced of the often-touted strength of China's influence in the global economy. Those belonging to the second camp, while convinced of the sustainability of the dynamism in China's economy in the long run, do not believe the renminbi really matters when it comes to deciding the fate of global imbalances, especially those contributed by the current account deficits of the US.

Three representatives from the first camp are Gordon Chang, Charles Wolf Jr and Minxin Pei. Gordon Chang (2001) in his provocative book, *The Coming Collapse of China*, put forward the argument that China's authoritarian political system is incapable of introducing and implementing the type of internal reform needed to solve the myriad of social and political problems brought about by economic reform, and the system could collapse within ten years. Wolf Jr et al. (2003), although less alarmist than Chang, believe that China faces potentially serious problems ranging from water shortages and major epidemics to high unemployment that could have a severe negative impact on economic growth. In a similar vein Minxin Pei argues that China's economic success has masked many of its problems – official corruption and decay of many of its public sector infrastructures – and there is no guarantee that its political system could withstand a severe shock; 'China may be rising, but no one really knows whether it can fly' (Pei 2006a).[18] Moreover, despite its post-Mao phenomenal economic growth, China's GDP per capita is still only a shade more than one-seventh of the US's (UNIDO 2005, Table 3.1).

In the second camp are bankers and analysts like Jonathan Anderson, Stephen Roach and Clyde Prestowitz. Anderson (2004), chief Asian economist at the investment bank UBS, and Roach (2003), Morgan Stanley's chief economist, are optimistic about the future of China's economy and may accept that the challenge from China to US power is real, but they believe that revaluing the renminbi will make little difference to the competitiveness of China's exports to the US because China's exports have high import content and low domestic value-added. Their beliefs are supported by the research of Lau (2003, p. 2), who estimated that the domestic value-added of China's exports to the world is low at 30 per cent, but it is even lower for China's exports to the US at only 20 per cent.

Additional support for the argument that the renminbi exchange rate is not crucial to the international competitiveness of the US and other developed countries comes from the work of Banister (2004, 2005) on the cost of manufacturing labour in China. Labour in China is extremely cheap compared to the cost of labour in the US. In her preliminary study on the costs of China's labour, prepared for the US Bureau of Labor Statistics (BLS), Judith Banister found that the 2002 hourly compensation cost of manufacturing workers in China was US$0.95 in urban areas and US$0.41 in township and village enterprises (TVEs), resulting in an all-China average of US$0.57 (Banister 2005, p. 32). This compared with US$21.11 in the US, US$2.53 in Brazil, US$2.60 in Mexico, US$0.49 in Sri Lanka, US$5.73 in Taiwan and an average of US$14.22 in a group including these five plus another 25 countries surveyed by the Bureau of Labor Statistics (BLS 2004, Table 2). China's manufacturing compensation cost was only about 3 per cent of that in the US and the EU,[19] a quarter of that in Brazil and Mexico and less than 10 per cent of the average cost of Hong Kong, South Korea, Singapore and Taiwan (Banister 2005, p. 32). China's extremely low labour cost has allowed it to compete very successfully, not only against manufacturing from the US with its high labour costs but also against manufacturing from other countries with low labour costs. Any conceivable revaluation of the renminbi will not be able to compensate for the high labour costs in the US and EU. As Prestowitz (2003), counsellor to the Secretary of Commerce in the first Reagan administration, points out, Chinese exports to the US are displacing exports from other developing countries rather than displacing US production.

Research by Fernald et al. (1999) indicates income growth is a significantly more powerful variable than real exchange rate changes for explaining export growth in China and other major East Asian exporter nations. Their research is consistent with the argument of Roach (2003) that US current account deficits are primarily caused by low national savings in the US. US net national saving fell to 0.7 per cent of GDP in the first half of 2003. This was due to a huge turnaround in fiscal balance, from a 2.5 per cent of GDP surplus in 2000 to a deficit of 4 per cent of GDP in 2003 – a fall in public savings of 6.5 per cent of GDP over three years (Roubini and Setser 2004, p. 22).[20] The turnaround in the fiscal balance was so dramatic that the US Congress had to raise the statutory federal debt limit in 2004 (OPA 2004a).[21] The deficits continued in 2004 and 2005, respectively at 3.6 per cent of GDP and 2.6 per cent of GDP. Official projections of the fiscal budget to 2011 indicate the US will continue to accumulate fiscal deficits in each year of the projection period (OMB 2006, p. 26). With continued deficits, the US Congress had to raise the statutory debt limit again in March 2006, this time by US$781 billion, which brought the debt limit to nearly US$9 trillion (Hulse 2006).

Against the accusation of Goldstein (2004) that China was manipulating the renminbi to keep it undervalued, both the International Monetary Fund and the US Treasury, while advocating a more flexible regime for the renminbi, did not believe that the renminbi was undervalued (OPA 2004b; ERD 2004). In the words of Steven Dunaway (ERD 2004), IMF mission chief to China: 'We still find it difficult to come up with evidence that would suggest that there's a substantial undervaluation of the currency [renminbi]'. The Omnibus Trade and Competitiveness Act of 1988 requires the US Treasury 'to consider whether countries manipulated the rate of exchange between their currency and the United States dollar for purposes of preventing effective balance of payments adjustments or gaining unfair competitive advantage in international trade'. Curiously, contrary to claims by the Treasury's boss John Snow, the Treasury's 3 December 2004 report to Congress states, 'it finds no major trading partner of the United States met the technical requirements for designation under the Omnibus Trade and Competitiveness Act of 1988'. The report makes the point that using a currency peg or intervening in currency markets 'does not in and of itself satisfy the statutory test' (OPA 2004b).

PERCEPTIONS AND POLICY DISAGREEMENTS

Regardless of the relative merits of the various arguments on China and the renminbi, ultimately what shapes international opinion is the image of China in the eyes of key foreign policymakers, especially those in the EU, Japan and the US. Domestic policymakers use the image of a foreign country as a key to interpret events and actions associated with that country, and perceived image is often critical in determining a nation's policy towards another nation (Boulding 1969; Hermann et al. 1997). Hermann et al. argue that perceptions of a nation's culture, capabilities and the threats or opportunities it represents are crucial factors in creating the image of that nation. China's abandonment of revolutionary communism and its embrace of globalization have not led to the demise of the 'China threat' syndrome but to a recasting of it (Yee and Storey 2002). There are sobering assessments of China voiced in international policy circles and the public media, but they are often drowned out by voices convinced of the resilience of China's 'rebirth' or 'reawakening' and of China's desire and mounting capacity to mount a serious challenge to US hegemony. Many in the George W. Bush administration see a link between the value of the renminbi and US national security in their calls for renminbi revaluation. They do not place any responsibility for the relative decline in US competitiveness on US inadequacy in investments in infrastructure, particularly human capital, or lack of savings. 'China has become [for many in the US] the poster child for those aspects of globalization that threaten the United States' (Lampton 2005, p. 67).[22]

Perceptions in the US of a challenge from China to US security interests did not begin with the George W. Bush administration. Comments on the US trade deficit and the renminbi in the 2004 report to Congress by the US–China Economic and Security Review Commission echoed comments of the US secretary of state under President Clinton, Madeline Albright, who famously warned China that it should take steps to reduce its trade surplus with the US before this surplus became 'a source of estrangement instead of engagement' between the two countries (Beck 1998). As long as key policymakers outside China believe that the value of the renminbi matters, the currency will be an issue in China's relations with the rest of the world. This is especially so with the US, which more often than not sees China as a strategic as well as economic competitor rather than a partner. In his testimony before the US Senate Committee on Banking, Housing and Urban affairs on 26 May 2005, Treasury Secretary John Snow made clear that the US Treasury's conclusion that no major trading partner of the US was found to manipulate their exchange rates to prevent balance of payments or gain unfair competitive trading advantage in international trade did not mean 'acquiescence with the foreign exchange policies of many of America's trading partners … Most notable among these is China' (OPA 2005a). His message seven months later was stronger. He expressed the view that although the US Treasury continued to find that none of the US's trading partners met the technical requirements for designation under the Omnibus Trade and Competitiveness Act, China's discontinuation of the renminbi–US dollar peg was an important factor in this decision and future decisions are contingent on China's progress in allowing greater exchange rate flexibility (OPA 2005b).

WHAT DETERMINES CHINA'S EXCHANGE RATE POLICY?

Between 1949 and the 1990s, China's domestic economic and political factors largely determined its exchange rate policy. As noted earlier, China's international economic engagements during that time were very limited. From the 1990s, external influences have become increasingly more important in China's exchange rate policymaking as a result of China's deepening engagement with and growing influence in the global economy. Yet external influences have not operated independently of domestic factors, especially the preferences of policy actors and their relative influences in the exchange rate policy arena. China did not devalue the renminbi during the Asian financial crisis – a decision that conformed to the desires of policymakers in the US, the EU and East Asia. But post-Asian crisis, the Chinese government for a long time steadfastly refused to allow the renminbi to float or revalue, despite not-so-subtle pressure from the US. The Chinese government finally ended China's pegged exchange rate system at 19:00 hours (Beijing time) on 21 July 2005, with a public announcement on the People's Bank of China (PBC) website that China was replacing the pegged exchange rate system with a managed floating exchange rate system referenced to a basket of currencies revaluing the renminbi immediately to RMB8.11 per US dollar (PBC 2005).

There is no doubt that foreign, especially US, pressures played some role in influencing China to discontinue the renminbi–US dollar peg. But international pressures, even if they are decisive, do not work in a vacuum that is completely detached from domestic influences. First, international pressures can be brought to bear in a tangible way at China's policy table only through policy actors representing domestic interest groups. Second, policy preferences of international actors on China's exchange rate may coincide with those of some domestic policymakers, but this is not always the case. Even if international and some domestic policy actors share a common policy preference, there will be uncertainty over the actual policy decision from the inevitable policy contest between these actors and other domestic policy actors.

Exchange Rate Policy Contests in Neo-liberal Regimes

Changes in exchange rate policy have great capacity to create winners and losers and therefore are political as well as economic instruments. They are usually not the result of purely rational economic analysis by policy planners acting in the national interest. Politics almost inevitably enters this picture. Frieden (1991) sees domestic sectors in neo-liberal economies that are directly affected by exchange rate changes as key actors influencing exchange rate policy. For Frieden, who emphasized the significance of fixed factors of production in industrial sectors, exchange rate policy outcomes can be understood by analysing the relative strengths of sectoral winners and losers of exchange rate policy in the domestic polity.[23] Frieden (1991, pp. 448–9), for example, argued that President Ronald Reagan's administration pursued a tight monetary policy and exchange rate appreciation against the opinion of most economists because President Reagan's main political support was based in non-traded sectors, like real estate, and among international investors, which benefited from a high US dollar.

Frieden's nomenclature of the exchange rate preferences of socio-economic actors can be presented in a simple matrix with two dimensions of exchange rate policy and two possible choices in each policy dimension (Figure 1.1). The first dimension of policy refers to the level of the exchange rate and the choice of policy is for either a high or a low level of exchange rate. In the second dimension of policy, the choice is between a high degree or a low degree of exchange rate flexibility and national monetary policy autonomy. On the rate of exchange, traded (export and import-competing) sectors face international competition and therefore prefer a low exchange rate (price of non-traded goods relative to the price of traded goods) that makes these sectors more competitive at home and in foreign markets.

Non-traded sectors, because they produce goods and services that are not sold abroad and face no competition from foreign goods and services at home, prefer a high exchange rate. On the flexibility of the exchange rate, import-competing and non-traded sectors depend heavily on domestic sales and therefore prefer national monetary policy autonomy, which requires exchange rate flexibility. This reasoning follows from the Mundell–Fleming proposition that in the presence of international capital mobility, monetary policy is more effective than fiscal policy in varying domestic demand under a flexible exchange rate regime, but fiscal policy is more effective than monetary policy under a fixed exchange rate regime (Fleming 1962; Mundell 1963). Conversely, exporters, international traders and investors depend more on foreign than on domestic markets and are exposed to greater commercial risk in the presence of exchange rate fluctuations. They therefore prefer a low degree of exchange rate flexibility.

Preferred degree of exchange rate flexibility
and national monetary policy autonomy

		High	Low
Preferred level of exchange rate	High	Producers of non-tradable goods and services	International traders and investors
	Low	Import-competing producers of tradable goods for the domestic market	Export-oriented producers of tradable goods

Source: Frieden (1991, p. 445).

Figure 1.1   Exchange rate policy preferences of socio-economic actors

Exchange Rate Policies in China

Frieden's schema is simple but provides useful insights into how exchange rate policies are determined in liberal industrialized market economies. His approach, however, cannot explain exchange rate policies in non-market economies nor in a country that does not have a well-developed civil society with political space. In liberal industrialized market economies, individual businesses, trade associations, professional bodies and learned societies often agitate openly for particular economic policies. This does not yet happen in China. China uses markets extensively but its civil society is still very weak and there is limited political space available that allows stakeholders to lobby for their preferred policy outcomes, despite more than two-and-a-half decades of economic reform.

One of the authors of this book (Liew) spent some weeks with a research assistant checking through several major Chinese national and sub-national newspapers published in 1998 and the first half of 1999. The papers include the *Jingji ribao* (Economic Daily), *Shanghai jingji bao* (Shanghai Economic Daily), *Shenzhen shang bao* (Shenzhen Commercial Daily) and *Xiamen ribao* (Xiamen Daily). The last three of these are published in localities highly dependent on exports, where one may expect to find significant opposition to the government's no-devaluation policy during the Asian financial crisis. However, the research produced not a single article that even questioned, let alone criticized the government's no-devaluation policy. The empirical study examined only a small proportion of the newspapers published in China, but its findings indicate uncritical acceptance of government policy and imply the absence of a strong independent media. These results are consistent with findings of other scholars working on China's civil society (for example Baum and Shevchenko 1999 and He 1997, pp. 147–77) that indicate poor development of civil society in China. With a weak civil society and a tightly controlled media, contestation over exchange rate policy in China is not played out in the public arena but largely among actors within the bureaucracy.

The remaining chapters examine the factors that shape exchange rate policymaking in China. Our starting point is central planning and socialist industrialization, when China's engagement with the world outside was minimal. It was the outcome of an economic strategy that had its origins in Mao's ideology of self-reliance and the US-led economic embargo against the PRC before the normalization of their relations during the Nixon presidency. The value of the renminbi was purely a domestic issue and international influences played only a very minor role in exchange rate policy. Our lens then moves to China's post-Mao economic reform, when international influences began to play a significant role in exchange rate policy and we conclude with China's post-WTO entry, where the renminbi has become an ever more consequential international issue and international influences are important considerations in exchange rate policy.

Chapter 2 explains how China's exchange rate policy was determined under central planning and in the period of socialist industrialization. We explain the reasons behind the replacement of the nationalist yuan with the renminbi and how the imperative of central planning determined China's exchange rate policy. During the period of socialist industrialization, the renminbi exchange rate was set simply with the objective of raising enough foreign exchange to pay for imports required to implement China's rapid industrialization policy. With the CCP's central plan, and not the market, chiefly responsible for allocating resources in the economy, the State Planning Commission was China's most influential exchange rate policymaking organ at that time.

Chapter 3 analyses the economics of post-Mao economic reform and how it influenced the management of China's foreign exchange from 1978 to 2005. This chapter analyses the major reforms in foreign exchange management in the period up to the end of the renminbi–US dollar peg. We explain how reform in foreign exchange management was linked to reform in foreign trade and investment and show how reform of China's foreign exchange management was driven by the desire of the authorities to promote exports and maintain price stability. The reforms analysed include the introduction of the foreign exchange retention system, the establishment of a dual exchange rate system for foreign exchange and swap centres, the unification of the dual exchange rate systems, and current account convertibility. Here we see how piecemeal reforms introduced to tackle one problem often created other problems. This chapter highlights in particular the difficulty of managing foreign exchange with a dual exchange rate system and maintaining macroeconomic stability after exchange rate unification under a pegged exchange rate regime.

In Chapter 4 we report results from several of our empirical investigations. In our first investigation we examined the historical domestic costs of earning foreign exchange from exports and found an inverse relationship between the renminbi return from each US dollar of exports and the balance of trade. The renminbi rate of return was significantly higher in the years when there were large deficits in the balance of trade and the authorities were trying to improve trade performance. The exchange rate and fiscal subsidies are important policy instruments that affect the renminbi rate of return from exports, but authorities when considering the use of these instruments have to consider their impacts on inflation and the fiscal budget. In our second investigation, we estimated an equation to examine what were the crucial variables that drove China's post-reform phenomenal growth in exports. We find that FDI and fiscal subsidies were more important than the renminbi exchange rate in explaining China's exports. Our third investigation provided evidence to support the view that if the renminbi was undervalued, it was more likely to be undervalued against the US dollar than the yen. Finally, we show that interest rate parity did not hold, which indicates that capital controls in China are effective to some degree.

Chapter 5 examines China's economic policymaking structure during the Asian financial crisis, explaining the roles of key individual and institutional policy actors that determine exchange rate policy. The chapter analyses the distribution of power and influence among key state and party bureaucratic organs in macroeconomic policymaking. We find the party was still paramount in macroeconomic policymaking; but influence of the State Planning Commission (SPC) (and its descendants) had diminished while that of the PBC had grown. This was a result of the market replacing planning to organize the domestic economy, and China's growing relations with the global economy. From our research on the relative power and influence among policy organs and the economic and international relations environment, we are able to explain China's devaluation of the official renminbi rate in 1990 and its no-devaluation policy during the Asian financial crisis.

Chapter 6 updates the economic policymaking structure described in Chapter 5 to take into account the changes in China's political leadership after the Chinese Communist Party Sixteenth Party Congress in November 2002 to examine the implications of China's 'rebirth' or 'awakening' and WTO entry on its exchange rate policy. In response to growing social instability from the pressures of globalization, China's new leaders after November 2002 began to focus more on the costs of globalization, which resulted in the reconfiguration and reassertion of authority of the renamed National Development and Reform Commission (last descendant of the SPC) in macroeconomic policymaking. This chapter focuses on the importance of poverty and income inequality, and WTO membership, on China's exchange rate policy, and explains the reasons behind the decision of the authorities to end the peg of the renminbi to the US dollar.

The concluding chapter contains a summary of the major findings in this book. In sum we find that domestic forces exert dominant influences over the making of China's exchange rate policy and although external influences are beginning to have more leverage since China's entry into the WTO, they are yet to be pivotal. China is continuing to engage globalization on its own terms. What remains pivotal are the bureaucratic hierarchy and the perceptions held by its key institutional and human policy actors of the nation's and their own bureaucratic interests.[24]

NOTES

1. At the Paris meeting of the G7 in February 2003, Japanese officials lobbied to increase pressure on China to revalue the renminbi (Karmin 2003). Calculated using data in 'Economic and financial indicators', *The Economist*, 26 January 2002 and 4 December 2004.
2. Not all policymakers decide policy. Policymakers include analysts who provide formal and/or informal advice to decision makers but who do not decide policy. This will be discussed in greater detail in Chapter 5.
3. Despite its decline after 1750, China's economy in 1820 was still 43 per cent larger than the economy of Western Europe and remained the largest in the world (Maddison 2005, Table 8b).

4. There are doubts over the reliability of China's official statistics. Annual growth rates may have been overestimated by up to 2 per cent, but even if growth rates are lower by 2 per cent, China's economic growth in the reform period remains very impressive and ranks comfortably among the world's ten fastest-growing economies (Lardy 2002, p. 12; World Bank 1997a, p. 3).
5. Available at http://www.oecd.org/document/15/0,2340,en_2649_34673_35363023_1_1_1 _1,00.html, accessed 19 September 2005.
6. The US–China Economic and Security Review Commission, using data in UNCTAD's 2003 *World Investment Report*, stated in its 2004 report to the US Congress (USCC 2004, p. 49) that China overtook the US in 2002 and was the world's largest recipient of FDI that year. However, the US 2002 FDI data were revised upwards from US$30 billion to US$62.9 billion in the 2004 *World Investment Report* and China ranked behind the US after the revision, even if one were to include FDI flows to Hong Kong.
7. In an important but relatively unknown paper, Fung and Lau (2003) argued that US and Chinese bilateral trade balance data are inaccurate, and a more accurate estimate of the 2002 US–China bilateral trade balance in goods and services, although large, is more than 25 per cent smaller than the official US estimate.
8. The share of manufacturing in China's GDP in 2002 was 34.5 per cent; in the US, it was 17.6 per cent (UNIDO 2005, Table A2.1).
9. For example, 75 per cent of China's electronic exports in 2003 are low-quality or low-price products. In high-technology electronic exports, 70 per cent belong to the low-quality or price range (Gaulier et al. 2006, p. 21).
10. One study estimated a loss of 100 000 jobs in 2004 to China. Another estimated a loss of almost 1.5 million jobs over 1989–2003 from US–China trade deficits (USCC 2005, p. 27).
11. NIIP = (Total stock of US claims on the rest of the world) – (Total stock of foreign claims on the US).
12. See Higgins and Klitgaard (2004, p. 8).
13. Total reserves minus gold, holdings of SDRs and reserve position in the IMF. Reserves totalled US$408.2 billion (IMF 2004a).
14. Calculated from data in IMF (2004a) and IMF (2004c, pp. 103–4).
15. This was due to the huge increase in China's balance of trade surplus in 2005. But China is not the only country that is holding a rising share of US federal debt. Between September 2005 and January 2006, the increase in the holdings of US federal debt of the United Kingdom was bigger than that of China. This will be discussed in Chapter 4.
16. Its CEO was Fu Chengyu and two members of its board were Evert Henkes, formerly of Shell, and Kenneth Courtis of Goldman Sachs; available at http://en.wikipedia.org/ wiki/CNOOC, accessed 21 September 2005. Information on CNOOC and UNOCAL is drawn largely from this source.
17. It is the holding company for Union Oil Company of California.
18. Pei expands this argument in his book (Pei 2006b).
19. China's manufacturing compensation was 3 per cent and 3.2 per cent of those in the US and the EU, respectively. 'The EU' refers to the 15 EU members prior to its expansion of its membership to 25 countries on 1 May 2004. See Banister (2005, Chart 1).
20. Revised figures indicate a 2.4 per cent GDP surplus in 2000 and a GDP deficit of 3.5 per cent in 2003 (OMB 2006, p. 26).
21. The US Treasury had to postpone its auction of four-week bills scheduled to settle on 18 November 2004 because it would have breached the US$7.38 trillion statutory debt limit. Republicans, who had a majority in Congress, were unwilling to vote to raise the debt limit before Congress adjourned in October because the US fiscal deficit was a politically sensitive issue in the 2 November elections.
22. Sino–US relations are also complicated by the centrality of moralism in US foreign policy. As Samuel Huntington (2005, pp. 80, 88, 91) pointed out in his provocative book, the US is a glaring exception among developed countries in terms of its high level of religiosity – 65 per cent of its population affirmed strong religiosity – and moralism as much as realism guides US foreign policy. Elsewhere in his book he argued that the collapse of communism and the Soviet Union left the US 'without any clear "other" against which to define itself'

(2005, p. 261). China is a likely candidate to fill this void. It looms large not merely as a strategic competitor but also as an atheist competitor, where only about 5 per cent of its population affirmed strong religiosity (Huntington 2005, pp. 91, 267).
23. If factors of production are highly mobile, industrial sectors cannot be units of analysis as policy actors.
24. NDRC is the new name of the former State Development and Planning Commission, which was previously known as the State Planning Commission.

2. Managing foreign exchange: from birth to decline of central planning

The history of the People's Republic of China's (PRC's) management of foreign exchange can be divided into four distinct periods. The first pre-dates the birth of the PRC and came with the dawn of the Chinese Communist Party's (CCP's) total victory over the Nationalists on mainland China as the CCP attempted to seize control of China's economy from the Nationalists. During this period, the CCP took action on currency in areas on the mainland under its control, replacing Nationalist and foreign currencies with the renminbi (RMB) that it created, and prohibiting the use of non-renminbi currencies. The second period covers the Rehabilitation Period (1949–52) (*huifu shiqi*) when the CCP consolidated its power on the mainland and mobilized and centralized resources to rehabilitate the war-torn Chinese economy. Efforts were made to increase state control over foreign trade and foreign exchange while simultaneously seeking to maximize flows of foreign exchange into China by stimulating exports and attracting overseas Chinese remittances.

The third period covers the period of central economic planning (1954–78) when the state monopolized the conduct of foreign trade and exercised virtual control over earning and use of foreign exchange. The last period refers to the years since 1978 when the state slowly liberalized the conduct of foreign trade and control over the administration of foreign exchange. In this chapter we consider the first three periods; the next chapter examines the last period.

FROM NATIONALIST YUAN TO PEOPLE'S CURRENCY

In 1948 with victory in the civil war in sight, the CCP began to plan how to manage a unified nation and reconstruct a devastated economy. The CCP's first step was to integrate and streamline the political and economic institutions in the areas under its control. In May 1948, the CCP Central Committee formed the North China Liberated Area (NCLA) (*Huabei jiefangqu*) by merging the two large liberated areas of Jin-Cha-Ji and

Jin-Ji-Lu-Xiang. In August 1948, the North China Provisional People's Congress (*Huabei linshi renmin daibiao dahui*) established the North China People's Government (NCPG) (*Huabei renmin zhengfu*) as a precursor to a national government (Dai 1998, pp. 2–3).

Many different types of currencies were in circulation in the areas under Communist control at that time. Miyashita (1976, p. 52) estimated there were at least 20 kinds of Communist currencies, each issued independently of the others, in circulation in the CCP Border Areas and Liberated Areas.[1] Thus the CCP saw the need in 1948 to plan for a central body to implement monetary integration – to replace all the Communist currencies, and later the currencies of the Nationalists, with a single national currency. At its third policy work meeting in November 1948, the NCPG decided to establish the People's Bank of China (PBC) as China's central bank. This involved merging several banks in Communist territories with the newly created Huabei Bank, itself a product of a merger of the Jinan Bank and Jin-Cha-Ji Border Region Bank, as the PBC's head office (Liu 1984, p. 29). Although the PBC functioned as a central bank in the CCP-held areas, it also performed the functions of a commercial bank. It was not until 1983 that the authorities divorced the PBC from its commercial functions, and from then on the PBC performed solely as a central bank (Chen 1994, p. 19).

The November 1948 meeting that established the PBC also decided to create a new currency, the people's currency – renminbi – as the new national currency to replace all the existing Communist and Nationalist currencies. PBC officially opened for business in the city of Shijiazhuang a month later on 1 December 1948. Nan Hanchen was appointed as its first head with the title of director general, and work was begun to exchange all the currencies in circulation with the renminbi (Cheng 1954, p. 13; Miyashita 1976, p. 60). Yet it was not until 1 October 1949, with the departure of Nationalist forces for Taiwan and the founding of the People's Republic, that the renminbi became a truly national currency.

Converting to a New Currency System

Because the old Communist currencies were issued independently by different Communist authorities, the currencies were valued differently in the market. Therefore different exchange rates had to be set for converting each of these currencies to the new renminbi. Some of these exchange rates are listed in Table 2.1.

The PBC had to replace not just the old Communist currencies with the renminbi but also the currencies of the Nationalist regime that were in circulation after the capture of Nationalist territories. The CCP's aim to replace all other currencies with the renminbi was not due entirely to its desire to lower transaction costs in trade by having just one medium of exchange. Another equally important reason was to control inflation. China's economy was in dire straits on the eve of the Communist victory. Gross product of heavy industry, light industry and agriculture in 1949 had fallen by 70, 30 and 25 per cent respectively compared to the historical high industrial and agricultural gross product levels in 1936 (Dai 1998, p. 3).[2]

Table 2.1   Renminbi conversion rates (per 1 RMB)

Beihai currency	100
Huazhong currency	100
Ji-Re-Liao border currency	5000
Jinan currency	100
Northeast currency	200
Northwest peasants' currency	2000
Jin-Cha-Ji border currency	1000
Shan-Gan-Ning border area	
Trading company notes	2000
Zhongzhou peasants' currency	3

Source: Miyashita (1976, pp. 60–61).

The loss in production paralleled the Nationalist government's increasing need to finance growing expenditure, which was made all the more urgent by the Nationalists' war effort against the CCP after the surrender of Japan. Thus, without a commensurate increase in the Nationalist government's capacity to raise revenue, fiscal deficits continued to mount. Monetary growth was used to finance these large deficits, but this soon gave rise to hyperinflation and resulted in a serious loss in confidence in the Nationalist government's currency. The average monthly rate of inflation for 1945–48 reached 26.3 per cent in Chongqing and 33.7 per cent in Shanghai (Chou 1963, pp. 24–5).[3] In September 1945, 1 yuan of the Shandong Liberated Area could be exchanged for 5 yuan of the nationalist legal tender notes (*fabi*) (GLTNs) and 1 yuan of the Jinan Liberated Area could be exchanged for 2 yuan of GLTNs. By August 1948, the Communist currencies had increased in relative value to between 800 and 2000 GLTNs for 1 yuan. At about this time, the Nationalist government implemented a currency reform, introducing the gold yuan note (GYN) to replace the GLTN at the rate of 3 million GLTN to 1 GYN in a futile attempt to slow the rate of inflation (Chou 1963, p. 25). In September 1948, 1 GYN was worth 3000 yuan of the Communist currencies of Shandong and Jinan, but by December its value had plummeted by more than 90 per cent to less than 300 yuan of these currencies (Miyashita

1976, p. 57). The Nationalist government faced the impossible task of reining in its fiscal deficits and dampening inflation in the remaining cities under its control. Instead of subsiding, inflation worsened after the Nationalists' currency reform. Between August 1948 and April 1949, prices increased by an average of 198 per cent per month in Chongqing and 300 per cent in Shanghai (Chou 1963, p. 26).

But no matter how serious the problem of inflation was for the CCP, the most pressing reason to unify the currency system on the eve of its victory over the Nationalists was to gain control of resources. By outlawing the use of all other currencies bar the renminbi, and mandating the compulsory conversion of GYNs into renminbi at rates well below the current market rates, the CCP was able indirectly to confiscate cash assets. It could also tax through seigniorage by controlling the only body (the PBC) that could create money. Moreover, as Miyashita (1976, p. 58) discovered, until the Nationalists retreated to Taiwan, CCP operatives would use GYNs obtained from newly captured Nationalist areas to buy rice, cotton, drugs and other daily necessities in the major cities of Beijing,[4] Shanghai, Tianjin and Qingdao. This worsened the shortages in these Nationalist-controlled cities, further fuelling the inflation there.

Table 2.2 shows the renminbi–GYN exchange rate in four major Chinese cities during various periods of conversion of the GYNs to renminbi. The average period of conversion was limited and the exchange rate became progressively unfavourable to holders of GYNs. The excess demand for goods relative to supply of GYNs increased as GYNs flooded into the remaining Nationalist-controlled territories following the CCP's capture of more and more of these territories, in the process gaining control over more and more GYNs. In one last desperate measure, the Nationalist government on 4 July 1949 issued silver yuan notes (SYNs) in Guangzhou to replace the GYNs at the exchange rate of 500 million GYN to 1 SYN. The CCP in response declared that it would not exchange renminbi for SYNs in the Liberated Areas in the future (Miyashita 1976, p. 66).

It did not take long for the renminbi to cement its status as the only legal tender currency in the PRC. However, the battle to control inflation was not won easily. Although the inflation of renminbi-denominated prices was far less serious than the inflation of GYN-denominated prices,[5] renminbi-denominated prices at the end of 1949 were still 75 times the levels at the beginning of that year (Miyashita 1976, p. 67). This was equivalent to an annual inflation rate of 7400 per cent. The CCP put in charge of battling inflation the Committee on Financial and Economic Affairs (CFEA) (*Caizheng jingji weiyyuanhui*), the highest economic and financial policy-making body, which oversaw the PBC and the Ministry of Finance (MOF) (Hsiao 1971, p. 20).

Table 2.2 Official GYN–renminbi conversion rates

City	Date of capture by CCP	Period of conversion	Exchange rate per RMB	Remarks
Tianjin	15 Jan	17 Jan – 4 Feb	At first 6, later 8 GYN	Preferential rates for workers and students
Beijing	24 Jan	2 Feb – 22 Feb	10 GYN	
Nanjing	24 Apr	28 Apr – 5 May	2500 GYN	
Shanghai	25 May	30 May – 5 June	100 000 GYN	
Guangzhou	15 Oct			No exchange made

Source: Miyashita (1976, p. 65).

In 1950 the CFEA drew up the Unified Policy for State Financial and Economic Work that had at its core a programme of 'three centralizations' to achieve 'three balances' (*santong sanping*) to break the inflation spiral. The 'three centralizations' were the centralization of money creation, public taxation and expenditure, and international trade in key commodities[6] in the hands of the central government, and the 'three balances' were fiscal, monetary and commodity balances (Dai 1998, p. 3). Balancing the government budget and controlling the money supply are standard tools of price stabilization. The move to centralize the control of essential commodities in 1950 was forced by the immediate problem of ensuring an adequate supply of food and other essential commodities to the cities that recently had been brought under CCP control. But the action also foreshadowed the impending socialization and implementation of central planning of the national economy.

The programme to stabilize prices was a success. By the end of 1952, the annual rate of increase in wholesale prices had fallen to 1 per cent in Shanghai and 5.4 per cent in Tianjin.[7] This was achieved despite a temporary resurgence of inflation in 1950 as a result of the outbreak of the Korean War in June 1950 and the PRC's entry into that war in October. Prices had peaked in March 1950 and fell continuously in April and May until the start of the Korean War, after which wholesale prices began to rise again, and by the end of 1950 they exceeded the April peak by about 30 per cent (Eckstein 1977, p. 167). The CCP's achievement in stabilizing prices was largely due to its success in reining in monetary growth.

Table 2.3 presents a comparison of the growth of currency in circulation between the fourth quarter and second quarter of 1949–51. The table shows that the growth in the amount of currency in circulation fell in 1951 and the absolute amount fell in 1952. But even then the amount of currency in circulation was still very large, causing prices of commodities to be denominated in large units. Policymakers decided to lower prices through reducing the enormous amount of currency in circulation by issuing a new renminbi in exchange for the old renminbi. The new renminbi was introduced on 1 March 1955 with the exchange rate set at one new renminbi for 10 000 of the old renminbi (Miyashita 1976, pp. 67–8). The conversion to the new renminbi went smoothly and the new renminbi remains in place today.

Table 2.3 Index of amount of currency in circulation

4th quarter of	2nd quarter of
1949 = 100	1950 = 233.7
1950 = 100	1951 = 161.0
1951 = 100	1952 = 93.3

Source: Hsiao (1971, p. 194).

The Foreign Exchange Regime in Transition

In 1945 Nationalist leaders believed that one of the factors responsible for the hyperinflation at that time was the shortage of commodities caused by World War II. They believed that with the end of the war, the reopening of seaports and resumption of overseas trade would bring in imports, which would check the rise in commodity prices. The GLTN was deliberately overvalued in an attempt to check the rise in prices. But its overvaluation led to excess demand for foreign exchange, which forced the Nationalist government to control the trade in foreign exchange. The Nationalist government introduced a series of measures that authorized only banks appointed by the Central Bank of China to trade in foreign exchange. The use of foreign currencies in domestic transactions was prohibited. All foreign currency export earnings had to be sold to the Central Bank at the rate fixed by the bank and foreign exchange could only be purchased from appointed banks for authorized imports and other payments (Chou 1963, pp. 130–31).

A black market in foreign currencies flourished as a consequence of overvaluation of the GLTN. GLTN overvaluation also discouraged exports, and combined with weak import controls led to a heavy drain on official foreign currency reserves. The foreign exchange regime was obviously untenable and before moving to Taiwan the Nationalist government made several attempts to reform this regime. These attempts centred on making the foreign exchange rate more flexible and tightening foreign trade controls. The Nationalist government's attempt to ban the circulation of foreign currencies in China was no more successful than its attempt to fix the GLTN rate above the free market rate. Hong Kong dollars circulated widely in southern China because of the close proximity to Hong Kong and a serious lack of confidence in the GLTN caused by its continuous depreciation (Chou 1963, pp. 133–49). The extent of the GLTN depreciation can be gauged by the erosion of its value from 7800 GLTN per Hong Kong dollar on 19 August 1947 to 88 505 GLTN per Hong Kong dollar on 17 May 1948, that is, 91 per cent in nine months (Chou 1963, p. 138).

On coming to power, the CCP, like the Nationalists before it, sought to control the circulation of and trade in foreign currencies within China. Here the behaviour of the CCP was similar to the earlier behaviour of many governments of developing and Eastern bloc countries and was motivated by the reasons behind its decision to force conversion of Nationalist currencies to renminbi. Outlawing the use of other currencies allowed the CCP to engage in seigniorage, and monopolizing the trade in foreign exchange gave the CCP a source of tax revenue, by providing it with a share of the margin between the buying and selling price of foreign exchange. Later, control of foreign exchange became part of the CCP's strategy for industrializing China. However, removing foreign currencies from circulation was difficult. Convincing the public to exchange their GLTNs for renminbi with the hyperinflation of GLTN-denominated prices was not too difficult, but it was a different matter convincing the public to give up their foreign currencies for renminbi.

The CCP promulgated its first national policy on foreign exchange in September 1949. The China People's Political Consultative Conference (*Zhongguo renmin xieshang huiyi*) passed the United Programme (*Gongtong gangling*), with clause 39 specifically outlawing the circulation of foreign currencies and restricting the trade in foreign exchange, gold and silver only to national banks (*guojia yinhang*). Meanwhile the North China, East China, Central China and South China People's Governments had appointed the PBC as the nation's sole body for administering foreign exchange (Wu and Song 1991, p. 24). In April 1949, the North China People's Government announced that the PBC had appointed the Bank of China (BOC) in Tianjin as the foreign currency exchange for north China. Twenty other Chinese and foreign banks were appointed members of the north China exchange, with licences to buy and sell foreign exchange on behalf of their customers. Although the authorities did not label them as such, these licensed banks were effectively members of an official inter-bank market in foreign exchange, with the BOC acting as the official administrator of the market. In June 1949 the East China People's Government repeated this move, announcing that the BOC in Shanghai had been appointed as the foreign currency exchange for east China.[8] The establishment of the BOC foreign currency exchanges for central and south China soon followed.

At the start of each trading day, the BOC at each exchange announced an opening price that it had set according to perceived market conditions and after approval by the PBC. The day's opening price was an indicative price only and banks that were designated members of the inter-bank market could settle their trade for the day at freely negotiated prices according to demand and supply (Shang 1999, pp. 337–8). All foreign exchange transactions outside the official markets were prohibited. Altogether there were 53 designated banks in the various inter-bank markets nationwide: 35 local banks, 3 overseas Chinese banks and 15 foreign banks (Wu and Song 1991, p. 26). However, the inter-bank foreign currency markets were short-lived. They were abolished within a year in April 1950, after which prices of foreign currencies were no longer negotiated freely among the designated banks and were instead fixed by the BOC. Although the inter-bank markets were abolished, the designated banks remained. These banks could no longer act as brokers of foreign exchange and free agents in an inter-bank foreign exchange market, and were instead made agents of the BOC, buying and selling foreign exchange on behalf of the BOC at a price set by the BOC.

The BOC has an interesting history. It was organized as a central bank under the Qing government in 1908, but under the Nationalist government it was made a public–private bank specializing in international banking with an international network of branches and correspondent banks (Hsiao 1971, p. 23). In 1949 the BOC's joint public–private ownership was retained, although the bank was placed under the leadership of the PBC as a specialized bank to control and conduct foreign exchange business (Hu and Wu 2000, p. 5). After nationalization of the finance industry, the BOC was appointed as the sole bank allowed to undertake foreign exchange transactions during the period of central planning. The BOC's monopoly over foreign exchange business lasted well into the post-central planning period and although it no longer holds monopolist status, in 2002 the BOC was still the dominant player in China's foreign exchange business.

Public access to and sale of foreign exchange was highly regulated during the Rehabilitation Period. Since foreign exchange transactions were mostly related to foreign trade, the authorities moved to control foreign trade at the same time as they began to control foreign exchange. All foreign exchange derived from exports of goods and services and from the remittances of overseas Chinese, and all foreign currencies held by Chinese citizens, had to be deposited with the BOC as foreign exchange deposits. Certificates with the equivalent value in renminbi were issued against these deposits, which depositors could sell to the designated banks. These certificates, however, could be purchased only for approved foreign exchange transactions: to conduct foreign trade, pay for living expenses of relatives living in another country, travel abroad, and other purposes approved by the provincial authorities (Cheng 1954, pp. 111–12).

Non-state enterprises had to obtain permission from the Foreign Trade Management Bureau (*Waimao guanli ju*) (FTMB) to import and export. After obtaining the relevant Permission to Import Certificate (*jinkou xuke zheng*) from the FTMB, the enterprise could then purchase the necessary foreign currency from an appropriate foreign currency exchange or, after April 1950, directly from one of the designated banks acting as an agent of the BOC. The bank that acted as the broker or directly sold the foreign exchange would also prepare the necessary Customs documentation. To export, an enterprise required a Permission to Export Certificate (*chukou xuke zheng*) and a Foreign Exchange Certificate of Transfer Deposit (FXCTD) (*waihui yicun zheng*) from the FTMB. A designated bank would then examine these documents, and if they were in order the bank would issue a permit that the enterprise would present to Customs, which would enable the goods to be shipped. The enterprise would then present the Customs-stamped copy of the FXCTD to the BOC in exchange for the Certificate of Foreign Exchange Deposit, which the enterprise could hold or sell through the foreign currency exchange. After April 1950 the enterprise had to sell the foreign currency directly to one of the designated banks, acting as an agent for the BOC, in exchange for renminbi. The enterprise would receive for the sale a Certificate of Foreign Exchange Settlement (*jiehui zhengmingshu*), which the enterprise had to present to the FTMB as proof that it had successfully executed its Permission to Export Certificate (Shang 1999, p. 489). The certificates for permission to import and export and foreign trade permits for designated banks were abolished and replaced by import and export Customs report forms when central planning came into operation (Shang 1999, p. 494; Wu and Song 1991, pp. 27–8).

As for the administration of foreign exchange in the state sector, in June 1950 the PBC entered into a contract with the Ministry of Foreign Trade allowing the latter's specialized foreign trading companies (SFCs) (*waimao zhuanye gongsi*) to retain a proportion of the foreign exchange earned from exports. These trading companies were required to deposit the retained foreign exchange in special foreign exchange accounts at the BOC, which the SFCs could use to finance imports. This arrangement did not last long. The foreign exchange retention contract was abolished after March 1951 (Shang 1999, p. 489) in line with the authorities' decision to have greater centralization of foreign trade and foreign exchange administration.

According to a promulgation issued on 6 October 1950 by the Government Administration Council (GAC), then the highest executive of the country, the CFEA was to be the sole official body responsible for the allocation of foreign exchange. The CFEA would allocate foreign exchange for imports to state-managed and private enterprises, and military and political organs, only after vetting the accompanying import plans. The CFEA was also responsible for vetting and making decisions on requests for foreign exchange quotas for non-imports. The CFEA adopted several general principles regarding the allocation of foreign exchange. First, the centre should take precedence over the local, and public should precede private. Second, approval would not be given to import a commodity that China also produced and where supply met existing demand. Third, approval would not be given where excess demand in one region could be met with excess supply in another. Finally, approval would not be given to import where there were substitutes available inside China (Shang 1999, pp. 488–9).

Foreign exchange administration before the First Five-Year Plan (FFYP) (1953–57) was increasingly centralized, but its design was kept simple. However, the system was made progressively complex as the CCP went about transforming China's economy into a socialist centrally planned economy. Centralizing control over the distribution of foreign exchange compounded the problems that foreign banks experienced with increasing state control over domestic and international trade, and made it difficult for them to continue trading in China after 1949. Conditions worsened for foreign banks during the Korean War (1950–53). The Chinese government froze the assets of US financial institutions, such as those of American Express and Chase, and placed their operations under state supervision in retaliation for the US government's freezing of financial and other assets owned by China or its nationals. During the first half of the twentieth century, foreign banks had a large presence in mainland China. Shanghai was the financial centre for the Far East, with more than 200 branches of foreign banks. At that time the financial market in Hong Kong was only just beginning to develop. Foreign banks in China for the most part enjoyed enormous freedom in their conduct of foreign exchange business and were able to capture a significant market share. For example, in 1948 foreign banks accounted for 53.7 per cent of the total value of foreign exchange business in Tianjin, joint foreign–local banks accounted for 36.4 per cent and local banks accounted for the remaining 9.9 per cent (Wu and Song 1991, pp. 23–4). After 1949 foreign banks steadily lost market share and soon became only agents for the BOC in conducting foreign exchange business. With the withdrawal of most foreign banks from China in the 1950s, when Deng Xiaoping's economic reform was begun in 1978 only four foreign banks – the Hong Kong & Shanghai Bank, Standard Chartered Bank, Bank of East Asia and Overseas Chinese Banking Corporation – had a presence in Shanghai; no joint-foreign bank remained (Yi 1996, pp. 37–8). Large numbers of foreign banks have commenced business in Shanghai with economic reform, but their share of foreign exchange business remains small.

Setting the Renminbi Exchange Rate during the Rehabilitation Period

Centralized state control and distribution of foreign exchange meant that the authorities had to fix the price at which they were prepared to buy and sell foreign exchange, instead of the market signalling the price of foreign exchange. Official renminbi exchange rates against foreign currencies were first announced in Tianjin on 18 January 1948. Later, authorities in Shanghai and Guangzhou under the management of the central authorities used the Tianjin renminbi–US dollar rate as a reference rate to set the official renminbi rate in their own city after taking into account the difference in commodity prices in the three cities. The result was that the lowest price for the renminbi (thus the highest price for the US dollar) was in Tianjin because it had the highest inflation rate. Guangzhou had the highest renminbi price, and the price in Shanghai was in between. A little over two years later on 8 July 1950, the task of setting a uniform renminbi exchange rate was centralized, with the PBC given the responsibility for announcing the renminbi rate for the whole country (Shang 1999, p. 491). The renminbi rate until 1952 was tied to the US dollar. But from 1952 onwards the renminbi rate was tied to the British pound and the renminbi–pound rate was fixed at the rate of (new) RMB6.893 to the pound for 15 years until the British government devalued the pound by 14.3 per cent in November 1967 (Shang 1999, p. 495). The Chinese government's decision to switch from pegging the renminbi with the US dollar to pegging it with the pound had to do with the British government's recognition of the CCP government and its willingness to trade with China, unlike the US government.

Official renminbi exchange rates against the US dollar, British pound and Hong Kong dollar from 1949 to 1978 are listed in Table 2.4. The massive devaluation of the renminbi in 1950 was a consequence of inflation brought about by the Korean War. Tight fiscal and monetary policies soon brought inflation under control and duly stabilized the renminbi rate in 1951. The rate was changed later by a factor of 10 000 in 1955 following the replacement of the old renminbi with the new renminbi at the conversion rate of 1:10 000. Until the Bretton Woods system of fixed exchange rates collapsed in 1972, the exchange rates between the world's major currencies were fixed but adjustable. It is therefore not surprising that China's exchange rate remained largely stable until 1972. However, as discussed later in this chapter, the Bretton Woods system was only partly responsible for China's stable exchange rate.

In the first three years of the PRC, known as the Rehabilitation Period, the renminbi exchange rate against Western currencies, including the Hong Kong dollar and yen, was set following the policy of 'encouraging exports but restricting imports' and 'looking after overseas Chinese' (*jiang chu, xian ru*;

zhaogu huaqiao) (Shang 1999, p. 491).[9] To achieve these two objectives, the exchange rate was set according to the principle of domestic and foreign purchasing power parity (*duinei duiwai goumaili*) (Wu and Chen 1992, pp. 154–5).

Table 2.4 Value of old renminbi per 1 unit of foreign currency (1949–54) and value of new renminbi per 100 units of foreign currency (1 March 1955–78) (official rates)

Year	US$	Br.£	HK$	Year	US$	Br.£	HK$
1949*	618.00			1964	246.18	689.30	42.90
1950*	42 000.00	98 708.00	6460.00	1965	246.18	689.30	42.90
1951	22 380.00	62 660.00	3900.00	1966	246.18	689.30	42.90
1952	26 170.00	68 930.00	4290.00	1967	246.18	690.80	40.40
1953	26 170.00	68 930.00	4290.00	1968	246.18	590.80	40.40
1954	26 170.00	68 930.00	4290.00	1969	246.18	590.80	40.40
1955	246.18	689.30	42.90	1970	246.18	590.80	40.40
1956	246.18	689.30	42.90	1971	226.73	590.80	40.40
1957	246.18	689.30	42.90	1972	224.01	524.63	38.99
1958	246.18	689.30	42.90	1973	201.02	468.39	39.47
1959	246.18	689.30	42.90	1974	183.97	431.50	37.67
1960	246.18	689.30	42.90	1975	196.63	396.91	38.65
1961	246.18	689.30	42.90	1976	188.03	319.80	39.33
1962	246.18	689.30	42.90	1977	173.00	328.13	37.85
1963	246.18	689.30	42.90	1978	157.71	319.27	30.66

Note: *10 April 1949, 11 March 1950. In 1955 the new RMB replaced the old RMB.

Sources: Cheng (1954, p. 120); Wu and Chen (1992, pp. 161–2); Wu and Song (1991, p. 26).

According to Wu and Chen, the first objective was to fix the exchange rate at a level that would provide a profit rate of 5 to 15 per cent on 75 to 80 per cent of the products exported by the remaining private enterprises. The other objective was to guarantee the purchasing power of the foreign remittances received by relatives of overseas Chinese living in China[10] when converted into renminbi. To help achieve the first objective, China's economic planners calculated what they referred to as theoretical relative export price (*chukou lilun bijia*) and theoretical relative import price (*jinkou lilun bijia*) for each of the major export and import commodities that together comprised more than 70 per cent of total foreign trade.[11] Each of these prices was calculated by dividing the estimated domestic cost of producing each commodity by the equivalent US dollar export or import price. The economic planners then weighted each theoretical export or import price so calculated by each commodity share in total exports and imports and summed them to derive two implicit renminbi–US dollar exchange rates – one for exports and one for imports.

To help achieve the second objective, Chinese economic planners divided the domestic cost of a basket of goods deemed to be daily necessities for a family of five in Fujian and Guangdong with the US dollar cost of the same basket of goods in Hong Kong to derive an implicit renminbi exchange rate. This implicit exchange rate when used to convert US dollars to renminbi theoretically could guarantee the purchasing power of foreign exchange remittances received by relatives of overseas Chinese living in China.

Chinese economic planners first set the official renminbi–US dollar exchange rate on the basis of the implicit renminbi rates described earlier. The planners would then use the official renminbi–US dollar rate and the official cross-rates between the Western currencies rates (including the Hong Kong dollar and yen) to set the official renminbi exchange rates against other Western currencies. All the rates have the common feature of being based on a simple form of purchasing power parity calculations, where the renminbi exchange rate linked the renminbi cost of a basket of domestic goods to the foreign currency cost of a similar basket of foreign goods. Although Wu and Chen did not point it out, to ensure that enterprises could make a minimum rate of return on exports, the renminbi exchange rate was set in a way that explicitly ensured sufficient incentives were provided to private enterprises to earn foreign exchange. Taking into account the domestic purchasing power of foreign exchange remittances received by relatives of overseas Chinese when setting the renminbi exchange rate was intended to ensure that an unfavourable exchange rate did not discourage overseas Chinese from sending foreign exchange remittances to their relatives in China. The official renminbi rate was technically a reference rate. To make it even more attractive for overseas Chinese to send remittances to China, special offers were also made to convert these funds to renminbi at preferential rates. One such offer was to convert these remittances at Tianjin's price, the highest for foreign exchange, regardless of where in China the remittances were converted into renminbi (Shang 1999, p. 491).

China's economic planners during the Rehabilitation Period were therefore conscious of the impact of the exchange rate both on domestic prices and on the international competitiveness of domestic enterprises, and planners accounted for these factors when setting the official renminbi exchange rate. The market was still operating and there were still large segments of private industry. Foreign trade was still conducted mainly by non-state enterprises. The economic planners were also aware of the incentive effects of the exchange rate on overseas Chinese remittances from abroad. This was in contrast with the way planners set the renminbi rate during what the CCP called the socialist transformation and construction period (*shehuizhuyi gaizao jianshe shiqi*), which lasted from 1953 until 1978. In the socialist transformation and construction period there was no longer private enterprise of any significance, foreign trade was completely monopolized by the state and central planning had replaced the market. Prices therefore no longer performed the primary role of directing resources as in a market economy, but served mainly as an instrument of accounting. Moreover, the politics of 'class struggle' featured prominently in the latter period and overseas Chinese became targets for political attacks rather than targets for preferential treatment. The link between foreign and domestic prices was therefore broken and the exchange rate could be set without the need to consider its effect on incentives to exporters or overseas Chinese remitting funds to China.

But even before 1953, increasing restrictions imposed by the authorities on the use of foreign exchange remittances had undermined the authorities' own efforts to attract overseas Chinese remittances with preferential exchange rates. In their efforts to raise foreign exchange, the Chinese authorities increasingly had to contend with US restrictions on economic exchanges with China. In December 1950, following the US government's freeze on Chinese funds deposited in the US, restrictions were imposed on overseas Chinese remittances from the US to China (Shang 1999, p. 492). The amount of remittances from overseas Chinese in 1951 was only 60 per cent of the US$100 million remitted in 1950 and the amount in 1952 was only about 67 per cent of the amount remitted in 1951.[12] Moreover, most of the remittances sent in 1952 were payments made by denounced landlords and other victims of the Five-Anti (*Wufan*) campaign (Cheng 1954, p. 125).

Although the authorities set the official renminbi exchange rate according to some purchasing power parity principle, the rate was often set above the market clearing rate. The resulting undervaluation of foreign exchange and the state's monopoly over foreign exchange inevitably gave rise to a black market in foreign exchange. Because of concerns over inflation, economic planners preferred a stable exchange rate to one that was adjusted according to market conditions, causing at times a significant divergence between the official and black market rates. During the early years of the PRC, the extent of overvaluation of the official renminbi rate sometimes became intolerably large and had to be reduced by devaluation when exports and overseas Chinese remittances became seriously affected (Cheng 1954, p. 122). The gap between the official and the black market rate, however, gradually diminished as the CCP progressively tightened its economic and political control over the nation. Moreover, with the imposition of central planning, the economic authorities were no longer concerned with the possible disincentive effects on foreign trade of an overvalued renminbi against the currencies of China's trading partners.

The renminbi rates of exchange with currencies of the Soviet bloc were not determined using the purchasing power parity principle. [13] This is understandable given that economies in the Soviet bloc (Union of Soviet Socialist Republics – USSR) were centrally planned and their prices were not market prices. Instead, the renminbi–rouble rate was determined through bilateral negotiations. Until 1957 there were two rates: one for trade and another for non-trade transactions. Renminbi rates against currencies of Eastern Europe and Outer Mongolia were cross-rates, calculated from the renminbi–rouble rate and the rates of the Eastern European and Outer Mongolia currencies against the rouble. These currencies were not convertible to hard currencies and payments in a given currency could only be used to purchase goods from, or settle payments with, the country that issued that currency. From 1970, PRC–USSR trade was conducted in Swiss francs. This practice was later extended to PRC trade with Eastern Europe and this continued until 1978 when the PRC, the USSR and governments of Eastern Europe agreed to liberalize the choice of foreign currency for trade and non-trade transactions.

CENTRAL PLANNING AND FOREIGN EXCHANGE

How foreign exchange is distributed and priced in an economy is decided first and foremost by the overarching economic strategy of the authorities running the economy. After rehabilitating China's war-torn economy, the CCP faced several policy choices in designing its long-term national economic strategy. First was the desired rate of economic growth. Second, financing the desired rate of economic growth: relying solely on domestic finance or partially relying on foreign finance. Third, the choice of system for allocating resources: plan or market, or something in between the two systems. Fourth, the choice of the pattern of investment: invest more on capital or on consumption goods, and pursue a strategy of inward-looking import substitution or outward-looking export promotion. Cutting across these four choices was the fundamental choice between current and future consumption.

China's economic development before the end of the 1970s was shaped partly by the ethos of Communist ideology and partly as a pragmatic response to necessity, brought by the US-instigated economic embargo on China at the outbreak of the Korean War and the break in relations with the Soviet Union in 1960. [14] The constant external threat to its rule in the early years of the PRC made the CCP eager to achieve industrialization as rapidly as possible. The CCP was especially eager to invest in heavy industry, recognized as the backbone of any credible defence industry. In 1952 China's industrial output was less than half of agricultural output (GTJ 1987, p. 43). Most of China's heavy industry had been located in Manchuria and when World War II ended Soviet troops briefly occupied Manchuria and systematically dismantled and transported more than half of the serviceable capital stock back to the Soviet Union (Riskin 1987, p. 33). Compared to the Soviet Union on the eve of its FFYP, in 1952 China's per capita railroad mileage was less than 10 per cent of the Soviet mileage and its per capita production of electric power and steel was less than half of the Soviet level (Chen and Galenson 1969, p. 35).[15] The CCP leadership recognized that China had to industrialize rapidly but it chose to finance the industrialization entirely from domestic sources. This strategy required a high savings rate, which forced sacrificing current consumption for the sake of investment. The consumption of urban residents was kept low through state-mandated low wages and rural consumption was repressed by taxing through the mechanism of the 'price scissors'[16] – fixing agricultural prices below world levels to transfer agricultural surplus to industry to promote industrialization. Its record on food consumption best sums up China's heavy commitment to saving and investment in the pre-reform period: China is the only country in the modern era that registered no increase in food consumption per capita, despite doubling its per capita income over a 20-year period (Lardy 1983, p. 159).

China's leaders, especially Mao Zedong, believed that market incentives would not be effective in generating the level of savings and human effort necessary to generate the high rate of investment needed to enable rapid industrialization. They felt that reliance on market incentives would increase production of consumer goods, thus reducing not only savings and the rate of investment but also, by consequence, the rate of economic growth. Imbued with Marxist philosophy and influenced by developments in the Soviet Union, they saw that market incentives had to be dispensed with. Instead, the main mechanism to allocate physical and human resources would be central planning backed up with moral reinforcement through rigorous teachings of socialist ideology and values. Agriculture was collectivized and a spirit of selflessness and nationalistic fervour was promoted to counter the disincentive effects of both the 'price scissors' in agriculture and low urban wages. Maximum resources were mobilized for industrialization while attempting to ensure that the basic needs of the population were satisfied.

The national leadership wanted China to industrialize quickly. However, particular impediments to this course were China's relations with the US and the Soviet Union at that time of the Cold War. The US pressured the

Coordinating Committee (Cocom) of the Western bloc, established in November 1949 to oversee strategic controls on Western trade with the Soviet bloc, to impose stringent prohibitions on trade with China (Riskin 1987, p. 47). The effects of these prohibitions can be gauged from data presented in Table 2.5. China's economic development was financed largely through domestic sources. Borrowing abroad and using foreign direct investment (FDI) were out of the question. China had zero foreign debt between 1968 and 1980 after repaying earlier loans to the Soviet Union (Hu and Wu 2000, p. 313). Nor could China implement export promotion, the strategy pursued so successfully by the newly industrialized countries (NICs) of East Asia. Maoist ideology was an important domestic preventive factor, but external circumstances also eliminated this option. The unfriendly international environment effectively dictated that China must rely on a self-reliant, import-substitution strategy.

This strategy is reflected in the data in Table 2.5 and illustrated clearly in Figure 2.1. As Figure 2.1 shows, from 1957 until the early 1970s, as a percentage of gross domestic product (GDP), imports, exports and thus foreign trade fell more or less continuously. During this period, outside financing was largely unavailable to China and with no foreign investment the country had to run a foreign trade surplus. In 1971 the US government ended the economic embargo it had enforced since 1950 (Roy 1998, p. 29). Ending the embargo foreshadowed the forthcoming rapprochement between China and the US, and the end of China's economic isolation. China's foreign trade took off in 1973 after relations with the US were normalized officially through the joint Shanghai Communiqué a year earlier. In 1973 China's foreign trade increased by two-thirds compared to its trade performance in the previous year. It declined slightly in 1976 but accelerated again in 1978 with the beginning of Deng's economic reform (Table 2.5).

Before 1978, China still required imports to industrialize despite its import-substitution strategy. No nation is endowed with, or can produce, all that it requires to sustain its economy. As a result of its heavy emphasis on heavy industry under central planning, China's economy intensified demands for heavy machinery and equipment, so that raw materials such as steel and other commodities were major import items. Imports of capital goods were also important as a major avenue through which China obtained advanced technology from abroad. In the 1950s imports of capital goods accounted for 40 per cent of the equipment component of investment. Eckstein (1977, p. 235) calculated that had China cut itself off completely from imports between 1953 and 1957, annual economic growth would have fallen from 6.5 per cent to between 3 and 5 per cent. China was forced to import even food. During the Great Leap Forward (1958–60) China's attempt at self-sufficiency in food was thwarted by ill-conceived economic policies that created a massive reduction in agricultural output, which forced China to import huge quantities of grain to alleviate a serious famine. From Table 2.5 we see that, despite the rhetoric of self-reliance, the value of imports actually increased during the Great Leap Forward compared to the previous eight years.

Inevitably, these imports had to be paid for with foreign exchange, which had to be earned through exports. This was an onerous task given that the unfriendly international environment at that time severely weakened China's export prospects and China faced a proverbial shortage of foreign exchange. At the end of 1950, China's foreign reserves were a relatively tiny US$199.8 million (Liu et al. 1997, p. 1). This shortage of foreign exchange had profound consequences for foreign exchange policy in China. Its deep psychological impact on the nation's leaders planted a legacy of a fear of foreign exchange shortage. Until WTO membership led to a huge influx of FDI flows in China, China's post-Mao leaders harboured this fear, even though China had access to funds through global financial markets, and it was a factor behind China's past somewhat mercantilist attitude towards international trade.

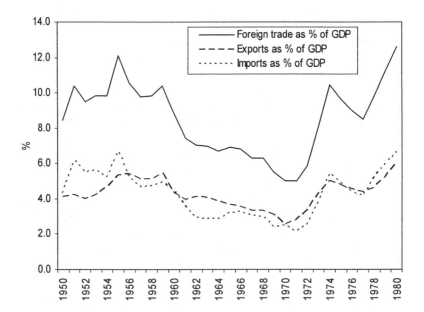

Figure 2.1 Significance of foreign trade (1950–80)

Table 2.5 *Foreign trade and GDP (1950–80)*

Year	Foreign trade (100 mil US$)	Foreign trade (100 mil RMB)	Imports (100 mil RMB)	GDP (100 mil RMB)	Foreign trade as % of GDP	Imports as % of GDP	Exports as % of GDP
1950	11.3	41.5	21.3	491.1	8.5	4.1	4.3
1951	19.6	59.5	35.3	572.9	10.4	4.2	6.2
1952	19.4	64.6	37.5	679.0	9.5	4.0	5.5
1953	23.7	80.9	46.1	824.0	9.8	4.2	5.6
1954	24.3	84.7	44.7	859.0	9.9	4.7	5.2
1955	31.5	109.8	61.1	910.0	12.1	5.4	6.7
1956	32.1	108.7	53.0	1028.0	10.6	5.4	5.2
1957	31.0	104.5	50.0	1068.0	9.8	5.1	4.7
1958	38.7	128.7	61.7	1307.0	9.8	5.1	4.7
1959	43.8	149.3	71.2	1439.0	10.4	5.4	4.9
1960	38.1	128.4	65.1	1457.0	8.8	4.3	4.5
1961	29.4	90.8	43.0	1220.0	7.4	3.9	3.5
1962	26.6	80.9	33.8	1149.3	7.0	4.1	2.9
1963	29.1	85.7	35.7	1233.3	6.9	4.1	2.9
1964	34.6	97.5	42.1	1454.0	6.7	3.8	2.9
1965	42.5	118.4	55.3	1716.1	6.9	3.7	3.2
1966	46.1	127.1	61.1	1868.0	6.8	3.5	3.3
1967	41.6	112.2	53.4	1773.9	6.3	3.3	3.0
1968	40.4	108.5	50.9	1723.1	6.3	3.3	3.0
1969	40.3	106.9	47.1	1937.9	5.5	3.1	2.4
1970	45.9	112.9	56.1	2252.7	5.0	2.5	2.5
1971	48.4	120.9	52.4	2426.4	5.0	2.8	2.2
1972	63.0	146.9	64.0	2518.1	5.8	3.3	2.5
1973	109.8	220.5	103.6	2720.9	8.1	4.3	3.8
1974	145.7	292.3	152.9	2789.9	10.5	5.0	5.5

47

Table 2.5 (continued)

Year	Foreign trade (100 mil US$)	Foreign trade (100 mil RMB)	Imports (100 mil RMB)	GDP (100 mil RMB)	Foreign trade as % of GDP	Imports as % of GDP	Exports as % of GDP
1975	147.5	290.4	147.4	2997.3	9.7	4.8	4.9
1976	134.4	264.1	129.3	2943.7	9.0	4.6	4.4
1977	148.0	272.5	132.8	3201.9	8.5	4.4	4.1
1978	206.4	355.0	187.4	3624.1	9.8	4.6	5.2
1979	293.3	454.6	242.9	4038.2	11.3	5.2	6.0
1980	378.2	563.8	291.4	4517.8	12.6	6.0	6.6

Source: Authors' calculations using data from GTJ (1987, pp. 50, 591) and DNEA (1997, p. 27).

Economic Planning and Foreign Exchange: a Brief Theoretical Exposition

The need to earn foreign exchange to pay for imports to help fuel industrialization made the foreign exchange plan an important component of the central economic plan. Investment and consumption determine final output. Production of final output requires intermediate inputs, which affects production. Thus the investment, production and consumption sub-plans in the central plan determined the quantity of foreign imports of various commodities required to achieve the targets in these plans. An estimate of how much foreign exchange had to be earned to pay for these imports was derived. Next, estimates of various commodities that had to be exported to obtain the required foreign exchange to pay for the imports in the plan were calculated. These export commodities had to be produced and might require imported intermediate inputs. Formulating the various production, investment, consumption and foreign trade plans was therefore a very complex task. The plans had to undergo several iterations before all the plans could become consistent with each other. As a prelude to understanding how foreign exchange was administered under central planning, let us first consider in greater detail how the central economic plan was formulated and implemented.

The CCP Central Committee decided broad economic policy guidelines that formed the parameters of the central plan. These guidelines were then transmitted to the State Council, the highest organ of state power in China. The State Council translated these broad policy guidelines into specific economic targets and policies, with inputs from particular ministries or commissions under the overall direction of the State Planning Commission (SPC). The SPC drew up long-term plans (10 to 20 years), medium-term plans (five years) and annual plans based on the 'two top-down and one bottom-up' (*liang xia yi shang*) principle. The SPC translated the State Council's economic growth targets into specific investment, saving and production targets after research and consultation with sub-national governments, ministries and basic-level units. Sub-national and ministry-level planning agencies coordinated to draw up individual sub-national and ministry plans based on production and investment plans and other targets negotiated at the enterprise level. These plans were submitted to the SPC, aggregated, and reconciled to ensure consistency across sub-national regions and ministries before release. Once consistency in the plans was achieved, provinces and ministries were called together for a consultative meeting to finalize the plan. After finalization, the plan was submitted to the State Council for discussion and approval, before being adopted formally by China's parliament, the National People's Congress (NPC).

Economic plans were formulated according to the Soviet materials balance approach. Export and import plans must be consistent with consumption and investment plans. For a simple illustration, assume that a hypothetical planned economy has only two goods, an export good and an import good. These are consumption goods as well as investment goods and they are also used as intermediate inputs to produce one another. In order that the annual economic plan for our hypothetical planned economy is consistent, the following two conditions must hold:

1. $Y - X = CX + IX$, that is:

    Output of export good (Y) minus exports of that good (X) equals consumption of that good (CX) and the use of that good in investment and production (IX).

2. $Q + M = CM + IM$, that is:

    Output of import good (Q) plus imports of that good (M) equals consumption of that good (CM) and the use of that good in investment and production (IM).

Since planning is based on the materials balance approach, all the variables, are measured in quantities. Any short-run gap between foreign exchange earnings and foreign cost of imports can be covered by foreign exchange reserves. But in the long run, the value of foreign exchange earned from X must be sufficient to pay for M.

For a more realistic illustration let us look at a hypothetical economy with 'g' number of industries producing 'g' number of commodities. As well as 'g' number of domestic commodities there are 'g' number of imported commodities. Figure 2.2 shows the flow of commodities in this hypothetical planned economy to various industries as intermediate inputs and for capital formation (investment), to households and exports. One industry produces only one commodity. Knowing the existing capital stock and amount of labour that are available in the economy, economic planners can specify the production target for each commodity (Q). The domestic (A) and imported inputs (A^*) required to produce the outputs Q are then calculated. Next planners calculate the quantities of domestic (B) and imported (B^*) commodities required for the amount of capital formation that they have planned for each industry (R). No labour and capital are used directly in capital formation. Labour and capital are embedded in the commodities that each industry obtains in the plan for capital formation.

Necessary imports for consumption (C^*), such as food, are calculated next. The total foreign cost of imports is obtained by multiplying the physical quantities of imports by their foreign prices. Given foreign prices of exports and the value of foreign exchange that has to be raised to pay for imports, the physical quantities of exports of different commodities that can pay for these imports (D) are then calculated. Household consumption of the various domestic commodities is calculated as a residual since $A + B + C + D$ must equal the production of domestic commodities.

Economic planners had to make a basic choice only over investment (R) or consumption (C, C^*). Domestic and imported commodities are not substitutes for each other. Available productive capacity and technology predetermine domestic and imported intermediate demands, and exports have to pay for imports. There is no labour mobility; labour is allocated by the plan. Capital is fixed for each industry and industries do not choose various inputs to minimize cost. Commodity flows are mechanistic, driven by economic planners' preferences and available technology. Once planners have chosen levels of investment and consumption, available technology determines commodity flows, without enterprises and consumers making any conscious economic decisions.

Intermediate demands		Final demands			
Domestic industries (current production)		Domestic industries (capital formation)	Household consumption	Exports	
Domestic commodities	$A\ (g \times g)$	$B\ (g \times g)$	$C\ (g \times 1)$	$D\ (g \times 1)$	Row sums = total use of domestic commodities
Imports	$A^*\ (g \times g)$	$B^*\ (g \times g)$	$C^*\ (g \times 1)$	0	Row sums = total imports
Labour			0	0	
Capital			0		
	$Q\ (1 \times g)$ Outputs of industries	$R\ (1 \times g)$ Investment by industry			

Figure 2.2 Economic planning and commodity flows

Exports are the difference between production and home consumption and investment. Governments in market economies can encourage exports by increasing domestic prices faced by consumers and producers. They can, for example, increase domestic prices to both consumers and producers through, say, an export subsidy or devaluation of the home currency; or increase prices paid by consumers with a consumption tax; or increase prices to producers with a production subsidy. In China's centrally planned economy, as in a market economy, production had to increase and/or domestic consumption fall for exports to increase. But, as pointed out earlier, factor immobility meant that production in each industry was predetermined by given technology and, instead of varying prices, China's economic planners mandated an export plan, which was derived sequentially within the central plan.

Prices play no role in determining the quantity of how much of each good is produced in a centrally planned economy. Prices do not function as signals to influence production. The plan dictates production. Although prices do not affect the supply of goods, they partially determine the demand for goods by households. Economic planners determine the wages of workers but planners cannot determine workers' exact demands for various goods. It is difficult even in an economy with only two goods to plan in detail the demand of every consumer; detailed consumer planning in an economy with millions of consumers and tens of thousands of goods is impossible. Ration tickets for each type of good could be given to each worker in lieu of wages but it would be difficult for households to save with ration tickets. How could the system cope with the introduction of new goods or the obsolescence of outdated goods? What about rationing the number of bus trips? Consumers would want to trade ration tickets of one good for another to satisfy their consumption preferences. The transaction costs of consumption and saving would be prohibitive.

The activity of economic planners in our hypothetical economy is not spelt out explicitly. In practice, their work demands real resources. Economic planners and other government workers sit in real offices, use office equipment and have to be paid. Their work is financed with taxes levied on enterprises. In a simple economy with two goods and two enterprises, taxes can be paid in kind. This is clearly not possible in a real economy with tens if not hundreds of thousands of enterprises. Thus, economic planning in a real economy with a large number of consumers and enterprises cannot do without money. Money serves as a store of value and medium of exchange, and with the use of money there are prices.

Planners of China's planned economy, like their counterparts in the economies of former Communist Eastern Europe, determined consumer demand through planned quantities and prices. Urban households were issued with ration tickets for essential consumer items like meat, grain, edible oils and cotton, which they had to use together with money to purchase these items. Although mostly unsuccessful, economic planners endeavoured to ensure that the quantity of a much-sought-after good, demanded as implied by the number of ration tickets pertaining to that good, was equal to or less than the planned supply of that good. Planners adjusted relative prices to influence consumer demand to equilibrate desired demand with planned supply for each good. Rationing was used to distribute consumer goods to guarantee the minimum basic needs of urban households, by making basic consumption independent of household income. The supplementary use of prices was to allow a limited role for consumer choice.

The plan's emphasis on heavy industry and its implicit tax on agriculture through the 'price scissors' were instrumental in making demand for consumer goods usually exceed supply. China's economic planners were influenced strongly by an aversion to open inflation and their desire to protect poor households, and so in practice they seldom adjusted consumer prices to equilibrate demand with supply. Instead, they set domestic prices according to their prevailing preferences for accommodating open inflation and forced savings. The planners used pricing of consumer goods to absorb money incomes paid to workers and agricultural producers. Low average prices did not always enable more goods to be consumed; excess demand could result, forcing a higher level of savings (Liew and Kawaguchi 1995).

Although China's economy was officially centrally planned, not all production in China came under the umbrella of the central plan and not all production was carried out in the state sector. The central plan covered only key commodities and the output of mostly state-owned enterprises. Just before Deng Xiaoping introduced his economic reforms in 1977–78, the central plan covered only 50–55 per cent of China's industrial output. The plan distributed almost all output of enterprises controlled by the centre, but less than 20 per cent of the output of rural collective enterprises (Wong 1987, p. 99). However, since all key inputs were controlled by the central plan, the share of commodities distributed according to the central plan indicated less than the actual extent of control that the state exercised over the national economy.

Commodities not distributed according to the central plan were allocated by provincial plans or by local agreements that had to be approved by the centre. Prices of these commodities were controlled, but they were more flexible than prices of commodities allocated by the central plan (Howe 1978, p. 53). Most agricultural production was directed by the plan, but depended very much on exogenous factors like the weather. In addition, agriculture was undertaken in non-state rural collectives and the state procured agricultural commodities from the collectives using cash payments. These purchases from non-state rural producers made agricultural output dependent on the procurement price, which was not the case for industrial output. Agricultural production shortfalls were met with accumulated stocks where possible and often with imports.

Hence monetary flows in China's planned economy consisted of passive and active money flows. Passive monetary flows are money flows that automatically accompany physical flows of goods designated in the plan. These money flows were transfers between bank accounts of state-owned enterprises and other state units. Active money flows were in the form of cash that flowed between the state and non-state sectors. Wages paid by state-owned enterprises or state bureaucracies to their workers were active money flows; so too were state payments to agricultural collectives for agricultural products. It is important to note that although these flows were active money flows, their incentive effects were limited by state control over most aspects of economic activity, especially the availability of consumer goods as designated in the central economic plan.

Since consumer prices were determined by planners' choice of preferences between inflation and forced saving, and since prices of intermediate and investment goods were part of passive money flows, the role of prices in distribution was very limited. The foreign exchange rate did not serve as a link between foreign and domestic prices. The state's economic planning came between domestic and foreign prices to eliminate the influence of the latter on the former. Thus, a change in foreign prices did not translate automatically into a change in domestic prices for consumers and users of imports.

China's Foreign Trade Plan

The Ministry of Foreign Trade (MOFT) (*Waimaobu*), which became the Ministry of Foreign Economic Relations and Trade (MOFERT) (*Duiwai jingji maoyibu*)[17] in 1982, was responsible for achieving the targets in the foreign trade plan drawn up by the SPC. Foreign trade was carried out through specialized foreign trade corporations (FTCs) (*waimao zhuanye zonggongsi*) and their branches, which were all under the control and direction of the MOFT.[18] There were 12 FTCs in 1978 (World Bank 1994, p. 24), but their number varied over time. Howe (1978, p. 142) counted nine FTCs in the 1970s, each specializing in a group of commodities: cereals, oils and foodstuffs; chemical products; light industrial products; machinery; metals and minerals; native products and animal by-products; textiles; the Export Packaging Corporation; and the Technical Import Corporation, responsible for importing complete plants. The FTCs had no choice in the type of commodities they exported or imported; they had to limit their trade to commodities that the responsible ministry had assigned to them according to their specialization. Trade volumes were all predetermined in the plan, with FTCs given little discretion. FTCs could not set export procurement prices or domestic prices of imports. The renminbi prices paid to enterprises for exports or renminbi prices charged to users and consumers of imports were determined in the mandatory export or import plans. Thus, volumes of exports and imports were determined only by what economic planners were willing to sell and buy at given world prices. Planners did not make a link between the procurement prices in the export plan that FTCs had to pay to domestic producers of export commodities and the foreign prices that FTCs received for exports with an appropriate exchange rate. The exchange rate was set largely independently of the export procurement prices paid to domestic producers. It was overvalued so that renminbi prices received by FTCs through converting foreign export prices using the exchange rate were less than domestic procurement prices and created a loss for FTCs in their exporting. Details of the overvaluation of the renminbi appear in Table 2.6, which displays the domestic currency cost of earning US$1 of exports and the official exchange rate for selected years. Losses per US$1 of exports are calculated by subtracting the exchange rate from the domestic currency cost of exports.

Table 2.6 Domestic currency losses per US$1 of exports (selected years)

	Domestic currency cost of earning US$1 of exports	RMB–US$ rate	Domestic currency losses per US$1 exports
Year*			
1952	3.08	2.26 (2.62)	0.82 (0.46)
1962	6.65	2.46	4.19
1963	>5.0	2.46	>2.54
1971	5.00	2.46 (2.27)	2.54 (2.73)
1975	3.00	1.85 (1.97)	1.15 (1.03)
1978	2.50	1.68 (1.58)	0.82 (0.92)
1979	2.40	1.55	0.85

Note: 1952 data are adjusted to account for converting old RMB to new RMB in 1955 to make the numbers of different years comparable. Numbers in brackets are based on exchange rates shown in Table 2.4.

Sources: Lardy (1992, p. 25) and Table 2.4.

Targets in foreign trade plans were not always met. Among many reasons were the failure of enterprises to meet their production quotas and the inability of planners to cut down actual consumption. In these circumstances FTCs had to seek export supplies from sources outside the central plan, creating additional active money flows and increasing the losses incurred by FTCs. Unlike prices paid to in-plan suppliers of export commodities, prices paid to out-of-plan suppliers had a direct impact on the quantity of commodities supplied and the prices of these out-of-plan suppliers were often higher than the procurement prices paid to state enterprises. In some instances planners offered highly desired industrial goods in exchange.

Central planning was never perfect. Administrative coordination is far less efficient than the market at resource allocation and shortages were common. Central planning also gave rise to the 'ratchet effect', where planners imposed even higher targets when enterprises exceeded production or export targets, providing enterprises with an incentive to disguise their true production capacity to seek lower production or export targets.

Prices played only a minor role in allocating resources. Enterprises could not choose a combination of inputs to minimize costs of production. Inputs were specified by the plan. Financial flows within the state sector had no real effect in the economy. Only subsidies for imported commodities sold to the non-state sector involved a net outflow of active money from the state sector and could have real effects. Similarly, prices paid to FTCs for exports were set low, but this did not matter even if procurement prices paid to state-owned enterprises (SOEs) for the export goods were higher. What mattered was if the procurement prices paid to out-of-plan producers for export goods were higher than the domestic export prices earned by FTCs. In the former transaction there was no net flow of active money out of the state sector; the financial transactions involved only those among state-sector units – FTCs and SOEs. In the latter transaction, there was a net outflow of active money from the state sector. Thus, the main role of prices was to ensure a balance between the value of commodities sold and the volume of active money, minimizing the amount of forced savings.

Until 1963 FTCs generally incurred losses on both imports and exports. In 1964 a levy of 103 per cent was imposed on the renminbi cost of about 20 per cent of imports that were converted at the official exchange rate, effectively devaluing the renminbi rate for these imports by approximately 50 per cent.[19] The objective of the levy was to make profits on imports to pay for losses on exports so as to reduce losses on foreign trade (Shang 1999, p. 495). However, losses on exports were not fully compensated for by profits on imports. Further, part of the net losses in foreign trade involved active money outflows to the non-state sector, which was a concern to the economic planners because of its inflationary consequences. Indeed, under central planning FTCs were significant contributors to the outflow of active money from the state to the non-state sector. As late as 1986, even after a series of significant price reforms and reform of foreign trade, direct fiscal subsidies to cover the losses of FTCs were still as high as 2 per cent of China's GDP (World Bank 1994, pp. 25–6).

China's planned economy, like other planned economies, could not avoid having active money flows and therefore control of the active money supply was important; too much cash chasing too few goods would lead to inflation. Because inflation was a constant concern for China's economic planners, they were often unwilling to raise consumer prices in the plan or to allow prices to increase for commodities outside the central plan. Planners, being unwilling to generate increases in prices or forced savings, had to ensure that the state sector did not run large fiscal deficits, which would significantly raise the volume of active money flows in the economy. The state did not issue any domestic bonds between 1959 and 1980, relying instead on a balanced fiscal budget to control inflation. The MOF therefore tried diligently to keep the state budget balanced. This meant making sure that state-owned enterprises as a group did not go into the red. But this strategy sometimes ran counter to the planners' unwillingness to raise prices, forcing planners to ration goods available to the non-state sector and to impose forced saving.

SOCIALIST ADMINISTRATION OF FOREIGN EXCHANGE

In our discussion earlier of Figure 2.2, we considered the physical mechanics formulating the central economic plan to make all the sub-plans consistent. Clearly this formulation required a huge amount of coordination among various state organs in the planning apparatus. This coordination was required not only to draw up the various plans but also to implement them. The process involved the SPC and ministries subservient to it that were responsible for production, the MOFT, the MOF and the PBC. The PBC was still needed to manage foreign exchange in the absence of active money flows in the economy, but without active money flows there would have been no role for the MOF. However the MOF did have a role in foreign exchange management. Since implementation of the foreign trade plan resulted in fiscal deficits and active money flows, the MOF played an active role in providing input to formulate the foreign trade and foreign exchange plans. Thus, under central planning in China, the management of foreign exchange was not just the responsibility of the MOFT and the PBC. The MOF, and especially the SPC, were also responsible, and together these four state organs were central in managing foreign exchange. Figure 2.3 shows the coordination among these four organs in formulating and implementing the central economic plan, particularly in controlling the flows of active money and foreign exchange.

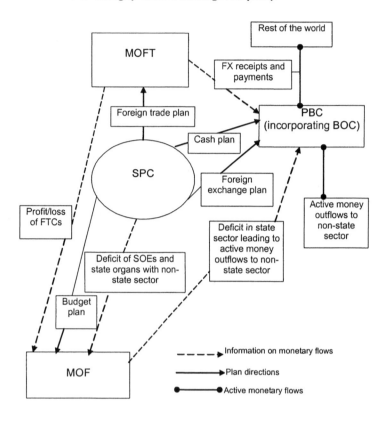

Figure 2.3 Management of active money flows and foreign exchange

The SPC was a commission and the MOF and the MOFT were ministries directly under the State Council.[20] The SPC was the key state organ in the economic planning apparatus. It had overall responsibility for formulating and implementing the central plan and its decisions determined the actions of other state organs like the various ministries associated with foreign exchange management. The MOF and the MOFT were subservient to the SPC; the PBC did not have ministry status and was subordinate to the MOF;[21] and the BOC operated as a department under the PBC.

Following the plans it had drawn up, the SPC would inform the PBC about the sources and amounts of foreign exchange that could be expected to be available and the various uses of foreign exchange that had been approved. This information enabled the PBC to monitor and supervise the inflows and outflows of foreign exchange. In implementing the foreign trade plan, the MOFT had to ensure that the value of foreign exchange earned from exports was sufficient to pay for imports in the plan. All foreign exchange earned was deposited with the BOC and was made available to SOEs and state organs for imports according to the import plan. The PBC managed and supervised the work of the BOC. Branches of the BOC helped the PBC to monitor implementation of the economic plan through supervision and control of money flows in the economy. The PBC also played a role in plan formulation. The PBC, together with the MOFT, advised the SPC on the potential value of foreign exchange available in any plan period. If necessary, the SPC would adjust the existing capital investment targets in the plan in the light of any revision to estimates of available foreign exchange. FTCs and other SOEs in the red were subsidized by the MOF, but only net deficits with the non-state sector involved active money outflows, part of which returned to the PBC through non-state purchases of commodities in the plan. If the SPC was unhappy with the resulting net active money outflows from the state sector, considering them too high for example, the SPC could raise commodity prices in the plan to reduce net active money outflows in the cash plan or, more likely, accept an increase in the volume of forced savings.

China's administration of foreign exchange under central planning was therefore enmeshed with the way the central plan and its composite budget, cash and foreign trade plans were formulated. Foreign exchange was mobilized at the centre to ensure sufficient foreign exchange was available to pay for necessary consumer imports and imports needed for current production and capital formation as designated in the plan. Foreign exchange cannot be allocated in a decentralized manner through the market when all key commodities are allocated centrally through the plan.

Therefore under central planning the system of foreign exchange management was highly centralized with tight controls over the use of foreign exchange. Formulation of foreign trade and foreign exchange plans, as discussed earlier, involved coordination among four key organs: the SPC, the MOFT, the MOF and the PBC. Coordination of these key organs was also required to implement the foreign trade and foreign exchange plans. Figure 2.4 shows the bureaucratic structure of coordination among the SPC, the MOFT, the MOF and the PBC for implementing the foreign exchange plan. These four organs and the BOC all had their own internal hierarchy, with offices at the provincial, municipal and county levels. SPC offices at each level in the hierarchy coordinated the work of the MOF, the MOFT and the PBC, and at each level the branch of the PBC led and managed branches of the BOC at that level.

FTCs under the MOFT monopolized foreign trade and traded commodities according to the central plan laid down by the SPC. The PBC through the BOC settled all foreign exchange transactions with foreign counterparts (payments and receipts) on behalf of the FTCs and all foreign contracts signed by the MOFT. The PBC thus played a crucial role in monitoring and supervising foreign trade and in administration of foreign exchange.

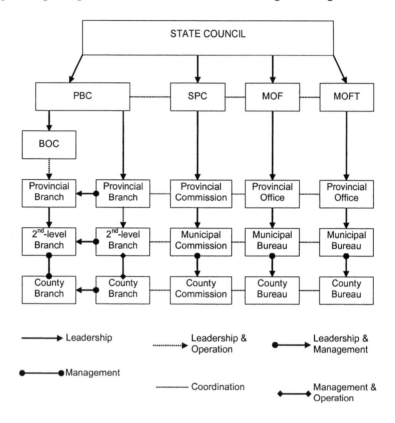

Source: Adapted from Wu and Song (1991, p. 38).

Figure 2.4   Foreign exchange administration under central planning

While imports and exports were under the jurisdiction of the MOFT, permission to engage in non-trade-related foreign exchange transactions had to come from the MOF and the PBC. Ministries approved their central units' non-trade-related foreign exchange plans before reporting to the MOF, and sub-national governments approved the plans of sub-national units before reporting to the MOF. All units had to report to the MOF and the PBC on any non-trade-related foreign exchange they possessed and had to sell the foreign exchange to the BOC. Neither unit nor individual was allowed to retain any foreign exchange. Foreign exchange allocated for use in any given year had to be used in that year; any foreign exchange left over in that year had to be returned; and non-trade-related foreign exchange could not be used for imports (Shang 1999, p. 494; Wu and Song 1991, p. 28).

Setting the Exchange Rate Under Central Planning

The renminbi exchange rate under central planning played a minor role in distribution within the national economy and setting of its value was not an important policy issue in the economic bureaucracy. The exchange rate was not varied according to demand and supply; instead, demand was adjusted in the plan to match the available supply of foreign exchange. The renminbi, as shown in Table 2.4, remained largely stable in the face of the introduction in the West of a system of flexible rates following the end of the Bretton Woods Agreement in March 1973, with only minor variations until 1980 when the renminbi was finally devalued significantly. The constant overvaluation of the renminbi during the central planning period, with resulting losses in foreign trade, did not concern the MOFT because the economic plan always provided the necessary fiscal subsidies from the MOF, or bank loans to cover any losses incurred by the FTCs. The performance of the FTCs and MOFT was not evaluated on the profit they generated but on whether they fulfilled the trade plan. The MOFT therefore had no view on what was a desirable exchange rate. This changed after 1978 during the reform period when central planning was relaxed and later abolished. From here, profits, not just achieving targets in the foreign trade plan, became a performance indicator.

SUMMARY

In this chapter we have considered management of China's foreign exchange through an historical lens. We discussed the history behind the introduction of the renminbi, how the renminbi became the national currency and early efforts by PRC economic planners to set its value in relation to foreign currencies. We compared the way the renminbi rate was set under central planning to the way it was set in the earlier Rehabilitation Period, highlighting how the imperative of central planning determined how foreign exchange was managed. China's foreign exchange administration from the mid-1950s remained largely unaltered until after the death of Mao Zedong and the return of Deng Xiaoping to power in 1977. During the years of central planning under Mao, the focus of foreign exchange policy was to raise enough foreign exchange to meet the foreign currency cost of essential imports, in line with the central plan and the leadership's notions of rapid industrialization.

It is clear from our discussion of the foreign exchange administration in this chapter that under central planning the SPC was the most powerful and influential of all the economic ministries. But as we explain in later chapters, progress on economic reform in the 1980s and 1990s worked to reduce the power and influence of the SPC and its descendant, the State Development and Planning Commission (SDPC). This was especially so as economic reform fostered the increasing integration of China's economy with the global economy. This development served to strengthen the power and the influence of the PBC over management of foreign exchange. It also made foreign exchange a more important instrument in national economic management, which by extension made foreign exchange policy an area of greater concern as the exchange rate now serves as an important bridge between the domestic and global economy by linking domestic and international commodity prices.

NOTES

1. Liberated Areas were areas captured from the Nationalists or taken from the departing Japanese army at the end of World War II. Border Areas were areas under Communist control before the end of the war.
2. Howe (1978, p. xxi) gave the figure of 33 per cent for the fall in agricultural output.
3. Chou's 1963 study provides a comprehensive analysis of China's inflation of 1937–49.
4. Beijing was known as Beiping at that time.
5. A monthly inflation rate of 200 per cent would compound into an annual inflation rate of just over 53 million per cent.
6. Especially raw cotton, cotton yarn, cotton cloth, grain and coal.
7. Calculations based on data in Miyashita (1976, p. 76).
8. In 1949 total foreign exchange trade in the Tianjin and Shanghai exchanges totalled US$32.3 million (Shang 1999, p. 338).
9. Another popular way of expressing this policy was 'encouraging exports and overseas Chinese remittances' (*jiangli chukou guli qiaohui*) (Shang 1999, p. 530).
10. Many relatives of overseas Chinese were themselves overseas Chinese who held foreign citizenships or had lived for a substantial period of time abroad. The PRC does not recognize dual citizenship and no longer considers all overseas Chinese as its citizens. It makes the distinction between overseas Chinese who are citizens of the PRC (*huaqiao*) and foreign citizens of Chinese decent (*huayi*).
11. Data were collected at the four major trading ports in Jin (Tianjin), Lu (Shandong), Hu (Shanghai) and Sui (Guangzhou).
12. Calculated from data given in Cheng (1954, pp. 124–5).
13. This paragraph is drawn largely from Liu (1984, pp. 104–5).
14. For a discussion on the Sino–Soviet split, see MacFarquhar (1983, pp. 255–92).
15. Cited by Riskin (1987, p. 53).
16. The Soviet economist Preobrazhensky was the first to suggest the use of the 'price scissors' to tax agriculture in order to finance industrialization. His ideas were very influential during the Soviet industrialization debates of the 1920s and they had a significant influence on Chinese economists in the 1950s (Liew 1997, pp. 12–25). See Sah and Stiglitz (1987, 1992) for a formal treatment of Preobrazhensky's ideas.
17. MOFERT became the Ministry of Foreign Trade and Economic Cooperation (MOFTEC) in 1984.

18. FTCs were formed from the earlier smaller specialized foreign trading companies.
19. Lardy (1992, p. 22) citing Chinese sources reported that the levy was reduced to 60 per cent in 1975 but was raised to 80 per cent in 1980.
20. A commission ranks higher than a ministry in the bureaucracy but it functions just like a ministry.
21. During the Cultural Revolution in 1969, the PBC and the rest of the banking system were absorbed by the MOF. The PBC only regained its independence from the MOF on 1 January 1978 (Dai 1998, p. 6).

3. Post-Mao reform of the foreign exchange regime

In pre-reform China, as in many other centrally planned economies, the foreign trade plan was an integrated component in the central plan and the foreign exchange management system was designed to serve the foreign trade plan. As discussed in Chapter 2, Maoist China pursued an import-substitution development strategy. Trade planning was designed, first, to identify key raw materials and commodities that had to be imported to meet the requirements of the import-substitution strategy, and then to ensure that sufficient foreign exchange was generated through exports to pay for these imports. Within this planning framework, the renminbi exchange rate was fixed and had a passive role in trade policy; export and import volumes were independent of the exchange rate.

While the exchange rate did not determine the volume of foreign trade, it affected the level of profit or loss of state foreign trade corporations (FTCs). It therefore affected the state budget, as we discuss in later chapters, and it became a serious issue in the course of economic reform and an important determinant of exchange rate policy. The exchange rate determined the renminbi prices that the FTCs had to pay for imports and the renminbi prices they received for exports, but economic planners set the renminbi prices that FTCs could charge users of imports or pay producers of exports independently of world prices and the exchange rate. The exchange rate was fixed and overvalued, which meant FTCs paid subsidized lower renminbi prices for imports and received taxed lower renminbi prices for exports. The FTCs made losses on exports as they had to pay much higher renminbi prices to secure the domestic products they exported compared to the renminbi prices they received from exports. Export losses were covered by profits on imports, where the renminbi prices that FTCs paid for imports were lower than the renminbi prices that they could sell to domestic users of imports.

In most centrally planned economies, primary products were underpriced and manufactured products were overpriced to finance rapid heavy industrialization. In the early 1950s, about 80 per cent of China's exports were agricultural and other primary products because its underdeveloped industrial sector produced few exportable manufactured goods. The losses from exports did not impose an unbearable burden on the state budget at that time because with low export levels the losses were generally small and could be subsidized easily by profits generated from imports. Nevertheless, subsidizing primary exports was inevitably inefficient and unsustainable, because China has no comparative advantage in producing primary products given its very low natural resource endowment (especially land) to population ratio. China's increasing need for foreign exchange earnings had to be met by expanding exports of manufactured goods. This resulted in the rapid decline in the share of primary products in total exports, from about 80 per cent in 1953 to 56 per cent in 1965–66 (Lardy 1992, p. 32).

After the failure of Mao's feverish Great Leap Forward (1958–60), the government found it had to raise the state procurement prices of agricultural products to maintain the incentive to work in agricultural collectives; socialist ideology could no longer elicit the necessary sacrifice from peasants working in collectives. In 1961–72, agricultural procurement prices were raised several times,[1] but the renminbi rate remained largely unchanged and overvalued.[2] As a result, there were huge losses on export sales.[3]

Export losses in the 1960s and 1970s were still manageable because prices of all commodities during that period were tightly controlled and export quotas were largely mandatory. But export losses grew in the late 1970s on the back of agricultural reform and became more serious in the 1980s with industrial reform. Relaxation of central planning and liberalization of the economy made production more sensitive to state procurement prices, increasing dramatically the export costs of FTCs. However, export revenues of the FTCs could not increase as rapidly because the exchange rate was fixed and overvalued. According to information cited by Lardy (1992, p. 27), in the years just prior to 1980, 70 per cent of China's exports posted heavy losses, which increased demands on the government's budget and exerted devaluation pressure on the renminbi. Pressure on China's exchange rate intensified in the mid-1980s when the government introduced industry reform, which for the first time since the beginning of central planning raised substantially the prices of key industrial input materials and increased the domestic costs of producing exportable manufactured goods for FTCs.

In this chapter we review the key reform measures in China's post-Mao foreign exchange management at each stage of national economic reform. Reform of foreign exchange management is linked not only to reform in international trade, but also, inevitably, to reforms in other sectors of China's economy. While we focus on the interdependence of reforms in foreign exchange and international trade, we will also examine reforms in other sectors that bear on foreign exchange and trade.

The Chinese authorities have to respond to new challenges brought on by globalization, and foreign exchange and trade reforms are inevitably part of globalizing China's economy. In this chapter we analyse a challenge that is especially daunting to the authorities: how to maintain macroeconomic stability given the enormous changes to China's foreign trade and investment, and foreign exchange management.

REFORMS WITHIN A PLANNING FRAMEWORK (1979–87)

China's reform of its foreign exchange management began with the decision of the authorities to introduce a foreign exchange retention system and an internal foreign exchange trading system in 1979–80. All reforms of the foreign exchange regime from that time until the eve of the official opening of China's first foreign exchange swap market in 1988 were attempts to improve the foreign exchange system within the old central planning framework. The authorities did not intend to transform completely the old foreign exchange rate regime. Yet in trying to solve its major problems they exposed serious weaknesses that are inherent in a plan-based foreign exchange system, which ultimately led them to replace it with an essentially market-determined exchange rate regime.

Initial Reforms

The foreign exchange retention system (*waihui liucheng zhidu*) that the State Council introduced in 1980 (State Council 1980) was similar to the foreign exchange retention systems adopted by some of the Eastern European countries in the 1950s (Plowiec 1988, p. 356) and by the former Soviet Union in 1987–88 (IMF 1990, p. 4). The system improved export incentives by allowing export-producing enterprises, state FTCs and their superordinate level of government administration the right to buy back a certain proportion of their foreign exchange earnings at the official rate. The foreign exchange retention rates were industry or commodity specific and varied according to geographic regions and the rank of the planning and administrative organs that oversaw the export-producing enterprises and FTCs. The retention rates were designed to provide greater incentives to enterprises and local governments to respond to new export opportunities and expand their above-plan exports (Table 3.1). The 1980 foreign exchange retention system was a milestone in exchange rate reform because it was the first attempt by the authorities in the reform period to allow the market to play a role, even though only at the margin, in determining the exchange rate (Wu 1998, p. 83).[4]

Table 3.1 Foreign exchange retention rates (1979 and 1985)

Category of export earnings	Retention rate
Implemented in 1979 by the State Council	
1. Exports under ministerial management	20% of the earnings above the 1978 level
2. Exports under local government	40% of the earnings above the 1978 level
3. Exports based on imports	15% of net earnings
4. Fees from processing and assembling foreign components	30% of all earnings
5. Medium and small-scale compensation trade	15% of net earnings
Implemented in 1985 by the State Council	
1. Export of machinery, electrical products, equipment sets and components	50% of all earnings
2. Export of military industry products	100% of all earnings
3. Export of crude oil and refined petroleum products under the MOFERT trade plan	3% of all earnings
4. Export of coal by agency as substitute for export of crude oil or refined petroleum products under the MOFERT trade plan	50% of all earnings
5. Export of crude oil and refined petroleum products by agent outside the MOFERT trade plan	100% of all earnings
6. Fees from processing and assembling foreign components earned by FTCs	30% of net earnings
7. All other exports not mentioned in Category 1–6 under the trade plan*	
From Guangdong and Fujian	70% of the earnings above the 1978 level
From Tibet (actual exports)	100% of all earnings
From all other autonomous regions plus Yunnan, Guizhou and Qinghai (actual exports)	50% of all earnings
8. All other exports not mentioned in Category 1–6 outside the trade plan	70% of all earnings
9. Export from special economic zones	100% of all earnings above the level as in the contract with the MOFERT

Note: * Provinces not listed should hand in all their export earnings under the trade plan.

Source: Lardy (1992, Table 3.2), Yang (2000, Table 2.11).

In 1980, with the introduction of the foreign exchange retention system, the Bank of China (BOC) began experimenting with a rudimentary foreign exchange trading system by establishing a foreign exchange adjustment centre (*waihui tiaoji zhongxin*) in Guangdong. The need for centres to trade retained foreign exchange arose from a situation where some enterprises with large retained foreign exchange entitlements lacked renminbi funds to buy back their entitled foreign exchange, while other enterprises had ample renminbi funds but small retained foreign exchange entitlements (Jing 1996, p. 63). In the foreign exchange retention system one unit of retained foreign exchange was set to equal one unit of foreign exchange trading rights and sellers of foreign exchange could sell at a premium above the official exchange rate. Only officially approved domestic enterprises were allowed to trade in the foreign retention system and foreign exchange adjustment centres were located typically in the internal trading rooms of the BOC. An internal foreign exchange trading room was established in Shanghai in 1981 after the establishment of the first foreign exchange adjustment centre in Guangdong, and more trading rooms were established later in other coastal cities.

Another important reform soon after establishment of the foreign exchange adjustment centre was the introduction of the internal foreign exchange settlement system (*neibu jiesuan zhi*) by the BOC at the beginning of 1981. Under this new system all trade transactions were to be settled at a unified internal settlement rate (*neibu jiesuan jia*) of RMB2.8 per US dollar,[5] parallel to the published official rate of RMB1.5 per US dollar that was applicable only for non-trade transactions. The internal settlement rate implies almost 50 per cent discount on the prevailing official rate.

China had established an internal settlement system as early as 1964 to tackle the problem of export losses. However, unlike the 1981 system that had a unified rate, the 1964 system had multiple internal rates, with premiums over the official rate ranging from 60 to above 100 per cent, that targeted imports of selected industries (Lardy 1992, p. 22; Bell et al. 1993). Instead of imports, the 1981 system targeted exports; it sought to boost the growth of China's exports while reducing the domestic currency losses on foreign trade.

Changes in the foreign exchange system were accompanied by significant changes to the foreign trade regime. In 1979, the central government decided to decentralize foreign trade, which for the first time since 1949 authorized industrial ministries, local governments and certain production enterprises to engage in foreign trade through individual arrangements with the central government. This decision ended a three-decade-long foreign trade monopoly of a dozen national FTCs and led to the mushrooming of various types of foreign trade organization nationwide in the early 1980s (Lardy 1992, p. 39). Meanwhile, the State Council began to reduce the scope of the national foreign trade plan by dividing it into two plans – mandatory and guidance.

The mandatory plan continued to specify trade by physical quantity. The guidance plan, however, specified some targets in value terms, giving FTCs more flexibility in determining the precise mix of imports and exports. According to the World Bank (1994), during the first few years of the 1980s, 20 per cent of China's foreign trade was already outside the national plan and, of the 80 per cent within the national plan, the ratio of the size of the mandatory to guidance plan was about 75:25.

A trade agency system was established to handle decentralized and non-plan exports and imports. FTCs in this agency system acted as intermediaries between domestic enterprises and international buyers and sellers, instead of buying export goods from or selling import goods to domestic enterprises. FTCs earned commissions from their role as intermediaries, but enterprises, not FTCs, were responsible for the profit and loss in these non-plan transactions. A significant outcome from the establishment of the trade agency system was that changes in international prices could now automatically affect domestic prices of imported and exported commodities via the exchange rate. Out-of-plan importers could increase the prices they charged domestic customers in line with rising international prices and were therefore not caught in a squeeze between rising import prices and fixed domestic prices. Similarly, out-of-plan exporters received a greater incentive to export in the form of higher domestic prices when international prices rose. The system cut domestic currency losses in foreign trade and reduced fiscal subsidies to foreign trade, but the improvement in state finances was modest, and linking domestic to international prices introduced the prospect of import-pushed inflation (Yang 2000, p. 90).

The Impact of Initial Reforms

Precise assessment of the impacts of the initial reforms is difficult because few details are available on the scale of planning control and official statistics on export and import transactions by industry and region are scarce. However, scattered data collected by Lardy (1992, pp. 69–74) show that the unified internal settlement rate's first year of operation raised more than RMB8 billion profits from exports but incurred about RMB9 billion losses on imports. The total value of exports was unprecedented, but export growth soon slowed and in 1982–83 was outstripped by the growth of imports (Figure 3.1). In 1980–83, financial losses in the trade sector as a whole amounted to RMB19.6 billion, which was more than the entire cumulative trade profits of the previous 26 years (Lardy 1992, p. 73).

The foreign exchange reforms and implied renminbi devaluation did not significantly improve the finances of foreign trade. First, the foreign exchange retention system and BOC internal foreign exchange trading rooms were barely effective in encouraging exports because the type of enterprises that could gain entry into the BOC internal trading rooms was tightly restricted. Second, the implied devaluation of the renminbi did not provide most producers with a stronger incentive to export. Devaluation of the renminbi did not reduce export costs to the extent suggested by the spread between the official and internal settlement rates (RMB1.5 versus RMB2.8 per US dollar). This is because before introduction of the unified internal settlement rate there were multiple internal rates that were already higher than the official rate (indicating renminbi devaluation) (Bell et al. 1993), and the government was also providing fiscal subsidies for many exports (Yang 1993; Chen 1987). In addition, the internal settlement rate of RMB2.8 per US dollar was initially allowed to 'float' with a 5–10 per cent margin in internal trading (Tsang 1994, p. 13).[6] Furthermore, the incentive to export was smaller via the agency system, where export subsidies were no longer available despite inflation increasing the cost of exporting (Figure 3.2).

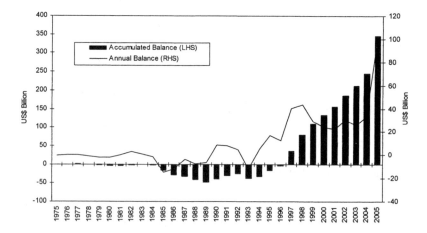

Source: Data up to 2004 are from NBS (1981–2006). Data for 2005 are based on preliminary reports published on the website of China's Ministry of Commerce, available at http://gcs.mofcom.gov.cn/tongji.shtml.

Figure 3.1   China's annual and accumulated trade balances (1975–2005)

The initial positive effect of renminbi devaluation on exports weakened quickly when price reform in the 1980s began to push up prices (Figure 3.2) and increased the domestic currency cost of exports. The extent of the rise in export costs can be gauged by examining changes in state procurement prices. In 1978–81 the average state procurement price for grain crops increased by 56 per cent. The price of soybeans, one of China's main farm products for export, rose by 170 per cent. The average price of cash crops, which were the basic inputs in many export-oriented light industries, increased by 57 per cent. The price of animal products increased by 29 per cent, of which the price of hides and skins rose by 34 per cent, and the price of silk cocoons increased by 24 per cent. Following price adjustments in the farm sector, many industrial materials experienced their most significant price increases since the mid-1960s. For example, between 1980 and 1984 the ex-factory price for basic metals rose by 15 per cent, building materials by 12 per cent, coal 16 per cent, petroleum 21 per cent and timber 27 per cent (NBS 2001, Tables 9-10, 9-12). In 1982–83 the number of commodities that posted export loses from increased export costs rose 70 per cent (Ma and Sun 1988, p. 307) over the previous year and exerted additional pressure on both the state budget and the exchange rate.

Devaluation of the renminbi internal exchange rate meant FTCs (or any importer under the agency system) had to pay more than before for foreign exchange to purchase the same amount of goods on the world market. But most of China's imports were exchange rate inelastic in the early 1980s. The share of imports set by mandatory import plans was still about 60 per cent of total imports and with severe shortages in the Chinese economy, the non-plan imports were exchange rate inelastic as well. Furthermore, the planning principle of setting prices of imported products at the same level as prices of comparable domestic goods continued to apply despite adoption of the internal settlement system. As a result, imported products comparable to domestic products that were in the national plan or judged to be 'required for the people's livelihood' remained underpriced. Importers were therefore not always able to pass on the increased cost of imports to users and devaluation of the renminbi inevitably reduced the profits or increased the losses of importers.

In 1979, the government granted greater autonomy to state-owned enterprises (SOEs) on a trial basis. This encouraged investment-hungry SOEs with soft budgets to increase imports despite higher import costs from renminbi devaluation. Imports were further stimulated by a new fiscal contract system introduced in 1984 that granted greater fiscal autonomy to local governments. The greater autonomy granted to local governments caused a boom in local projects that relied on imported machinery. Foreign trade decentralization accompanied the greater fiscal autonomy granted to enterprises and local governments. The greater autonomy created opportunities for the importation of commodities that were not subject to price controls, particularly those commodities where there were no comparable domestic products, such as automobiles and luxury consumer goods. It also facilitated the importation of machinery used in assembly lines to produce highly profitable household electrical appliances (ACFB 1986, part III, p. 9).

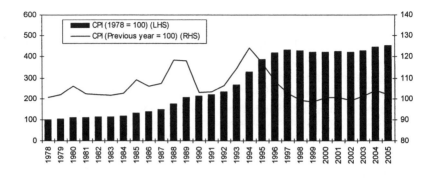

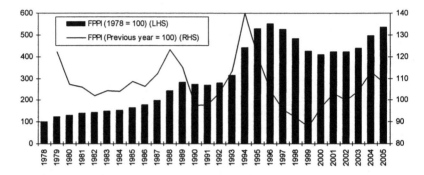

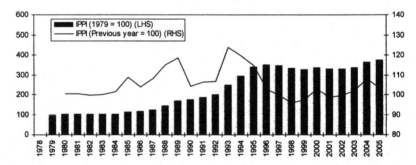

Sources: Data up to 2003 are from NBS (1981–2006). Data for 2004 are from Guomin jingji he shehui fazhan tongji gongbao (*National Economy and Social Development Statistical Bulletin*) for 2004, from the website of NBS, available at www.stats.gov.cn/tjgb/index.htm. CPI data for 2005 are up to November, available at www.stats.gov.cn/tjsj/index.htm; FPPI data for 2005 are from the website of the Ministry of Agriculture, available at www.agri.gov.cn/xxfb/jgxxfb.htm; IPPI data for 2005 were unavailable when this chapter was completed.

Figure 3.2 China's consumer price index (CPI), farm procurement price index (FPPI) and industrial producer price index (IPPI) (1978–2005)

Official Response to the Impacts of Initial Reforms

Having decided not to abandon trade planning, the authorities were caught in a dilemma. On the one hand, the authorities introduced higher foreign exchange retention rates and trade liberalization to provide greater incentive to exporters. But on the other hand, the authorities attempted to retain control over the use of foreign exchange to secure foreign exchange for imports that were under state planning, which served only to reduce the incentive to export. The main aim of the authorities in introducing foreign exchange and trade reform was to increase foreign exchange earnings to make more foreign exchange available to finance the national import plan. However, the authorities did not anticipate that decentralization and deregulation of foreign exchange and trade would provide greater incentives to exporters to bypass planning controls on foreign exchange earnings in search of higher profits, making it more difficult for the state to retain control over the supply of foreign exchange.

In 1985, the government abolished the internal settlement system and unified the dual exchange rates for trade at the internal settlement rate. Some observers (for example Lardy 1992, p. 73) explained that this move was due largely to the pressure from the international community on China to abolish its dual exchange rate system. The International Monetary Fund (IMF) had pointed out that the dual exchange rate was in violation of IMF standards, and US enterprises facing competition from Chinese imports complained that the internal settlement rate was equivalent to an export subsidy. However, it is more likely that the devaluation of the official renminbi rate to the internal rate was designed to encourage higher domestic earnings in non-trade foreign exchange incomes, such as income from tourism and remittances from overseas Chinese, which before devaluation were converted into renminbi at the official rate. It must be pointed out that abolishing the internal settlement system did not mean that China had only one exchange rate. Trade of retained foreign exchange earnings among domestic enterprises in foreign exchange adjustment centres continued to be priced at a premium above the 'official unified rate'.

In the year that the government abolished the internal settlement system, the government revised the foreign exchange retention scheme it had introduced in 1979 to offer greater incentive to exporters, especially those in special economic zones, by increasing above-plan-quota export prices and the share of non-plan exports. The 1979 scheme distributed retained foreign exchange more or less equally among all central and local government bodies involved in export, FTCs and enterprises that produced for export. On average, the revision to the scheme in 1985 distributed 80 per cent of retained foreign exchange earnings to local governments and enterprises that produced for export, leaving 20 per cent for central ministries and FTCs (State Council 1985).

In 1985–86 two foreign exchange adjustment centres (FEAC) (*waihui tiaoji zhongxin*) or 'swap markets' were opened in Shenzhen and Shanghai to handle foreign exchange transactions of joint ventures. The aim of the authorities was to achieve surplus in the foreign exchange accounts of joint ventures so that joint ventures would make a positive contribution to the country's stock of foreign exchange. Joint ventures contributing positively to China's foreign exchange holdings is an important principle that China's authorities had followed strictly since China opened its doors to foreign direct investment (FDI). Without the need to meet plan targets, the swap centres functioned better than the foreign exchange retention scheme in distributing foreign exchange to those who valued it most. The swap centres provided a marketplace where those in joint ventures with excess foreign exchange earnings could sell to those in joint ventures that lacked hard currency to meet their foreign currency obligations. Sellers of foreign exchange had the incentive to use the swap market because here they could acquire renminbi on terms more favourable than the official rate, allowing them to purchase inputs from the domestic market at a lower foreign exchange cost.

Meanwhile, the internal foreign exchange trading rooms for domestic enterprises were transformed slowly into larger and more open foreign exchange adjustment centres to facilitate trading of retained foreign exchange in line with the national import plan. Nevertheless, restrictions on foreign exchange remained. Only importers holding an approved import licence could buy foreign exchange. Once these funds were purchased they had to be used to finance imports within six months, and no buyer of foreign exchange was allowed to resell for a profit (Lardy 1992, p. 63).

Foreign exchange and trade reform did not, however, eliminate shortages in foreign exchange. The State Administration of Foreign Exchange (SAFE) reported that a lack of foreign exchange continued to impact adversely on national import and export plans. Imports of materials used in export production were particularly affected (ACFB 1986, part III, p. 9; 1988, p. 141). China's annual trade surplus declined from US\$3 billion in 1982 to merely US\$0.8 billion in 1983, and became a deficit of US\$32 billion in 1984–87 (NBS 2001, Table 17-3) (Figure 3.1). Realizing that there were still substantial loopholes in their control of foreign exchange, in 1986 the authorities decided to freeze all retained foreign exchange. However, as they admitted later, some ministries and localities still managed to circumvent the import restrictions and their imports exceeded the central plan quotas (ACFB 1987, part III, p. 17).

The price of foreign exchange in the less tightly controlled swap centres for foreign-invested enterprises was generally higher than that in the swap centres for domestic enterprises (Ba 1999, pp. 4–5). This provided the incentive for domestic enterprises with large amounts of retained foreign exchange to exploit loopholes through false joint ventures – so-called 'round-tripping investment' – that sent their foreign exchange earnings illegally out of China and returned them disguised as investments in foreign-invested enterprises. Controls in the swap centres for domestic enterprises also nurtured foreign exchange black market activities and encouraged the illegal holdings of foreign exchange earnings outside China (ACFB 1986, part III, p. 9).

The official renminbi rate was devalued gradually by 12.5 per cent to RMB3.2 per US dollar by the end of 1985 and devalued by a further 13.5 per cent to RMB3.7 per US dollar in July 1986 to give additional encouragement to exporters (ACFB 1987, part III, pp. 17–18). Although the government did not allow supply and demand to determine freely the price of foreign exchange in the swap centres, the swap rate of the renminbi surprised the authorities by slipping quickly to RMB5.7 per US dollar in 1987.

The reform measures were undertaken largely under the rubric of central planning. Nevertheless, these measures were the first milestone in the transition of China's foreign exchange system to a market regime. For the first time in the reform period, the market was allowed to play a role, although only at the margin, in determining the price of the renminbi. However, as we discuss in the next section, when the authorities began to allow the market to play a greater role, they faced an increasingly difficult challenge to maintain a balance between plan and market.

REFORM IN A PLAN–MARKET SYSTEM (1988–93)

It became clear between 1988 and 1993 that controls over the use of retained foreign exchange reduced the effectiveness of both the foreign exchange swap system and renminbi devaluation in promoting exports. Moreover, with continued overvaluation of the renminbi, the controls encouraged exporters to delay their foreign exchange settlement or increase their illegal holdings of foreign exchange earnings outside China.[7] There was mounting pressure on state FTCs as a result of domestic price liberalization. Primary products were vastly underpriced under central planning in order to finance heavy industrialization. These prices were gradually liberalized from the late 1970s, but export prices of primary products remained relatively low with an overvalued renminbi. Fiscal subsidies to exports had to be increased to boost export performance. However, it soon became increasingly clear to the authorities that continuous increases in export subsidies were undermining the national budget and could not be continued indefinitely. A lower value renminbi through official devaluation and/or further liberalization of control over foreign exchange became inevitable.

The authorities understood that to promote exports they would have to allow the market to play a greater role. In 1988 significant changes were made to China's plan–market or dual-track foreign exchange system. That year, along with further reductions in the scope of national trade planning, the authorities relaxed their control over the use of retained foreign exchange and improved the access of domestic enterprises, particularly those in labour-intensive sectors, to the foreign exchange swap system.[8] In September 1988, in an important move to merge the foreign exchange swap system for foreign-invested enterprises[9] with the foreign exchange rate system for domestic enterprises to form one integrated open foreign exchange market system, China's first foreign exchange market for domestic enterprises was opened in Shanghai. Following Shanghai, more open foreign exchange swap markets were opened in 1989, in Xiamen and Fujian and later in several other coastal cities including Shenzhen (ACFB 1990, p. 216). In August 1992, China's National Foreign Exchange Open Market was opened in Beijing (*Jingji ribao*, 10 August 1992). By the end of 1992, this national open market consisted of a chain of 26 regional markets, all linked electronically (ACFB 1993, p. 50).

The price of foreign exchange trading rights – equivalent to the premium over the official exchange rate – had been tightly regulated since the internal trading system was established. The benchmark rate was fixed at RMB1 per US dollar in 1985 and RMB2 per US dollar in 1988, and the authorities usually intervened in the market if the benchmark rate could not be maintained. The Shanghai swap market became the country's first foreign exchange swap centre that allowed supply and demand to determine the price of foreign exchange (Ba 1999, p. 6).

The objective of the market reform in foreign exchange was to make importers subsidize losses from exports through the depreciated swap market rate of the renminbi and to reduce out-of-plan imports through the higher cost of foreign exchange. The authorities also anticipated that the foreign exchange market would facilitate implementation of the foreign exchange and investment plans. They rationalized that the higher renminbi price of foreign exchange in the market would increase the incentive to export and lift the amount of foreign exchange earnings available for the planned imports required for state investment projects, which authorities continued to cost at a lower official exchange rate.

Two years of economic austerity following the Tiananmen crackdown in June 1989 provided the authorities with an opportunity to devalue the official exchange rate without the need to worry about inflation (Figure 3.2). In December 1989 the renminbi was devalued by 21.2 per cent from RMB3.7 to RMB4.7 per US dollar, which was its biggest devaluation in a decade. In November 1990, the renminbi was devalued by a further 9.6 per cent to RMB5.2 per US dollar. In April 1991, the authorities announced the adoption of a 'managed float system' to allow timely adjustments to the official rate so that adjustments would be less abrupt and more in line with changes to the exchange rate in the swap market (Ba 1999, p. 116). Authorities hoped they could use this new system to forge a closer link between the official and swap exchange rates (Tsang 1994). Yet as we discuss later, this system proved to be too difficult to manage in an inflationary situation (see Wu 1998, pp. 86–9) and was abolished with the unification of the official and swap systems in January 1994.

Reform of the trade regime accompanied foreign exchange reform. In January 1991, China's central government announced a new round of foreign trade reform that ended all fiscal subsidies on export losses (ACFB 1992, p. 71). This round of trade reform brought all foreign trading operations under the trade contract system that was introduced in 1988 to selected light manufacturing industries on a trial basis. This new arrangement did not mean the end of national trade planning. State trade plans were incorporated into trade contracts and the only significant change was that enterprises, industries and localities were able to negotiate details of trade contracts with the planning authorities, which gave exporting firms greater incentive to implement state trade plans.

Along with the new trade reform, there was a new foreign exchange retention arrangement that unified existing foreign exchange retention rates and reduced the share of foreign exchange earnings that was delivered to the state at the official rate. Export earnings were no longer identified as in-plan or above-plan. The new system allowed local governments to retain 10 per cent, export-producing enterprises to retain 10 per cent and FTCs to retain 60 per cent of their foreign exchange earnings. However, in this new arrangement all of an enterprise's entitled foreign exchange and one-third of an FTC's entitled foreign exchange must be settled for renminbi at the average swap rate. As a result, shares of foreign exchange earnings were 50 per cent for the central government, 10 per cent for local government and 40 per cent for FTCs (Cao 1991, pp. 43–4; ACFB 1992, p. 71).

The apparently greater incentive to export offered by the new foreign exchange retention system was in fact compensation to enterprises for terminating direct export subsidies. Nevertheless, unified retention rates removed the long-standing and troublesome practice of bargaining between exporters and authorities over industry or case-specific retention rates, thus allowing the swap market to play a bigger role in foreign exchange allocation. However, the new arrangement also introduced a controversial change that disadvantaged export-producing enterprises. They no longer received their entitled foreign exchange in the form of retained foreign exchange trading rights as before, but in renminbi payments. They now had to purchase any foreign exchange that they required for imports from the swap market. This new arrangement tightened state control over the use of foreign exchange. Moreover, as documented in official publications, many export-producing enterprises did not welcome the change because it increased their costs and the risks they undertook in foreign exchange transactions – including outstanding foreign exchange debts – and tightened state control over their use of foreign exchange (ACFB 1992, pp. 71–2).

Devaluation–Inflation Circles

The international community welcomed the introduction of the plan–market or dual-track foreign exchange system, which was considered to be a positive step towards transforming China's foreign exchange regime into a market system (World Bank 1994). However, the transformation was not smooth and its biggest challenge was inflation. Introduction of the dual-track foreign exchange system was accompanied by the highest rates of inflation since the early 1960s. In 1988–89 China's general retail price level increased by about 40 per cent (Figure 3.2) and caused the renminbi exchange rate in the swap market to depreciate from RMB5.7 to an all time high of RMB7–8 per US dollar at the end of 1988,[10] resulting in about 46–53 per cent discount under the official rate of RMB3.75 (Table 3A.1). High inflation was due to competitive money creation among China's local governments, which sought to take advantage of weak central control over local bank officials in order to expand credit in their localities beyond what was stipulated in the credit plan, to compete for additional resources from the market (Liew 1997, pp. 127–36).

  While high inflation in the late 1980s was driven largely by competitive money creation, renminbi devaluation also played a role.[11] Devaluation raised the domestic currency cost of imports. Whether imports were purchased with retained foreign exchange or not did not decide whether their prices were controlled. Except for a few imported commodities, where comparable domestic products were still subject to stringent price control, most commodities – including many in the import plan – were sold at higher prices in the domestic market. Prices of imports purchased using retained foreign exchange and marketed through non-plan channels were not controlled, and contributed to a higher general price level. Another factor contributing to inflation was the official permission granted to regions that enjoyed preferential treatment for conducting reform experiments to raise funds independently by importing commodities in great demand and selling them at market prices. It must be noted, however, that although the increase in non-plan imports contributed to a higher general price level because non-plan imports were sold at market prices, the increase in imports absorbed some of the forced savings in the banking system, which helped to stabilize prices in the longer term.

Devaluation-induced export growth increased aggregate demand in the economy, but supply elasticity is less than infinite. Existing planning controls and institutional barriers to factor mobility caused price increases even when the economy was not operating on its production possibilities frontier. Devaluation encouraged competition among exporters for primary goods to export, and foreign trade reform gave FTCs a stronger incentive to fulfil export plans so they could increase their more lucrative non-plan exports. FTCs that managed to set up offices in the special economic zone of Shenzhen were able to enjoy a higher foreign exchange retention rate and were keen to offer high prices when procuring products for export. To fulfil their export plans, FTCs in other localities had to compete with them by offering even higher prices to secure supplies, causing the infamous 'price wars' all over China.[12] As a result of this competition, prices of primary products rocketed and farmers rushed to increase production, leading eventually to overproduction. Towards the end of the 1980s, oversupply of these products eventually caused their prices to crash and the government had to bail out the troubled FTCs at a huge financial cost.[13] The fiscal impact of the devaluation was one of the main reasons for the government putting a stop to all export subsidies in 1991.

Finally, an important factor often ignored by analysts and policymakers in the 1980s and 1990s was the expectation of devaluation, a factor that China never experienced under central planning. Yang (2000, p. 15) suggests that around 1986–87, people in China began to expect the renminbi to devalue which, together with rising inflation expectation, exacerbated what he called vicious devaluation–inflation circles. According to Yang, from 1986–87 until unification of the renminbi official and market rates in January 1994, international buyers offered lower prices to China's FTCs and domestic producers asked for higher prices from the FTCs whenever devaluation was expected. Consequently, the benefit of devaluation to the state FTCs diminished rather quickly, usually less than one year after devaluation, and the authorities soon felt the pressure for higher export subsidies, or further devaluation, or both.

Inflation expectations translated into increases in the renminbi price for foreign exchange in the swap market, enlarging the gap between the official and swap rates, which made it more difficult for the authorities to secure control over foreign exchange. State enterprises sought import projects funded at the official rate and were in a stronger position to bargain with the state for higher export subsidies to achieve plan targets, but they also became more reluctant to hand over their export earnings to the authorities at the official rate because they expected depreciation of the swap market rate. Authorities were therefore forced to consider another round of devaluation of the official rate, but this induced higher inflation and further expectations of depreciation of the swap rate and hence further devaluation expectations of the official rate.

Devaluation–inflation circles were deeply rooted in China's transition economy. National export plans were considered essential to earn the foreign exchange required for fulfilling import plans deemed crucial for economic development, so the government was not confident to give up these plans quickly. This situation aroused continuous debates from the late 1980s till the mid-1990s among state bodies involved in foreign trade. The Ministry of Foreign Economic Relations and Trade (MOFERT) argued strongly in favour of a continuous devaluation policy largely because it had to fulfil the highly rigid foreign exchange earnings plan. The State Price Bureau (SPB), State Planning Commission (SPC), and Ministry of Finance (MOF) took the opposite position and opposed devaluation. The SPB was worried about price instability and the SPC was concerned that devaluation–inflation circles could jeopardize the overall national plan. The MOF did not support devaluation because as long as there were mandatory export and import plans, it could end up paying out more subsidies, with ever-increasing inflation. The MOFERT, with its strong bargaining chip of 'no devaluation, no guaranteed foreign exchange earnings', seemed always to be the winner in any State Council's roundtable debate over renminbi policy (Yang 2000, p. 15).[14]

The only way to break the devaluation–inflation circle was to concentrate on attacking inflation. Since competitive money creation was the major cause of inflation, the cure had to come from reform of the central banking system. A plan to reform the central banking system was proposed in 1994, but did not come into operation until 1998. Nevertheless, as discussed earlier, the authorities made good use of the opportunity created by the austerity programme in 1989–91. They managed to reassert monetary control and imposed a contractionary fiscal policy. The contractionary fiscal policy slowed the growth of fiscal revenue and forced all levels of government to cut price subsidies (Ba 1999, p. 116; Yang 2000, p. 90). The central government also took the opportunity to reduce its budgetary burdens created by the partial reforms in the 1980s. For example, the authorities reduced substantially the number of producer goods that remained in the plan in the dual-track price system introduced in 1984. By 1992, the transition of the price system into a fully market-based system was almost completed with only 89 items left in the plan, down from a level at which virtually all producer goods were subject to strict central planning control. In 1992 the government also liberalized state retail grain prices, putting a stop to a 15-year-old fiscal black hole whereby grain bought from farmers at higher procurement prices that were largely in line with market prices was sold at lower subsidized state prices (Shea 2003, pp. 52–3; Wu 1997, p. 14).

Price reform reduced substantially the scope of state pricing. By 1994, 80 per cent of sales of producer goods, 79.3 per cent of sales of farm products and 90.4 per cent of retail sales were through the market (PYC 1995, pp. 18–21). The effects of devaluation and the austerity programme on foreign trade began to appear at the end of 1990 when a significant and unprecedented trade surplus (US$8.7 billion) was recorded. With an improved current account and low inflation (below 3 per cent), the gap between the official and swap market exchange rates shrank to about RMB0.5–0.6 in 1991 (Figure 3.3). This gap was far more sustainable than the over RMB3 gap in 1988–89. The small gap indicated that it was the appropriate time for authorities to introduce the managed float system for the renminbi, which the authorities hoped would establish a closer link between the official and swap rates (Tsang 1994).

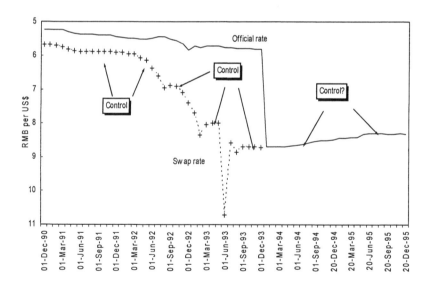

Source: Adapted from Wu (1998, Figure 3).

Figure 3.3   Official and swap market renminbi rates (1990–95)

To Control or Not to Control?

The fundamental problems of the Chinese economy at this time were structural rather than cyclical, stemming from the economic distortions under central planning which could not be removed without deeper economic reform. By 1992 prices had stabilized and the Chinese government saw that it could end its austerity programme. Even so conservatives among China's leadership remained concerned that further economic reform could reactivate inflation. Deng Xiaoping's call for 'bolder reforms' spurred the government to end its austerity programme, but as the expansionary policy took hold, the old dilemmas quickly resurfaced with great force.

Economic expansion led to strong demand for capital construction, stimulating a significant rise in imports. This created a surge in the demand for foreign exchange in the swap market. From May to July 1992, the renminbi depreciated by 20 per cent from about RMB6 to RMB7.5 per US dollar in the swap market. As is evident from Figure 3.3, from August to October 1992 the authorities had to intervene in the swap market to keep the exchange rate from depreciating beyond RMB7 per US dollar. When control on the exchange rate was lifted in November, the renminbi depreciated and by the beginning of 1993 the swap rate had fallen to RMB8 per US dollar. During 1992 the consumer price index rose by 14.7 per cent (Figure 3.2) and China recorded a trade deficit of US$12.2 billion (Figure 3.1), raising expectations that the official renminbi rate would be devalued. Devaluation expectations encouraged capital flight through multiple channels: import over-invoicing, export under-invoicing, fake import documents, and transfer pricing by foreign-invested enterprises (Li 1998; Song 1999; Ren 2001), which in turn encouraged black market activities in foreign exchange (Zhang 2001).

For two years prior to unifying the two exchange systems in January 1994, China's authorities struggled with the choice: to control or not to control? Control would be a retrogressive step away from reform, but without control the gap between the official and swap rates would be too large to be sustainable and pressure to devalue the official rate would become too strong to resist. The authorities' response was to intervene. Figure 3.3 indicates that the largest intervention occurred in June 1993 when the swap rate fell to over RMB11 per US dollar, which was a discount of almost 50 per cent under the official rate of RMB5.7 per US dollar. The authorities fixed the swap rate at RMB8.7 per US dollar, which lasted till the unification of the official and swap markets at the prevailing swap market rate of RMB8.7 per US dollar on 1 January 1994.

UNIFICATION AND CURRENT ACCOUNT CONVERTIBILITY (1994–2002)

Although unification of the official and swap rates was widely thought of as further liberalization of foreign exchange, Tsang (1994, p. 31) views the move as an attempt by the authorities to recentralize foreign exchange and gain greater control over it. The main motivation for unification was to eliminate contradictions in the dual-track foreign exchange system in order to exercise better control over the demand for and supply of foreign exchange. The authorities realized from their experiences in 1992–93 that the dual-track system was unsustainable in the long term. The dual rates provided incentive for actors to engage in arbitrage and encouraged rent-seeking, but the system did not allow the authorities to control foreign exchange effectively. The central government's immediate objectives with unification were to increase foreign exchange earnings, reduce foreign exchange spending, and gain control over a larger stock of foreign exchange through regulating foreign exchange purchases and sales. A bonus to the authorities from unification was the implied devaluation of the unified official and swap renminbi exchange rate, as the lower swap rate was adopted as the unified rate, which reduced the encouragement to capital flight.

However, it was the difficulties in managing the dual-track foreign exchange system in a highly inflationary and unstable environment that forced the authorities to make the unification decision. All available information suggests that the decision was made rather unexpectedly and within a very short time. Less than 18 months before the decision was announced, it seemed that all efforts were being made to develop a more integrated nationwide foreign exchange market. In August 1992, the so-called National Foreign Exchange Open Market (*Quanguo waihui gongkai shichang*) was opened in Beijing, which for the first time allowed members of the market to trade foreign exchange via an electronic network. At about the same time, Yin Jieyan, the head of the SAFE, disclosed that there was an ongoing trial in selected regions on foreign exchange cash retention that aimed further to improve foreign exchange swap market transactions (ACFB 1993, p. 22). By the end of 1992, according to the SAFE, 11 cities were included in the cash retention trial (ACFB 1993, p. 48). In April, the SAFE issued its first regulations on foreign exchange swap markets, Regulations on Foreign Exchange Adjustment Markets. The regulations emphasized that 'no administrative measures should be used by any region or any government office to intervene in foreign exchange market transactions' (Clause 13) (ACFB 1994, pp. 352–3).

The decision to unify the dual exchange rates was also driven to some extent by the authorities' desire to move China's foreign exchange and trade systems closer to the international standards set by the IMF and the World Trade Organization (WTO) (formerly GATT – General Agreement on Tariffs and Trade). By the time of unification, the renminbi had become conditionally convertible for current account transactions, indicating that China's trade and foreign exchange regimes were closer to achieving the standards set by the WTO and the IMF.

According to Ba (1999, p. 163), the architects of the 1994 unification never expected what they managed to achieve after unification – a very stable renminbi (Appendix Table 3A.2), and accumulation of one of the world's largest foreign exchange reserves. They were conservative and concerned mainly with how to gain effective control over the foreign exchange market in order to prevent massive capital flight and a big decline in foreign reserves, to keep the renminbi stable. Official measures adopted after unification followed the principle of 'easy to get in, tough to get out' (*kuan jin yan chu*) for foreign exchange transactions (ACFB 1995, pp. 380–81). The concerns of the authorities turned out to be unfounded and later in this chapter we show that China's overcautious post-unification foreign exchange *kuan jin yan chu* principle made the implementation of sensible macroeconomic policy more difficult.

Unification and Increased Control

Following unification of the official and swap market exchange rates, the authorities implemented a series of measures to gain greater control over foreign exchange. Domestic enterprises, units and organizations were allocated a limited number of designated banks that were granted rights to handle sales and purchases of foreign exchange. A compulsory foreign exchange sales system (*qiangpo jiehui zhi*) replaced the foreign exchange retention and foreign exchange trading rights management system. Domestic enterprises, units and organizations could sell their foreign exchange export earnings only to their designated banks and had to purchase their foreign exchange required for imports or non-trade payments exclusively from their designated banks. This rule covered virtually all foreign exchange sales and purchases with only a few exceptions, and the use of foreign currency in any pricing and settlement in the domestic market was formally banned (PBC 1993).

To ensure some banks did not have excess foreign exchange while other banks were unable to meet the demand for foreign exchange, an inter-bank foreign exchange market was established and started operations on 4 April 1994. In the first quarter of 1994, the exchange rate was based on a weighted average of prices in 18 major swap markets around the country, then still operating for foreign-invested enterprises (ACFB 1995, pp. 55–6). The initial operations of China's inter-bank foreign exchange market reflected the government's effort at recentralizing foreign exchange. The inter-bank market was a highly controlled market with two giant players – the central bank (People's Bank of China, PBC) and the BOC – that participated asymmetrically in foreign exchange sales and purchases. A 1996 survey shows that the BOC was the largest seller, accounting for 70–80 per cent of total foreign exchange sales, and the PBC was the largest buyer, accounting for 70–80 per cent of total foreign exchange purchases (Lin 1996, pp. 47–8). Only 13 designated state banks among the participating banks and non-bank institutions had permission to conduct both foreign exchange sales and purchases;[15] others were allowed only to sell but not to buy foreign exchange in the inter-bank foreign exchange market.

Banks traded foreign exchange according to the PBC's benchmark rate or median rate (*zhongjian jia*) for the US dollar that was based on the rate of the previous day and changes in the international foreign exchange market, which was published daily. The exchange rates of individual banks were allowed to vary but only within a given range. The prices of foreign exchange for transactions between banks were not allowed to move above or below 0.3 per cent of the median price quoted by the PBC. For transactions between enterprises and their designated banks, the range was set at +/– 0.25 per cent of the median price (Lin 1996). Furthermore, the PBC introduced a proportional limitation management rule to prevent speculative activity by banks in the foreign exchange market. The rule specified that the amount of foreign exchange held by a given bank should be proportional to the total amount of foreign exchange settled with this bank plus the bank's own foreign exchange assets; any foreign exchange above the amount allowed by the rule must be sold in the inter-bank market (Tao 1998).

Some transitional arrangements for the existing accounts for retained foreign exchange held by enterprises were made.[16] The swap system was retained for foreign-invested enterprises for a transition period after unification. Swap markets for foreign-invested enterprises were integrated into the inter-bank–market system and pricing in swap markets was based on the inter-bank–market exchange rate plus a 0.15 per cent service charge (ACFB 1995, p. 59).

Unresolved Problems

Unification did not signal the end of the process of transforming China's foreign exchange regime from a centrally planned to a market system.

Foreign-invested enterprises continued to trade separately from other enterprises in the swap market and domestic enterprises were still not allowed to trade freely in foreign exchange. As unification of the exchange rates was an attempt at recentralization, the reforms were more conservative than the earlier recommendation of granting export enterprises the right to retain 100 per cent foreign exchange in cash.

Export enterprises had to sell all their foreign exchange earnings to their designated banks at the exchange rate offered by the banks under the compulsory foreign exchange settlement system. Enterprises were not allowed to keep foreign exchange cash accounts from which they could withdraw foreign exchange at will (Shi 1995, p. 34). They could not change their designated banks without permission and the PBC's control of the exchange rate ensured that the exchange rates quoted by different banks were virtually the same or very similar. These banks played no role in the exchange market and had to accept passively any rate published by the PBC.

Although enterprises were entitled to purchase foreign exchange up to the amount they had settled with the banking system and held in their foreign exchange accounts, they had to obtain various approvals from the authorities by presenting valid documents for imports.[17] Any foreign exchange purchase that was over 50 per cent of an enterprise's entitled foreign exchange was subject to more restrictions, indicating that there were still disguised dual exchange rates (Tao 1995). The system made it difficult for enterprises to manage foreign exchange risks. For example, an enterprise had to sell its foreign exchange earnings even if it expected a likely rise in the price of foreign exchange in the near future.

Domestic enterprises, because they were prohibited from having foreign exchange cash accounts and faced difficult and complicated procedures when they tried to purchase foreign exchange, had a powerful incentive to exploit any loophole in the system. A major loophole available to domestic enterprises was the foreign exchange cash accounts of foreign-invested enterprises, which were not integrated into the new system prior to July 1996. Domestic enterprises illegally traded with foreign-invested enterprises to obtain foreign exchange in cash and established false joint ventures with foreign partners to keep their foreign exchange earnings in cash (Tao 1995).

Towards Current Account Convertibility

To close these loopholes and to clear the remaining obstacles to current account convertibility for the renminbi, the government decided to bring foreign-invested enterprises into the unified foreign exchange system. From July 1996, foreign-invested enterprises could choose which system to use for their foreign exchange transactions. According to Chen Yuan, then deputy governor of the PBC, the procedures involved in foreign exchange sales and purchase for foreign-invested enterprises were almost identical to those for domestic enterprises; the key difference was in the new system – foreign-invested enterprises could retain a proportion of their foreign exchange in a cash account. [18] The preferential treatment granted to foreign-invested enterprises was to encourage them to settle their foreign exchange with the banking system.

In another move to achieve WTO and IMF compatibility, foreign-invested enterprises that still chose to trade foreign exchange in the swap system were no longer required to have their licence to trade in the swap market verified and approved by the SAFE (*Renmin ribao* 21 June 1996). In December 1996, the Chinese government announced that it had lifted the remaining restrictions on non-trade transactions in the current account, including private transactions, and formally accepted all the IMF provisions in Article 8 covering current account convertibility. Full current account convertibility was thus achieved four years ahead of the previously announced schedule. Two years later in December 1998 the authorities closed all swap centres. Their closure marked the end of a two-decade transition from a centrally planned, essentially multiple exchange rate system, to an inter-bank market-based single exchange rate system (ACFB 1999, p. 76).

Further efforts were made to encourage domestic enterprises not to delay their sales of foreign exchange earnings to the banking system, or divert their foreign exchange current account earnings illegally to the capital account, or hold foreign exchange illegally abroad. In a significant move, the authorities decided to allow, from 15 October 1997, selected domestic enterprises to keep a proportion of their foreign exchange earnings (ACFB 1998, pp. 52–3). As stated in the PBC Circular No. 402 (1997) (ACFB 1998, p. 382), to qualify to keep a foreign exchange cash account in a designated bank, an enterprise should satisfy the following criteria: (1) have total value of trade (export and import) above US$30 million and have at least RMB10 million registered capital for a trade corporation; or (2) have total value of trade above US$10 million and have at least RMB30 million registered capital for a production enterprise that has a trade permit. The amount of foreign exchange that could be kept in a cash account for use at an enterprise's discretion was equivalent to 15 per cent of its total trade value for the previous year. This rule favoured large SOEs but it nevertheless facilitated development of the foreign exchange market by allowing some domestic enterprises together with foreign-invested enterprises to participate actively, though only at the margin, in the foreign exchange market.

On the eve of China's accession to the WTO and four years after introducing the above measures, the authorities relaxed foreign exchange regulations further. Effective from 1 December 2001, the total trade value required for opening a foreign exchange account was reduced to US$2 million for exports and US$0.2 million for imports, and the amount of foreign exchange that an enterprise was allowed to retain was increased to 25 per cent of either its export or import value, whichever was smaller. However, export value was no longer based on the total value of export transactions, but on export earnings sold to an enterprise's designated bank, indicating that an important objective of the relaxation was to encourage enterprises to sell their foreign exchange earnings promptly and completely to their designated banks (SAFE 2001 No. 184).

While further liberalizing the state's management of foreign exchange, the authorities were making additional efforts to enforce the remaining rules. Significant devaluations of Asian currencies during the Asian financial crisis raised devaluation expectations for the renminbi and caused disguised capital flight through misinvoicing and fake transactions. Faced with a massive capital flight, the SAFE strengthened measures to verify foreign exchange payments and earnings (ACFB 1999, pp. 298–301). In its 1999 No. 103 Circular, the SAFE announced an annual check-up and appraisal system on foreign exchange sales under which export enterprises would be rewarded or penalized according to their 'foreign exchange settlement rate', measured as a ratio of settled export earnings to verified export transactions (ACFB 2000, pp. 312–14).[19] Towards the end of the 1990s, while implementing more stringent measures to verify foreign exchange earnings from exports, the SAFE reinforced its verification measures on import transactions. In the second half of 1998, the SAFE worked with other government bodies to conduct a nationwide campaign targeting fake import documents submitted to Customs, during which 13 800 forged papers with a combined written value of RMB11 billion were found among import claims with individual values of over RMB0.2 million (SAFE 1998, p. 25).

Defying most projections at the beginning of unification, the renminbi did not depreciate but actually appreciated after unification. By 1996 the renminbi had appreciated 4.8 per cent from RMB8.7 to RMB8.3 per US dollar and had remained very stable within the range of RMB8.30 to RMB8.28 until China unpegged the currency from the US dollar. The PBC managed to keep the renminbi rate stable during the Asian financial crisis in 1997–98 when most of the currencies of China's Asian neighbours depreciated substantially. It appeared that the government was determined to defend the renminbi for political reasons, but in reality, renminbi depreciation might not have benefited China significantly as its exports are highly dependent on imported materials.[20] Instead of renminbi devaluation, it was fiscal support to exports, especially tax rebates on exports, that minimized the negative impact of Asia's financial crisis on China's exports.

MACROECONOMIC PROBLEMS

In a centrally planned economy, the foreign trade plan is an integrated component of the central plan and the foreign exchange regime is designed to facilitate foreign trade planning. The domestic currency is typically overvalued so the government can subsidize imports by taxing exports, a policy that is in line with pursuit of an import-substitution strategy. However, taxing exports to subsidize imports has limits. Sooner or later taxing exports will affect the incentive to export, and direct fiscal subsidies are required to compensate for the overvalued exchange rate. When foreign trade becomes a significant share of gross domestic product (GDP), the size of fiscal subsidies required will be prohibitive and cannot be sustained in the long run.

In China, when market-oriented reform began to correct price distortions and increase prices of primary products that were underpriced significantly under central planning, it inevitably increased the cost to FTCs of exporting, which required a change in foreign exchange and trade policies. Exchange rate policy becomes more complicated when an economy becomes liberalized and policymakers can no longer ignore the response of external actors to their policies. For example, with the Chinese economy becoming increasingly open and reliant on inflows of foreign investment, the government has to consider the effect of the price of the renminbi on capital account transactions. However, in the early years of reform China's authorities were still used to relying on material balances to manage the economy and were not yet ready to manage an economy that had become increasingly monetized.

China's Foreign Exchange Reserves

From 1997 onwards, current account convertibility and capital account inconvertibility are the main features of China's post-unification foreign exchange system. China's government had significant problems working with this foreign exchange system to coordinate foreign exchange policy and macroeconomic management. The most serious problem that this foreign exchange system created for the government is difficulty with the conduct of monetary policy.

Figure 3.4 shows the significant build-up of China's foreign exchange reserves after exchange rate unification. From 1993 to September 2004, China's foreign exchange reserves increased from US$21.2 billion to US$514.5 billion or about 34 per cent per annum.[21] Almost all policy measures after unification have tended to exacerbate the imbalance in the foreign exchange market, or more precisely, to make the supply of foreign exchange continuously outstrip the demand for foreign exchange.

After unification a one-off policy effect increased China's foreign exchange reserves when domestic enterprises were forced to sell all their previously accumulated foreign exchange within a three-month period before their foreign exchange accounts were closed. Some of the foreign exchange that was forcibly sold included foreign exchange purchased by domestic enterprises before unification in anticipation of renminbi devaluation (Sun 1995, pp. 32–3). Foreign exchange sales also included a large amount of foreign exchange held by residents (Ba 1999, p. 171). As a result of these sales in 1994, China's foreign reserves increased by 144 per cent (US$30.4 billion) that year (Figure 3.4), which was the largest annual increase in foreign exchange reserves ever recorded in China. The stock of foreign reserves increased steadily until the Asian financial crisis, when it stabilized; but it resumed rapid growth after 2001. The scale of China's foreign exchange reserves can be seen from Figure 3.4. Since 1995, the stock of China's foreign exchange reserves has been continuously above 50 per cent of annual imports, or more than sufficient to cover six months of imports. Between 1997–98 and 2003–04, China's foreign reserves were equal to or more than 100 per cent of annual imports.

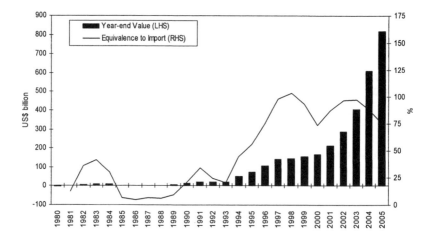

Source: Data to 2004 are from NBS (1981–2006). Data for 2005 are from the website of SAFE, available at www.safe.gov.cn/Statistics/Reserve_data_05.htm.

Figure 3.4   Build-up of China's foreign exchange reserves and its equivalence to imports (1981–2005)

Most researchers (for example Ba 1999; Yi and Fan 1997; Sun 1997; Zhang 1997) agree that surpluses in both the current and capital accounts have contributed to the post-unification rapid increase in China's foreign exchange reserves, with surpluses in the capital account becoming increasingly important. These researchers have based their studies mainly on data in China's balance of payments (BOP) accounts. Their research approach is controversial. The SAFE released its accounts on foreign exchange sales and purchases for the first time in 1997 and these accounts tell a story that is the opposite of what is shown in the BOP accounts. For example, as Yang calculated, between 1994 and 1996, the huge capital account 'surplus' of US$112.7 billion reported in the BOP accounts turns into a 'deficit' of US$7.8 billion in the SAFE's accounts on foreign exchange sales and purchases, which seems to suggest that the current account surplus could explain almost the entire increase in China's foreign exchange reserves during that period (Yang 2000, Tables 3.6 and 3.7).[22]

However, the SAFE's foreign exchange sales and purchases accounts are not exactly comparable to the BOP accounts because some items in the latter do not involve actual foreign exchange sales or purchases. For example, the reinvestment of renminbi profits by foreign-invested enterprises does not appear in the SAFE's foreign exchange sales and purchases accounts but is included in the BOP accounts as a 'debt' item under the current account (profit remittance) and a 'credit' item under the capital account (that is, inflow of foreign direct investment).[23] After reconciling the two accounts and using other data, Yang (2000, pp. 121–5) estimated that 88 per cent of China's foreign exchange reserves in 1994–96 were attributed to surplus in the current account, which challenges the view of other researchers who calculated a far lower figure and attributed a greater proportion of the increase in foreign reserves to foreign investment.[24]

Even if China's current account surplus is largely responsible for the increase in China's foreign reserves, capital inflow in the form of FDI played a significant role in creating this surplus. FDI inflows into China promote China's exports, and China's accumulation of foreign exchange reserves since 1994 (Figure 3.4) is closely associated with both improvements in trade balances (Figure 3.1) and increases in FDI (Figure 3.5). Figure 3.5 shows that the impact of exchange rate unification with a 35 per cent devaluation of the official renminbi rate on FDI in 1994 was enormous but temporary. The impact on FDI after 1994 is small after the unprecedented annual increase in FDI of 150 per cent in 1992 and 1993; but continuous FDI inflows into China since exchange rate unification have resulted in a significant build-up of accumulated FDI (Figure 3.5). Official statistics show that along with the steady growth in FDI since the 1990s, China's exports attributed to foreign-invested enterprises increased from 29 per cent of total exports in 1994 (NBS 1998) to a much more significant share of 57 per cent in November 2004.[25]

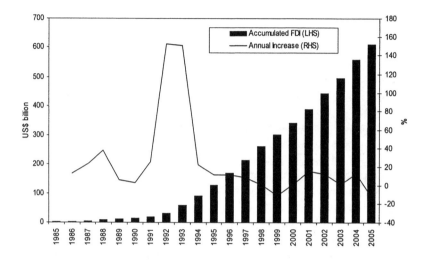

Source: Data to 2004 are from NBS (various issues). Data for 2005 cover only to November and are published on the website of the Ministry of Commerce, available at www.fdi.gov.cn.

Figure 3.5   Foreign direct investment in China (1985–2005)

Dilemma in Fiscal Policy

Chinese authorities tend to use fiscal subsidies rather than manipulate the exchange rate to promote exports.[26] The types of subsidies used include direct subsidies to export losses, writing off bank loans of export-producing enterprises, and de facto excess tax rebate for exports. As pointed out earlier, direct fiscal subsidies to export losses ceased in 1991. However, informal or indirect subsidies remained. For example, the government has granted preferential interest treatment to exporting industries and enterprises. With fiscal support, banks also wrote off most of the RMB15 billion debt that FTCs incurred in 1988–90 (Yang 2000, p. 63). However, the most significant fiscal support to exports is financial subsidies from excess tax rebates to exporters (Xu and Lin 2004).

In principle, export tax rebate is a neutral instrument if it rebates only the amount of value-added taxes (VAT) paid on inputs in the production of commodities for export, which is the standard practice in international trade. Strictly speaking, China has never used explicit excess rebate rate or higher-than-VAT rebate rate to promote exports. When China introduced its new taxation system in 1994, the general rebate rates to manufacturers, resource-based goods producers and small businesses were respectively 17, 13 and 6 per cent, which were the general VAT rates imposed on these producers (Liu 2001, pp. 52–7). In reality, inadequate verification of exports and rebate claims in the context of an overall policy environment favouring exports led to a de facto excess rebate rate paid to exports. Fabricated rebate claims surged in the first two years of the new fiscal system. From 1994 to mid-1995, 5770 fabricated cases were reported, involving RMB6.8 billion or almost 10 per cent of total rebates of about RMB70 billion for that period (Yang 2000, p. 65).

The central government, which received 75 per cent of VAT but was solely responsible for VAT rebates to exporters, faced a difficult situation with the growth in the value of export rebates significantly outstripping the growth in VAT revenue. In 1995, while VAT revenue rose by only 12.7 per cent, the value of export rebates increased by 22 per cent. In 1996, export rebates jumped by over 50 per cent but growth in VAT revenue was only 13.8 per cent (NBS 2003, p. 283). Local governments received 25 per cent of VAT revenues but were not responsible for paying the export rebates. They were therefore tolerant of local efforts to exaggerate the value of export rebates payable.

The imbalance between VAT revenue and export rebates placed the central government in a dilemma. The imbalance clearly was evidence of fraud but it also indicated de facto subsidization of exports. The central government had tried without success to improve markedly the administration of export rebates, but for fiscal reasons was forced instead to reduce export rebate rates. It reduced rebate rates twice, in July 1995 and January 1996, lowering the average rebate rate of 16.3 per cent in 1994 to 8.3 per cent in 1996 (State Council 1995a, 1995b). But export growth fell 20 per cent in 1995 and 1 per cent in 1996 (NBS 2003, p. 654) and the central government responded by instructing the taxation authorities to relax export verification and speed up payment of export rebates. As expected, the government's instruction encouraged fabricated rebate claims.

Between 1997 and 1999, the Asian financial crisis raised the prospect of renminbi devaluation. This prospect encouraged enterprises to send capital overseas illegally through over-invoicing of imports and under-invoicing of exports and delay settlement of their export earnings with their designated banks. As rebates could be paid only after foreign exchange settlement, the value of rebates declined sharply during this period, which was followed by a considerable decline in export growth in 1998 (Figure 3.6). To compete with Asian neighbours that had more competitive exchange rates, the government raised rebate rates by an average of 2.58 percentage points in 1999 (MOC and SAT 1999a, 1999b), which could be considered a de facto devaluation of the renminbi for exports. In 2001, the rebate rate for textile products was raised from 15 to 17 per cent (SAT 2001).

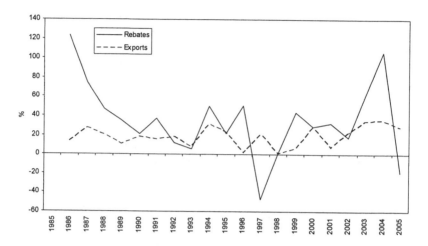

Source: See Figure 3.1 for export data. Data on the tax rebates for exports are from the website of SAT, available at www.chinatax.gov.cn.

Figure 3.6   Annual changes in exports and export rebates (1986–2005)

Exports boomed in response to the increase in the rebate rates, but the problem of an excessive rebate worsened, putting pressure on the national budget. By the end of 2003, unpaid rebates totalled RMB200 billion, and some Chinese analysts referred to these as 'disguised fiscal expenditure' (Sui 2004). Pressure on China's national budget and from the US government over the increasing US trade deficit with China propelled China in 2004 to reform its export rebate system. The 2004 reform significantly cut the average rebate rate for most manufacturing industries from 15 or 17 per cent to 13 per cent. More importantly, a centre–local rebate-sharing system was introduced, under which the local export value of 2003 was set as the benchmark value for future rebate arrangements after 2004. The central government would be responsible for paying all rebates for exports valued below the benchmark, but both the central (75 per cent) and local (25 per cent) governments would pay the rebates for exports valued above the benchmark. In implementing this export rebate split, as explained in official documents (MOF and SAT 2003) and by trade officials in Guangdong Province, local governments had to pay the 25 per cent rebate first before the central government would pay the remaining 75 per cent.

The implication of this new rebate system was obvious. With the new system, local governments had a greater incentive to verify export rebate entitlements since in theory they were responsible for paying a portion of the rebate, which they did not have to do before. This would reduce the 'real' as opposed to the 'nominal' rate of export rebates to enterprises and lower the incentive of enterprises to export. But there were also doubts as to whether local governments had the financial resources to pay the export rebates. Trade officials in China's most export-oriented province, Guangdong, voiced concerns that local export growth might suffer from the introduction of the new export rebate system. Local governments complained that they found it difficult to balance their budgets with the additional burden of funding their share of the rebates. In some localities exporting enterprises agreed to 'lend' the local government the 25 per cent rebate even though the prospect of the local government ever being able to repay the loan was poor, because these enterprises could receive at least 75 per cent of their rebate entitlements from the central government.[27]

The above-entitlement export rebates paid by the centre to enterprises had supplemented the export subsidies that local governments often paid to encourage exports to promote local development. The new rebate system altered the way local governments viewed local industry support. Many local governments, while they might be willing to continue to subsidize local enterprises manufacturing for export, were now lukewarm towards FTCs. A city mayor in southern China was reported to express the view that he no longer welcomed FTCs in his city because the city could not afford to pay the export rebates (NDRC 2005). FTCs, unlike manufacturing enterprises producing for export, do not generate significant local employment.

Despite complaints from local governments, all outstanding rebates were paid by the end of 2004. These rebates included RMB200 billion of unpaid rebates at the end of 2003 and RMB220 billion of rebates incurred in 2004 (reported on New China Web, 11 January 2005). Due to complaints from local governments, the central government changed the 75:25 per cent share of responsibility for above-benchmark export rebates between the central and local governments to 92.5:7.5 per cent, from 1 January 2005 (NDRC 2005). Despite this change, US pressure on China over China's booming trade surplus and China's fiscal deficits combined to induce Chinese policymakers to reduce the export rebates paid in 2005 (Figure 3.6) and caused a fall in the renminbi rate of return per US dollar of exports.[28]

Dilemma in Monetary Policy

The ever-increasing supply of foreign exchange created for China's monetary authorities a huge dilemma that they did not experience before unifying the dual exchange rate regime. With the overriding policy target of a stable renminbi exchange rate – where the renminbi was virtually pegged to the US dollar – the PBC's ability to control the money supply and hence conduct monetary policy was highly circumscribed. Since the PBC had to buy all excess foreign exchange in the inter-bank market to stabilize the value of the renminbi, a substantial increase in the supply of foreign exchange translated into a substantial increase in the domestic money supply.

There was an unusual structural change in the PBC's monetary base after unification of the exchange rates. In 1990–93, the ratio of foreign exchange (renminbi equivalent value) to the reserve money was less than 10 per cent on average, with 11 per cent for 1993.[29] As shown in Table 3.2, this more than doubled to 25 per cent in 1994 and increased further to about 33 per cent in 1995–96. From 1997 to 2002 it remained at around 44 per cent on average. For the first ten months of 2005 it jumped to nearly 100 per cent, adding fuel to the international debate over whether China was manipulating the renminbi to keep it undervalued.

The significant increase in the foreign exchange component in China's monetary base (see the ratio of foreign exchange to reserve money in Table 3.2) implies that the PBC's ability to control money supply has weakened. The PBC's own researchers recognized this problem and have written about it in numerous publications (see for example Lü 1996, pp. 53–4; Yi and Fan 1997, pp. 33–4; Ba 1999, pp. 237–8). In Table 3.2 we estimate the likely impact of the increase in foreign exchange on the money supply that is measured as 'money and quasi-money' or M2 in the PBC's regular 'Money Survey' tables. In estimating this impact we remove the effect of the PBC's sterilization efforts on M2 and show in the last column of Table 3.2 the share of the total increase in M2 that is due to the increase in foreign exchange that the PBC passively purchased to maintain the renminbi exchange rate.[30]

We first estimate the money multiplier based on M2 and the monetary base, which the PBC defines as reserve money (H). The multiplier has been increasing gradually, indicating an economy growing in sophistication, which is relying proportionately less on cash and more on bank deposits. In the second step we use this multiplier and stock of outstanding PBC bills to calculate the amount of money supply reduced by the stock of outstanding PBC bills (sterilization) and add this to M2 to derive 'M2 without PBC sterilization (I). This is then used to calculate the impact of sterilization (J). Finally we use the change in foreign reserves to estimate the share of the increase in non-sterilized M2 from the PBC's passive purchase of foreign exchange (K) or foreign exchange impact factor.

As Table 3.2 shows, reform of the foreign exchange regime in 1994 was immediately followed by a significant increase in the foreign exchange–reserve money ratio. This is largely because there was no longer an expectation of renminbi devaluation after the official renminbi rate was devalued by over 30 per cent at unification. During 1994–97, about 44 per cent of the increase in the non-sterilized money supply was attributed to the

Table 3.2 Foreign exchange reserves and money supply in China (RMB100 million) (1993–2006)

	Monetary base				Adjusted monetary base			Money supply			Share of foreign exchange component in increase in M2[8]
	Reserve money	M0[1]	Foreign exchange[2]	PBC bills outstanding	Foreign exchange-reserve money ratio	Adjusted reserve money[3]	M2[4]	Underlying money multiplier[5]	M2 without sterilization[6]	Impact of sterilization (%)[7]	
	A	B	C	D	E=C/A	F=A+D	G	H=G/A	I=H*F	J=G/I-1	K=H*dC/dI
1993	13 147	5 865	1 432	0	10.9	13 147	34 880	2.7	34 880	0.0	0.64
1994	17 218	7 289	4 264	0	24.8	17 218	46 924	2.7	46 924	0.0	0.46
1995	20 760	7 885	6 511	197	31.4	20 957	60 751	2.9	61 328	-0.9	0.54
1996	26 889	8 802	9 330	0	34.7	26 889	76 095	2.8	76 095	0.0	0.65
1997	30 633	10 178	12 649	119	41.3	30 752	90 995	3.0	91 348	-0.4	0.11
1998	31 335	11 204	13 088	119	41.8	31 453	104 499	3.3	104 896	-0.4	0.22
1999	33 620	13 456	14 061	119	41.8	33 739	119 898	3.6	120 322	-0.4	0.19
2000	36 491	14 653	14 815	0	40.6	36 491	134 610	3.7	134 610	0.0	0.68
2001	39 852	15 689	18 850	0	47.3	39 852	158 302	4.0	158 302	0.0	0.41
2002	45 138	17 278	22 107	1 488	49.0	46 626	185 007	4.1	191 104	-3.2	0.76
2003	52 841	19 746	29 842	3 032	56.5	55 873	221 223	4.2	233 915	-5.4	1.03
2004	58 856	21 468	45 940	11 079	78.1	69 935	253 208	4.3	300 871	-15.8	0.82
2005	64 343	24 032	62 140	20 296	96.6	84 639	298 755	4.6	392 993	-24.0	1.17
2006	77 758	27 073	84 361	29 741	108.5	107 498	345 578	4.4	477 754	-27.7	

Notes:
1 M0 is currency in circulation.
2 All foreign exchange figures are denoted in renminbi. See Appendix 3.2 for the US$-RMB exchange rate.
3 Adjusted reserve money is reserve money plus value of outstanding PBC bills (i.e. no sterilization). The PBC treats reserve money as the monetary base.
4 M2 includes M1 (M0 plus demand deposits) and all other deposits.
5 Derived by dividing the annual M2 by the annual reserve money.
6 Adjusted reserve money multiplied by the money multiplier.
7 Fall in M2 as a result of sterilization.

Table 3.2 (continued)

[8] Annual change in foreign exchange multiplied by the multiplier and then divided by annual change in the pre-sterilization M2. Result for 1993 is for reference only, since it is not directly compatible with the other years (see endnote 29 for details).

Source: 1993–2004 data are from PBC (1994-2005), updated data for 2005 and 2006 are from the PBC website: www.pbc.gov.cn. Original data are year-end values.

increase in foreign exchange reserves. This dropped to 17 per cent on average during the Asian financial crisis and its aftermath (1998–2000) because of strong expectations of renminbi devaluation. After 2000 the accumulation of foreign exchange accelerated, supported by excessive export rebates, and once again posed problems for China's monetary authorities. The impact factor increased to more than 60 per cent on average in 2001–03 and jumped to 100 per cent in 2004 and 82 per cent in 2005.[31] In response, the PBC substantially increased the sale of bills to sterilize the foreign exchange effect on the money supply in 2004 and during the first ten months of 2005. In the two years since 2003, the value of PBC bills outstanding increased by more than RMB1.7 trillion.

Identified and unidentified capital flows explain the changes in the foreign exchange impact on China's money supply. Following the Asian financial crisis, between 1998 and 2000, there was a significant slowdown in the increase in foreign exchange reserves, which reduced the impact of foreign exchange on the money supply. The reason for the slowdown was large-scale capital flight by speculators in anticipation of renminbi devaluation, which did not eventuate. The situation changed in 2003–05. Large inflows of FDI followed China's entry into the WTO in 2001 and speculation about possible revaluation of the renminbi, which was fuelled by the US government's claims that the renminbi was undervalued. There is strong evidence to support the view that a large part of the capital inflow has been foreign exchange earnings held illegally outside China. According to a report by Mei Xinyu, a researcher in the Chinese Academy of International Trade and Economic Cooperation (CAITEC) of China's Ministry of Commerce (MOC),[32] offshore financial centres, where 'tens of thousands' of Chinese companies are registered, are sources of significant investment flows into the PRC (excluding Hong Kong and Macao) (Zhong Jing 2004). In 2003, actual investment flows into the PRC (excluding Hong Kong and Macao) from the British Virgin Islands and Bermuda were exceeded only by investments from, in order, Japan, South Korea, the US and Taiwan. Singapore ranked fifth as a source of investment after this latter group of countries, followed by West Samoa and the Cayman Islands. More investments flowed into the PRC (excluding Hong Kong and Macao) from the British Virgin Islands, Bermuda, Western Samoa and the Cayman Islands than from Germany, the UK or France (NBS 2004, pp. 732–4).

In 1994–96, the PBC had two monetary policy targets: exchange rate stability and control of inflation. However, substantial sales of renminbi required to keep the exchange rate stable were a major factor behind the record inflation in 1994 (Figure 3.2). Exchange rate stability was at the expense of price stability. To preserve price stability, the PBC had to sterilize the rise in money supply from its passive purchase of foreign exchange. But since the bond market was still underdeveloped, the PBC was unable to conduct open market operations to sterilize the increase in money supply, which became possible only in 2003. In the absence of open market operations, the PBC had to rely on recalling loans from commercial banks as well as requiring commercial banks to increase their ad hoc deposits with the PBC (Ba 1999; Tao 1998; Yi and Fan 1997). These actions enabled significant tightening of credit in the economy and eventually brought inflation under control in 1996 (Figure 3.2).

Having achieved its monetary targets, the PBC now faced a new problem. The credit squeeze caused a severe shortage of working capital in the economy. Non-exporting SOEs were the worst affected. State banks are the designated banks for SOEs and monetary sterilization affected mainly these banks. Foreign-invested enterprises and exporting SOEs were protected somewhat from the credit squeeze. The former could obtain renminbi by selling foreign exchange and the latter had guaranteed access to renminbi from the system of compulsory foreign exchange sales. The credit squeeze made obvious what had been happening to the supply of working capital – most were going to export-oriented enterprises or foreign-invested enterprises after unification. The credit squeeze unintentionally stimulated exports by forcing Chinese enterprises to sell to the international market to gain working capital.

Ironically, it was the increasing unpredictability of foreign exchange supply that eventually forced the PBC to abolish credit-planning control in 1998. China had relied on credit planning as a key monetary instrument for a long time, even from the mid-1990s when most commodities were distributed by the market. The PBC's substantial passive purchases of foreign exchange had made credit planning difficult, because these purchases could not be planned in advance and the size of its purchases in a year could easily be more than half of the annual planned credit allocation (Table 3.2).[33]

The problem for the monetary authorities was that the more foreign exchange the central bank purchased, the more renminbi funds were directed to foreign-invested enterprises or domestic export-oriented enterprises and away from non-exporting domestic enterprises. For non-exporting domestic enterprises, there were two possible solutions to their shortage of working capital. The first solution was to borrow renminbi from domestic export-oriented enterprises or foreign-invested enterprises, but this would lead to illegal renminbi trading among these enterprises. The second solution was to set up joint ventures with foreign enterprises, which would lead to more inflows of foreign exchange and, given a fixed quota of credit in the credit plan, larger diversion of renminbi funds away from non-exporting domestic enterprises. Both solutions were undesirable from the PBC's perspective. The problem worsened when increasing numbers of fake joint ventures were set up with the sole aim of gaining access to renminbi funds. In this method of fundraising, foreign partners in joint ventures were offered a guaranteed risk-free return. Renminbi funds raised in this way were not covered by any renminbi lending policy and bypassed the PBC's administrative control. This increased uncertainties in money creation in the eyes of the monetary authorities and created difficulties in macroeconomic management. Some Chinese economists have described this phenomenon as *waibi benbihua* (foreign money is the root of domestic money) (Ba 1999, p. 236).

These policy dilemmas indicated that foreign exchange policy had to be changed to enable better macroeconomic management. The 'easy to get in and tough to get out' principle of foreign exchange management had caused enormous problems in macroeconomic management and was unsustainable. The authorities decided to modify the principle by making it 'not too easy to get in and not too tough to get out'. To check the rapid rise in capital inflows, which set off speculation over renminbi appreciation, the SAFE tightened the regulations over foreign exchange settlement for renminbi (SAFE 2004). To make it easier for capital to flow out, in 2003 overseas investment by domestic firms was deregulated and approval procedures including the verification of source of capital were simplified. In particular, approval of overseas investment projects of less than US$3 million was decentralized (SAFE 2003a, 2003b). Yet changes in foreign exchange management did not end with these small steps toward greater liberalization. Derivatives trading was liberalized following the discontinuation of the renminbi–US dollar peg in 2005 in favour of a managed float exchange rate regime.

SUMMARY

We have reviewed critically in this chapter the major official efforts at reforming the exchange rate regime in China and the impacts of these efforts on macroeconomic management. Reform of the foreign exchange regime is a major challenge for any centrally planned economy (CPE) in transition towards a market economy. It is inevitably tied to reform in other sectors of the economy, including foreign trade and investment, and has a major bearing on macroeconomic management. The success or otherwise of economic reform depends on macroeconomic stability during the transition period (Borensztein and Masson 1993), and macroeconomic stability depends on financial stability, which cannot easily be achieved without developed financial markets (Calvo and Kumar 1993). For China, in the absence of developed financial markets, the primary post-1994 objective of exchange rate policy has been to maintain macroeconomic stability, leaving the role of promoting exports primarily to export rebates. But after China joined the WTO, the renminbi–US dollar peg, which was the anchor for China's macroeconomic stability, made macroeconomic management difficult for the authorities in the face of significant capital flows and current account surpluses. Examination of post-Mao reform of China's exchange rate regime continues in the next chapter where we empirically investigate China's exchange rate regime in the light of foreign trade and investment.

NOTES

1. State procurement prices for agricultural products were raised by 25 per cent in 1961. In 1960 the government introduced a 10 per cent price premium on above-quota delivery of grains. After being abolished in 1961 and reinstated in 1965 in some low-yield regions, the price premium was raised to 30 per cent in 1972 and had remained until 1978 (Shea 2003, pp. 26, 30).
2. From 1955 to 1970 the renminbi–US dollar rate was unchanged at the rate of US$100 = RMB246.18. See Table 2.4.
3. See Table 2.6. It should be noted that the further appreciation of the renminbi from the 1970s was mainly the consequence of abandonment of the Bretton Woods system in 1971, which resulted in appreciation of the major currencies in the West against the US dollar and the 17 per cent devaluation of the US dollar against gold in 1973 (Appleyard and Field 1998, pp. 679–80). This change shifted China's foreign exchange rate setting from a 'compatible commodity price approach', which was a compromise between the cost of earning foreign exchange in trade transactions and the purchasing power of the Chinese currency, to a new approach that was based on 'a basket of major currencies' (Ba 1999, p. 113; Lardy 1992, p. 28).
4. For a discussion on the significance of the foreign exchange retention system, see the theoretical model discussed in Wu (1998). See also Desai and Bhagwati (1979), Anderson (1990) and Martin (1991).
5. Largely based on the then RMB2.65 cost of earning a dollar (Wang 1985, p. 21).
6. The limited variability in the internal rate was later abolished.
7. According to the head of SAFE, Yin Jieyan, the foreign exchange settlement rate (measured as settled foreign exchange to total exports) declined in 1988–90, even though the value of exports grew (ACFB 1992, p. 68).
8. Enhanced access to swap centres was provided to light manufacturing industries including garments and crafts in an export contract system with an increased retention rate of 40 per cent for planned exports (Wang 1993, p. 16) and 80 per cent for above-plan exports (Lardy 1992, p. 56).
9. Enterprises that have foreign equity.
10. No reliable information is available on the renminbi exchange rate in FEACs for the 1980s, especially for the highest spot rate during that period. According to the study by Ba (1999, p. 155), the renminbi exchange rate reached RMB8 per US dollar in 1988, but from a graphical demonstration by Pang (1996, Figure 2), the highest spot rate should be around 7.3 towards the end of 1988.
11. A study by China's State Price Bureau (SPB) on imported industrial producer goods showed that a 1 per cent increase in the price of imports due to devaluation of the renminbi would cause the general price level to rise by 1.55 per cent (Yang 2000, pp. 13–14).
12. See Yang (2000, Tables 19 and 20) for a list of the 'price wars' between 1986 and 1989 and a list of export prices over the 1988–89 period.
13. Farmers suffered huge losses too but the government did not bail them out.

14. The roles and influence of various policy actors in policymaking are examined in greater depth in Chapter 5.
15. The 13 designated state banks include the so-called 'big four', that is, Industrial and Commercial Bank of China (ICBC), Agricultural Bank of China (ABC), Bank of China (BOC), People's Construction Bank of China (PCBC), plus the Bank of Communication, CITIC Industrial Bank, Huaxia Bank, China Everbright Bank, Guangdong Development Bank, Shenzhen Development Bank, Shenzhen Merchants Bank, Shanghai Pudong Development Bank, and Fujian Industrial Bank.
16. For example, enterprises that had settled their foreign exchange earnings by the unification date could use their retained foreign exchange at the pre-unification rate. Enterprises with any unsettled foreign exchange earnings by unification could still have their entitled foreign exchange trading rights at the pre-unification rate as long as they settled their accounts by the end of January 1994 (ACFB 1993, p. 17).
17. According to the regulations on foreign exchange transactions issued by the Bank of China, foreign exchange purchases could be approved by the FEAC and the designated bank only if import enterprises could present documents on import licence, quotas, certificate and registration and passed all prerequisite examinations. These documents had to be obtained from different authorities including the State Planning Commission (SPC), State Economic Commission (SEC) and State Economic and Trade Commission (SETC) (Tao 1995).
18. The maximum amount of foreign exchange cash that a foreign-invested firm could keep depended on the firm's normal current account transactions, which were approved by the SAFE (*Renmin ribao*, 21 June 1996).
19. In the SAFE's 1999 No. 103 Circular, export enterprises are distinguished by four categories according to their foreign exchange settlement performance, that is, 'credit' with 95 per cent or above settlement rate, 'pass' with 70–94 per cent settlement rate, 'risk' with 50–69 per cent settlement rate, and 'high risk' with a rate of below 50 per cent. In a new decision jointly made by the PBC, SAFE, MOFTEC and SAT in 2000 (ACFB 2001, pp. 282–3), a 'credit' firm could receive various preferential treatments as rewards, including low interest rate for a renminbi loan and high limit for a foreign exchange cash account. But a 'risk' or 'high risk' firm could lose its export permit.
20. This point is discussed in greater depth in Chapter 5.
21. The 2004 figure has not been adjusted to take into account likely additional increases in foreign exchange reserves from September to the end of 2004.
22. The SAFE stopped publishing data on its foreign exchange sales and purchase account after 1998 and so we can no longer compare the SAFE's figures with figures in the BOP accounts.
23. Another example is foreign direct investment in kind (machinery and equipment) that almost every foreign direct investment project involves. Such items are excluded in the SAFE's foreign exchange sales and purchases account, but recorded as a 'debt' item under the current account (imported goods) and a 'credit' item under the capital account (foreign direct investment).
24. However, as Yang does not report all the details of his estimation, it is difficult to judge the plausibility of his results.
25. For 2004 figures, see the MOC website on FDI, www.fdi.gov.cn.
26. We present econometric evidence on the importance of subsidies in explaining China's exports in Chapter 4.
27. This information is based on discussions with senior trade officials in Guangdong Province on 7 January 2005.
28. This is discussed extensively in Chapter 4. See Table 4.1.
29. A compatibility problem for some data should be noted here. The PBC started to publish a quarterly 'Balance Sheet of Monetary Authorities' in 1996, covering all deposit banks, non-monetary financial institutions and non-financial sectors with historical data from the first quarter of 1993. In contrast, data in the PBC's Balance Sheet, which is available for 1983–93, include only those of state banks.
30. We ignore that most but not all changes to the stock of foreign exchange reserves affect the monetary base. This explains why we can have estimates greater than 1.

31. Some Chinese researchers suggested the impact of foreign exchange increase on money supply was 75 per cent in 1994 compared with only 7 per cent in 1993, but they provided no details of how they came up with these figures (see, for example, Tao 1998, p. 26; Ba 1999, p. 238).
32. We are unable to obtain the original report (Mei 2004). Its contents are reported in Ho and Fong (2004, pp. 11–12) and in Zhong (2004).
33. As pointed out by Ba (1999, p. 239), this was the major reason for the central bank to shift to the balance sheet approach in its administration of commercial banks. See Gong and Dai (2000, pp. 266–7) for details of the balance sheet approach adopted by the PBC for administration of commercial banks.

APPENDIX

Table 3A.1   A chronicle of the reform of China's foreign exchange regime (1978–2005)

Year	Reform measures and major adjustments to the official exchange rate
1978	• Following the ambitious 1976–1985 National Economic Development Plan under the Hua Guofeng government, the renminbi was revalued by 9.6% to 1.5771 per US dollar from 1.7300 at the end of 1977, which was the third major revaluation since 1975 (Lardy 1992; Zhou and Xie 1993). • In February, the State Council approved an SPC proposal for resuming the foreign exchange retention system for overseas remittance. Local governments could retain 6% of the remittance for family support and 15% of the remittance for housing repair (Bai 2002, p. 2).
1979	• A system of foreign exchange retention was introduced, under which foreign exchange earnings could be shared between the state and provincial governments and export-producing enterprises (Han 1991; Panagariya 1993). • By the end of this year, the renminbi had been further revalued by 5.1% to RMB1.4962 per US dollar (Lardy 1992; Zhou and Xie 1993).
1980	• The foreign exchange adjustment system was introduced, under which enterprises were allowed to trade foreign exchange through SAFE (State Administration of Foreign Exchange) or the Bank of China (BOC). China's first foreign exchange trading room was set up in the Guangzhou branch of the BOC (Han 1991; Lardy 1992). • Effective from 1 April, following the State Council's decision, foreign visitors began to use the newly issued, renminbi-equivalent foreign exchange certificates (FECs) for their purchases in China. • On 18 December, the State Council issued 'Interim Regulations on Foreign Exchange Administration of the People's Republic of China' (ACFB 1986, section VI, pp. 4–5).
1981	• The foreign exchange internal settlement system was introduced, which started a two-tiered pricing system of foreign exchange with an official open rate (RMB1.7/US dollar) for non-trade transactions and an internal rate for trade transactions (RMB2.8/US dollar). The trading prices were allowed to vary from this rate by 5% to 10% (Han 1991). • As announced by SAFE on 31 December, 10% of foreign exchange brought into China by Chinese citizens and foreigners and 30% of overseas remittance by overseas Chinese could be retained in personal foreign exchange accounts (ACFB 1986, section VI, pp. 6–7).
1982–84	• SAFE sought to keep the trading price of foreign exchanges at the level of the internal settlement rate, RMB2.8 per US dollar (Lardy 1992; Yang 1993).

Table 3A.1 (continued)

Year	Reform measures and major adjustments to the official exchange rate
	• The official renminbi exchange rate was devalued to RMB1.9227/US dollar by the end of 1982, to RMB1.9809/US dollar by the end of 1983, and to 2.7957/US dollar by the end of 1984.
	• Residents in China were allowed to open personal foreign exchange accounts from the beginning of 1984.
1985	• The internal settlement system was abolished from the beginning of 1985. The two official foreign exchange rates, open and internal, were unified at the 1984 year-end internal rate of RMB2.8 per US dollar (Han 1991).
	• On 13 March, the State Council announced additional controls over the uses of retained foreign exchange (State Council 1985).
	• The first foreign exchange swap market, officially named a foreign exchange adjustment centre (FEAC), was opened to foreign-invested enterprises (FIEs) in the Shenzhen Special Economic Zone (Lardy 1992).
	• On 30 October, the renminbi was devalued by 12.5% to RMB3.2 per US dollar.
1986	• On 5 July, the renminbi was devalued by 13.6% to RMB3.7 per US dollar.
	• On 15 January, the State Council made the decision to allow foreign exchange adjustment among FIEs (ACFB 1987, section IX, pp. 5–6).
	• In October, the cap on the swap rate of transactions among FIEs was lifted. In November, the second foreign exchange swap market opened in Shanghai (Lardy 1992). Meanwhile, the SAFE formally took over the swap business, and the BOC concentrated only on accounting and settlement (Tsang 1994).
1987	• Some domestic manufacturing enterprises, especially those engaged in labour-intensive manufacturing, were allowed access to the foreign exchange swap market (Lardy 1992).
	• In 1987, US$4.264 billion were traded nationwide at FEACs (Lardy 1992).
1988	• The State Council abolished the special controls over the uses of retained foreign exchange (State Council 1988).
	• The Shanghai swap centre was opened to all domestic enterprises for the first time in April. Meanwhile, the State Council gave official blessing to the establishment of FEACs nationwide (Tsang 1994).
	• In 1988, US$6.264 billion were traded nationwide at FEACs (ACFB 1990, p. 215).
1989	• On 16 December, the official renminbi exchange rate was devalued by 21.2% from RMB3.7221 to RMB4.7221 per US dollar, the biggest devaluation in 10 years (Lin 1990; Ba 1999; ACFB 1991, p. 270).
	• In 1989, US$8.566 billion were traded nationwide at FEACs, up 37% on the previous year (ACFB 1990, p. 215).

Table 3A.1 (continued)

Year	Reform measures and major adjustments to the official exchange rate
1990	• On 17 November, the official renminbi exchange rate was further devalued by 9.7% to RMB5.2221 per US dollar (Tsang 1994). • On 9 December, the State Council approved a regulation on verifying export foreign exchange earnings (ACFB 1991, pp. 563–4). • In 1990, US$13.164 billion were traded nationwide at FEACs, up 54% on the previous year (ACFB 1991, p. 270).
1991	• On 9 April, a 'managed float' system was adopted, under which the official rate was to be adjusted 'continuously' and 'in small steps' (Tsang 1994). By the end of the year, the official rate had depreciated to RMB5.4342 per US dollar. • As the actual foreign exchange earnings from exports settled with the banking system were increasingly less than the value of exports (ACFB 1992, pp. 69–70), regulations on verification of foreign exchange earnings from exports were further tightened by a supplementary circular on 10 June issued jointly by the PBC, SAFE, MOFERT, GAC (General Administration of Customs) and BOC (ACFB 1992, p. 375). • Effective from 1 January, a new, unified foreign exchange retention system was introduced, under which 20% of export foreign exchange earnings was handed over to the central government at the official rate, 10% was retained by local governments, 10% by producing enterprises and 60% by export-producing enterprises. However, all foreign exchange retained by producing enterprises and one third of foreign exchange retained by export-producing enterprises had to be sold to the central government at the average FEAC rate (ACFERT 1991, p. 43; ACFB 1992, p. 71). • In 1991, US$20.451 billion were traded in FEACs nationwide, up 55% on the previous year (ACFB 1992, p. 67).
1992	• On 27 July, the RMB0.15 daily variation limit on the foreign exchange rate was lifted in the swap centres (*Jiefang ribao*, 20 August 1992). On 8 August, the national FEAC was opened in Beijing (*Jinrong shibao*, 10 August 1992). • On 8 August, the National Foreign Exchange Open Market was opened in Beijing to integrate the swap markets electronically nationwide (ACFB 1993, p. 23). • 11 cities participated in an experiment to shift from the prevailing foreign exchange quota retention to a cash retention system (ACFB 1993, p. 48). • US$25.105 billion were traded nationwide at FEACs, up 22% on the previous year (ACFB 1993, p. 48). • By the end of the year, the official rate depreciated to RMB5.7518 per US dollar (Ba 1999, p. 246).
1993	• As required by SAFE, price caps were introduced in FEACs in February. In March–May, the price cap was set at RMB8.135 per US dollar on average (Tsang 1994).

Table 3A.1 (continued)

Year	Reform measures and major adjustments to the official exchange rate
	• On 14 April, following the approval by PBC in February, SAFE issued 'Regulations on Foreign Exchange Adjustment Markets' to regulate foreign exchange transactions in FEACs (ACFB 1994, pp. 352–3).
	• On 1 June, the price ceiling on the swap rate was abolished. The swap rates of all FEACs rose sharply. In Shanghai, the swap rate shot up to RMB10.47 per US dollar, a devaluation of 26 per cent from the level early in the year (*Jingji ribao*, 8 June 1993).
	• On 12 July, following the imposition of a new financial adjustment policy, China's central bank for the first time sold tens of millions of US dollars on the swap market in Shanghai and Beijing to stabilize the renminbi. In the following month, hundreds of millions of US dollars were sold in all major swap markets around the country (*Zhongguo xinxibao*, 24 November 1993).
	• When unification was announced at the end of the year, the official rate stayed at RMB5.8 per US dollar, a small depreciation from the 1992 end-year level (Ba 1999, p. 246).
1994	• On 1 January, following the State Council's decision, the official and swap market exchange rates were unified at the prevailing swap rate of RMB8.7 per US dollar. All domestic enterprises were to be shifted to an inter-bank foreign exchange market system after a three-month transition period, under which a compulsory settlement of all foreign exchange earnings with designated banks was imposed, while the foreign exchange retention system was abolished (ACFB 1994, pp. 17–18).
	• On 24 March, the PBC (No. 3 Decree) issued 'Interim Regulations on Foreign Exchange Sales, Purchases and Payments' to regulate the new foreign exchange system (ACFB 1995, pp. 377–8). The transfer of domestic enterprises to the new system was completed, while all FIEs remained under the old system, trading foreign exchange in 18 major swap centres.
	• On 11 July, SAFE issued a regulation on verification of import payments, effective on 1 August (ACFB 1995, p. 60).
	• At the end of this year, the renminbi appreciated slightly to RMB8.45 per US dollar (ACFB 1995, p. 56).
1995	• Effective on 1 January, the circulation of foreign exchange certificates was terminated. Remaining FECs could be exchanged for US dollars by 30 June at the official rate published on 31 December, 1993 (ACFB 1995, p. 63).
	• At the end of the year, the exchange rate appreciated further to RMB8.32 per US dollar (Ba 1999, p. 246).
1996	• On 29 January, the State Council issued 'Regulations on Foreign Exchange Administration of the People's Republic of China' (ACFB 1997, pp. 311–13).

Table 3A.1 (continued)

Year	Reform measures and major adjustments to the official exchange rate
	• On 1 July, the PBC's 'Regulations on Foreign Exchange Sales, Purchases and Payments' were implemented (Gong and Dai 2000, p. 355). At the same time, all FIEs were allowed access to the designated banks-based foreign exchange system.
	• Also effective from 1 July, the limit on the individual purchase of foreign exchange for private purposes was increased from US\$20–60 to US\$500–1000, following new regulations issued by SAFE on 13 May (ACFB 1997, pp. 17–18).
	• On 27 November, China formally accepted IMF provisions covering currency convertibility and announced that the renminbi had become fully convertible under the current account from 1 December 1996. Meanwhile FEACs remained available to FIEs that chose to stay outside the banking system (Gong and Dai 2000, p. 352).
1997	• On 13 July, as instructed by the State Council, China's first monetary policy committee was set up under the administration of the PBC, headed by the governor of the PBC, Dai Xianglong (ACFB 1998, p. 55).
	• Starting from 1 March, SAFE replaced designated banks in conducting import payment verification. This was said to be an important move from prior supervision to afterward supervision (ACFB 1998, pp. 387–8).
	• Effective from 15 October, domestic enterprises could retain a certain amount of their foreign exchange earnings, to be no more than 15% of their last previous year's total trade amount (ACFB 1998, p. 382).
	• Over the past two years, the renminbi exchange rate had remained fairly stable at around RMB8.3 per US dollar.
1998	• On 22 June, the Financial Work Commission of the CCP's Central Committee was established and vice-premier Wen Jiabao was appointed its head (Bai 2002, p. 479).
	• Also on 22 June, SAFE issued new regulations (Circular No. 012; No. 199) on the verification of import payments and export earnings for authenticity and legality (ACFB 1999, pp. 297–330).
	• Effective from 15 September, after necessary verification up to the equivalent of US\$2000 of foreign exchange could be purchased for personal use according to the new regulations issued by SAFE (Circular No. 11) (ACFB 1999, p. 301).
	• On 1 December, all FEACs were closed and all FIEs transferred to the designated banks-based system of foreign exchange sales, purchases and payments (ACFB 1999, p. 76).
1999	• On 23 March, as instructed by SAFE (Circular No. 103), a check-up and appraisal system was set up on a trial basis to better enforce rules covering the sales of export foreign exchange earnings (ACFB 2000, pp. 313–14).

Table 3A.1 (continued)

Year	Reform measures and major adjustments to the official exchange rate
	• On 1 April, the PBC implemented its revised 'Regulations on the Administration of Renminbi Interest Rate' to clarify administrative duties on handling interest rates of financial products among the PBC headquarters, PBC branches and other financial institutions (Bai 2002, p. 499).
2000	• On 17 February, the PBC, SAFE, MOFTEC and SAT jointly implemented detailed measures specified in the check-up and appraisal system for the sales of export foreign exchange earnings (PBC Circular No. 58) (ACFB 2001, p. 283).
	• On 29 May, the PBC granted approval to the BOC to significantly increase deposit and lending interest rates of major foreign currencies (Bai 2002, p. 538).
2001	• Effective from 26 February, the CSRC (China Securities Regulatory Commission) and SAFE lifted restrictions on Chinese residents investing in B shares (foreign-owned shares in China's stock market).
	• On 19 September, the PBC and SAFE jointly issued a circular to relax foreign exchange purchases related to capital account transactions (PBC Circular No. 304).
	• On 12 November, SAFE issued a circular to relax the criteria that allow domestic enterprises to open foreign exchange cash accounts (SAFE Circular No. 184) (ACFB 2002, p. 391).
	• On 12 November, the PBC's ninth interest cut on major foreign currencies was announced. This decision lowered the US dollar one-year deposit rate from 5% on 29 May 2000 to 1.25%.
	• On 11 December, China became a member of the World Trade Organization.
2002	• On 28 November, SAFE issued detailed regulations on foreign exchange related to the Qualified Foreign Institutional Investor (QFII) scheme, opening the domestic A-share and bound markets to foreign institutional investors (ACFB 2003, p. 416).
	• On 29 May, SAFE announced that a unified domestic inter-bank foreign exchange lending market, the China Foreign Exchange Trading Centre, would start operations from 1 June, aiming to improve the operational efficiency and promote the development of China's foreign exchange market (*Renmin ribao*, 20 May 2003).
2003	• Following SAFE's No. 104 Circular on 1 September, SAFE and GAC jointly issued an interim regulation, increasing the amount of foreign currencies that Chinese residents are allowed to take in and out of China without reporting, from the equivalent of US$2000 to US$5000.
	• Effective from 1 October, member banks were allowed to conduct mutual trading of foreign exchange (SAFE Circular No. 109, 9 September), a decision that was said to improve the inter-bank foreign exchange market (www.safe.gov.cn).

Table 3A.1 (continued)

Year	Reform measures and major adjustments to the official exchange rate
	• Following SAFE's Circulars No. 43 and No. 120, verification of the sources of capital for overseas investment was simplified and procedures for overseas investment approval were decentralized. Local SAFE offices were allowed to approve overseas investments by domestic firms of projects worth less than US$3 million.
2004	• On 30 March, foreign exchange credit cards issued within China could be used to withdraw foreign exchange at up to US$1000 per day in cash overseas, US$5000 per month, and US$20 000 per year (SAFE 2003, Circular No. 19).
	• On 11 November, SAFE strengthened regulations over foreign exchange inflows and settlement for renminbi.
2005	• On 21 July, the PBC announced the renminbi would no longer be pegged to the US dollar, and instead would be pegged against a basket of currencies. This had the immediate effect of appreciating the renminbi by 2.1 per cent to RMB8.11 per US dollar.

*Table 3A.2   Officially published renminbi–US dollar exchange rate
(1952–2005)*

Year	US$–RMB	Year	US$–RMB
1952	226.45	1979	155.49
1953	261.70	1980	149.84
1954	261.70	1981	170.50
1955	246.76	1982	189.25
1956	246.18	1983	197.57
1957	246.18	1984	232.70
1958	246.18	1985	293.66
1959	246.18	1986	345.28
1960	246.18	1987	372.21
1961	246.18	1988	372.21
1962	246.18	1989	376.51
1963	246.18	1990	478.32
1964	246.18	1991	532.33
1965	246.18	1992	551.46
1966	246.18	1993	576.20
1967	246.18	1994	861.87
1968	246.18	1995	835.10
1969	246.18	1996	831.42
1970	246.18	1997	828.98
1971	246.11	1998	827.91
1972	224.51	1999	827.83
1973	198.94	2000	827.84
1974	196.12	2001	827.70
1975	185.98	2002	827.69
1976	194.14	2003	827.70
1977	185.78	2004	827.70
1978	168.36	2005	811.00*

Note: * 21 July.

Sources: Ba (1999, p. 246), NBS (2001, p. 586), PBC (www.pbc.gov.cn) and SAFE
(www.safe.gov.cn).

4. Foreign trade, prices and the exchange rate

INTRODUCTION

In this chapter we investigate important empirical issues that influence China's exchange rate policy. We have three principal objectives. First, to assess the relative importance of China's exchange rate as a trade policy instrument; second, to explore how prices in China and in its major trading partners affect renminbi exchange rates; and third, to examine the effectiveness of China's capital controls and effects of market expectations on China's exchange rate. The results of this investigation will feed into our analyses in the following two chapters of China's post-Mao exchange rate policies, focusing on the devaluation policy of 1989, the no-devaluation policy during the Asian financial crisis and the end of the renminbi–US dollar peg.

Before we proceed in this chapter, we need to emphasize that a lack of reliable data is the biggest obstacle to any empirical study on China's external economy. The data available for analysis are limited and often inconsistent. The available time series data are usually not for a period of time long enough for in-depth empirical investigations; in most cases, annual data are available only from the mid- or late 1980s, while quarterly data are available only from the mid- or late 1990s. Moreover, one has to bear in mind that official interventions regulate changes in the exchange rate and interest rate, so these economic variables could move only within a very narrow band, which can lead to unreliable empirical results.

We begin with discussion of the role of domestic currency cost of exports in China's exchange rate policymaking. The tradition in central planning is to price foreign exchange, like most commodities, according to the cost-plus principle. Following this tradition, the domestic currency cost of exports or cost of earning foreign exchange has always been at the centre of exchange rate policy debate and received significant attention from Chinese scholars and policymakers. Using various data on the cost of earning US dollars from exports and changes in producer prices we construct a time series of data for fiscal subsidies to exports and renminbi return per US dollar of exports and show how these returns vary with the balance of trade.

In the following section we examine the importance of the exchange rate in explaining China's export performance by comparing its impact on exports with the impacts of: (1) the cost of earning foreign exchange; (2) imports, which is a proxy for foreign investment inflows into China's fast-growing 'export processing' sector; and (3) export subsidies and rebates. We then apply the theory of purchasing power parity (PPP) to see if the renminbi exchange rate has reflected changes in the relative prices of China and its major trading partners. Finally, we examine the relationship between the forward renminbi exchange rate and interest differentials between China and its major trading partners to see whether interest parity holds for China. If interest parity holds, this will indicate official controls on capital movements are ineffective. We find that interest parity does not hold, indicating that official controls on capital movements have been effective in preventing the free flow of capital in and out of China.

RENMINBI COST OF EARNING FOREIGN EXCHANGE

Domestic currency cost of exporting is referred to by the Ministry of Foreign Economic Relations and Trade (MOFERT) and other officials commenting on China's trade performance as *chuanghui chengben*, the cost of foreign exchange earnings. It has always been an important factor in China's foreign exchange rate policymaking. Before the 1994 unification of the official and swap market exchange rates, MOFERT officials used the rising domestic cost of earning foreign exchange as a powerful argument for devaluing the renminbi. After the 1994 unification, this cost continued to be one of the key factors determining exchange rate policymaking.

Under the trade planning system, the official exchange rate was set according to the average renminbi cost for one unit of foreign exchange earnings. However, this did not mean that the official exchange rate reflected the real cost of exports. As discussed in Chapters 2 and 3, in China's centrally planned economy, the foreign exchange regime acted in tandem with the domestic price system to transfer resources from the agricultural sector to the manufacturing sector. The renminbi was deliberately overvalued and agricultural and other primary products, which made up most of China's exports, were priced well below their real factor costs. The official exchange rate did not fully cover the nominal cost of exports (Lardy 1992, pp. 25–6) and foreign trade corporations (FTCs), which purchased goods from domestic producers for exports, often posted losses.

One of two consequences could follow from an increase in the real input cost of exports. If procurement prices paid to producers for exporting products remained unchanged, this would further discourage producers from producing goods for exports. But if procurement prices were raised, FTCs would experience a drop in their profits or incur heavier losses. In either case, the authorities would have to devalue the renminbi, increase fiscal subsidies to exports, or do both just to maintain past levels of exports. During the years of central planning, because of the fear that renminbi devaluation might jeopardize their ambitious industrial plans that relied on imported machinery and equipment, the authorities resorted to various fiscal subsidies rather than devaluing the renminbi to support exports. The use of fiscal subsidies, which set the real exchange rate on a product-by-product basis, meant that for years China actually had a de facto multiple exchange rate regime (Lardy 1992, pp. 28–9; Mah 1971, p. 37).

Introduction of economic reform in agriculture in 1978 and gradual price reform to correct price distortions in the commodity and factor markets caused China's export costs to rise. As a result, the authorities had to not only adjust the renminbi exchange rate but also reform the foreign exchange regime. Most Chinese trade officials and scholars studying China's foreign trade believe that concern over the renminbi cost of exports was the major factor behind introduction of the internal settlement rate for current account transactions in 1981, adoption of the dual-track exchange regime in 1988, and unification of the official and swap exchange rates in 1994. In making exchange rate policy, Chinese officials had to consider whether to price the renminbi to cover sufficiently the domestic currency cost of exports or rely on subsidies to cover the domestic currency cost of exports.

There are no official statistics on China's domestic currency costs of earning foreign exchange, nor is any systematic estimate of these costs available. Lardy (1992, p. 25) managed to construct a time series of these costs based on information from various studies in Chinese, but it was Yang (2000, pp. 71–8) who made the first attempt to construct a series of renminbi costs of exports using internal data that took into account fiscal subsidies for exports. Lardy's and Yang's calculations of the renminbi cost of earning US$1 in export sales are presented in Table 4.1. Yang calculated two cost-of-exports series: Series 1 that includes central subsidies and Series 2 that excludes them. It is difficult to interpret fully these estimates of export cost because information about how they were calculated is not provided. Moreover, since some of the arguments in Yang (2000) are not always clear, readers must interpret what some of his data actually inform us of. [1] Nevertheless, his study is one of only a few detailed Chinese studies on renminbi policy and makes an important contribution to shedding light on the relationship between China's export and exchange rate policies.

In Table 4.1 we present the official and swap market exchange rates. The official exchange rate incorporates the pre-1994 posted rate and post-1994 inter-bank market rate, and the swap market rate incorporates the pre-1985 internal settlement rate and post-1985 swap rate. The weighted nominal exchange rate (WNER) is a weighted average of the official and swap rates. Based on scattered information on the share of China's total foreign exchange transactions conducted in the swap market in the early 1990s,[2] we calculate a series of 'weighted nominal exchange rates' by assigning appropriate weights to the official and swap rates. WNER, instead of the official or swap rate, is a more appropriate variable to explain foreign trade. Since export costs in Yang's Series 1 contain fiscal subsidies, which are not taken into account in Yang's Series 2, export costs in Yang's Series 1 should be larger than the export costs in Series 2. This is the case for all years except 1983, suggesting that the 1983 figure could be incorrect. Furthermore, Lardy's data as shown in Table 4.1 appear to be inconsistent; they are similar to Yang's Series 2 for 1978–84 but closer to Yang's Series 1 for 1985–88.

Data in Table 4.1 make it clear that in many of the 28 years included in the table even the higher swap market rate did not cover export costs. The gap between exchange rate and export costs widens further if we compare the 'weighted nominal exchange rate' with Yang's Series 1. Other studies have also indicated that China's exchange rate could not have covered the actual cost of exports. In his 1993 study, Yang gave an example from a foreign trade officials' viewpoint showing that to earn US$1 of export sales in 1990 the government had to pay: (1) RMB4.72 based on the prevailing official exchange rate;[3] (2) RMB0.35 through the central tax rebate; (3) RMB0.86 as the 'quota price' for every retained dollar, which is considered a bonus to exporters by the authorities;[4] and (4) over RMB3 through various local government subsidies. In total, an average exporter in 1990 received about RMB9, of which over 33 per cent was fiscal subsidies (Yang 1993, p. 5). A study by Chen (1987) found that on average the authorities paid RMB4.5 for every US dollar export earned in 1985. On the basis of the cost of exports of RMB3.52 indicated by Yang's Series 1, local government subsidies would have to make up the gap of RMB1, or 22 per cent of the unit export cost.

Lin (1996, pp. 44–5), in a comment on the 1994 unified rate, pointed out that the unified rate should not be considered as an equilibrium rate. Not only did controls over the use of foreign exchange continue after 1994, but the unified exchange rate was unable to cover the cost of exports and the gap had to be bridged by tax rebates and subsidies. Given the size of fiscal subsidies paid by local government to stimulate exports, it is highly likely that a major factor behind the 33 per cent devaluation of the renminbi official exchange rate from RMB5.8 to RMB8.6 in 1994 was an attempt by the central authorities to alleviate the fiscal burdens of local governments.

Table 4.1 Renminbi exchange rate and cost of per unit US dollar exports (1977–2005)

	Officially published rate (indirect quotes)		Internal rate or swap market rate[1] (indirect quotes)		Weighted nominal rate[2] (indirect quotes)		IPPI	Return to exports[5] (fiscal subsidies[6])	Renminbi cost of exports (RMB cost per US$ exports)			
	US$/RMB	% change	US$/RMB	% change	US$/RMB	% change	last year =100	RMB per US$ exports	Lardy	Yang 1[3]	Yang 2[3]	IPPI-implied[4]
1977	1.858		2.980		2.980							
1978	1.684	10.35	2.690	10.78	2.690	10.78	100.1	0.63 (0.47)	2.50	3.00	2.53	3.05
1979	1.555	8.28	2.640	1.89	2.640	1.89	101.5	0.61 (0.37)	2.40	2.77	2.40	3.09
1980	1.498	3.77	2.700	-2.22	2.700	-2.22	100.5	0.88 (0.49)	–	2.80	2.31	3.11
1981	1.705	-12.12	2.800	-3.57	2.800	-3.57	100.2	0.76 (0.38)	2.31	2.80	2.42	3.12
1982	1.893	-9.91	2.800	0.00	2.800	0.00	99.8	0.26 (0.13)	2.66	2.80	2.67	3.11
1983	1.976	-4.21	2.800	0.00	2.800	0.00	99.9	-0.39(-0.07)	3.02	3.05	3.12	3.11
1984	2.327	-15.10	2.800	0.00	2.800	0.00	101.4	0.50 (0.50)	2.79	3.30	2.80	3.15
1985	2.937	-20.76	3.940	-28.93	3.238	-13.52	108.7	0.76 (0.52)	3.67	3.52	3.00	3.42
1986	3.453	-14.95	4.450	-11.46	3.752	-13.71	103.8	-0.36(-0.18)	3.90	3.75	3.93	3.55
1987	3.722	-7.24	5.700	-21.93	4.513	-16.87	107.9	0.91 (0.40)	4.20	4.40	4.00	3.83
1988	3.722	0.00	6.800	-16.18	4.953	-8.88	115.0	2.25 (1.60)	5.80	5.90	4.30	4.41
1989	3.765	-1.14	6.380	6.58	5.073	-2.35	118.6	1.32 (1.10)		5.95	4.85	5.23
1990	4.783	-21.28	5.800	10.00	5.292	-4.14	104.1	0.86 (0.81)		6.05	5.24	5.44
1991	5.323	-10.15	5.830	-0.51	5.627	-5.97	106.2	1.17 (0.92)		6.30	5.38	5.78
1992	5.515	-3.47	6.520	-10.58	6.218	-9.51	106.8	1.04 (0.81)		6.80	5.99	6.17
1993	5.762	-4.29	8.590	-24.10	8.024	-22.51	124.0	3.42 (1.90)		8.40	6.50	7.66
1994	8.619	-33.15			8.619	-6.90	119.5	1.11 (0.82)		9.15	8.33	9.15
1995	8.351	3.21			8.351	3.21	114.9	0.52 (0.56)		8.95	8.39	10.51
1996	8.314	0.44			8.314	0.44	102.9	0.51 (0.83)		9.30	8.63	10.82
1997	8.290	0.29			8.290	0.29	99.7	0.04 (0.36)			8.61	10.79
1998	8.279	0.13			8.279	0.13	95.9	0.39 (0.36)		9.00	8.25	10.34
1999	8.278	0.01			8.278	0.01	97.6	0.71 (0.49)		10.00	8.06	10.10
2000	8.267	0.13			8.267	0.13	102.8	0.49 (0.50)		10.28	8.28	10.38

Table 4.1 (continued)

	Officially published rate (indirect quotes)		Internal rate or swap market rate[1] (indirect quotes)		Weighted nominal rate[2] (indirect quotes)		IPPI	Return to exports[5] (fiscal subsidies[6])	Renminbi cost of exports (RMB cost per US$ exports)			
	US$/RMB	% change	US$/RMB	% change	US$/RMB	% change	last year =100	RMB per US$ exports	Lardy	Yang 1[3]	Yang 2[3]	IPPI-implied[4]
2001	8.268	-0.01			8.268	-0.01	98.7	0.72 (0.62)		10.15	8.17	10.24
2002	8.252	0.20			8.252	0.20	99.5	0.74 (0.59)		10.10	8.13	10.02
2003	8.281	-0.35			8.281	-0.35	102.0	0.70 (0.71)		10.30	8.38	10.25
2004	8.270	0.13			8.270	0.13	108.2	0.38 (1.08)		11.14	8.98	10.86
2005	8.075	2.42			8.075	2.42	103.1	-0.49 (0.69)		11.49	9.25	10.35

Notes:
1 Refer to average of various 'internal settlement rates' till 1980, an identical 'internal settlement rate' in 1981–84, and swap market rates for 1985–93.
2 Weights are applied to the period 1985–93 when there were parallel official and swap market rates. See text for details.
3 'Yang 1' is export cost per US$ with fiscal subsidies and 'Yang 2' is export cost without fiscal subsidies. 'Yang 1' after 1998 and 'Yang 2' after 1995 are estimated using the IPPI.
4 Calculated using IPPI with the renminbi cost of exports per US$ in 1994 of 'Yang 1' as the 'control limit' (see discussion in text).
5 'Yang 1' – 'Yang 2' + weighted nominal rate – 'Yang 2' (1978–1995).
6 'Yang 1' – 'Yang 2' (1978–1995).

Source: Renminbi exchange rates are from Tables 3A.1 and 3A.2 of this book, truncated to 3 decimal places; differences exist between spot rates and average rate of a year. Estimates of renminbi cost of exports are from Lardy (1992, p. 25) and Yang (2000, pp. 71–3, 78). IPPI is the NBS ex-factory price index (NBS 2003, Tables 9–10; other issues for filling gaps and updates).

Local government export subsidies to producers have been a crucial factor in China's exporting success. There is no consistency in the way regions allocate export subsidies because production costs vary across regions and export targets of local governments differ from one to another. Local governments use export subsidies to meet other economic performance targets as well as export targets set by the central government, as many localities are dependent on export-oriented industries to generate economic growth and employment within the locality. But as we noted in the previous chapter, the fiscal capacity of local governments to subsidize exports was reduced by central efforts to reduce its spending in the 2000s.

In the last column of Table 4.1 are our estimates of the 1978–2005 industrial producer price index (IPPI) implied renminbi costs of US$1 of export earnings. We assume that the producer costs of export products vary with changes in the IPPI. We further assume that Yang's Series 1 for the benchmark year of 1994 can be used as our 'control limit' for this estimation. This is because 1994 was the year when the dual exchange rate regime was unified and the 33 per cent devaluation would have made the exchange rate closer to the underlying export costs. But despite the devaluation, after 1994 the cost of exports was always higher than the exchange rate, regardless of which cost of exports series was used to compare with the exchange rate.

Yang's original Series 1 and Series 2 end in 1999 and 1995, respectively. We extended these series to 2005 using the IPPI index series. The differences in Yang's Series 1 and 2 are fiscal subsidies.[5] We add the subsidies to the exchange rate and minus Yang's Series 2 to derive the renminbi return to exporters of each US dollar of exports. We adopt this method to calculate fiscal subsidies to exports and the rate of return to exporters only for the years from 1978 up to and including 1995. We could not subtract Yang's Series 2 from Yang's Series 1 to derive the post-1995 estimates of fiscal subsidies to exports because this would assume the authorities varied fiscal subsidies to exports after 1995 strictly according to the rate of inflation.

We adopt the following method to estimate the fiscal subsidies and rate of return to exports for the years after 1995. First, we calculate the ratio of export rebates to exports. Assuming fiscal subsidies to exports vary at the same rate as export rebates, we derive estimates of the 1996–2005 fiscal subsidies using the 1995 estimate of fiscal subsidies (Yang's Series 1 and 2) as base. Next we add these estimates of fiscal subsidies to the exchange rate and subtract the estimates of export costs for the post-1995 years in Yang's Series 2 to derive our remaining estimates of the rate of return to exports.

In Figure 4.1 we plot the renminbi return per US dollar of exports and China's trade balances against time. This figure reveals an important determinant of China's export policy. The years of low turning points in

China's trade balance when it was in deficit (1980, 1985, 1988 and 1993) coincided with the years of high turning points in return to exports. The two highest returns to exports were in 1988 and 1993, when China recorded two of its largest balance of trade deficits since 1978. The high return to exports and large balance of trade deficits in 1988 and 1993 were followed by significant devaluations of the official exchange rate in 1990 and 1991, and unification of the swap and official exchange rates in 1994 that produced a 6.9 per cent devaluation of the weighted exchange rate. Examining the 1993 fiscal subsidies in Table 4.1 makes it clear why the exchange rates were unified. Renminbi fiscal subsidies per US dollar of exports in 1993 (RMB1.9) were the highest of all the years since 1977; they were 18.8 per cent higher than in 1988 (RMB1.6), which came second behind 1993. Fiscal subsidies were a significant component in the return to exports in 1988 and 1993 and devaluations of the official exchange rate and later unification of the exchange rates were clearly attempts to shift the burden of promoting exports away from fiscal subsidies to the exchange rate.

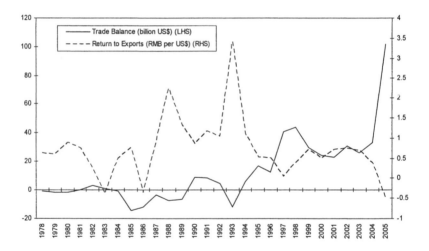

Sources: Figure 3.1 and Table 4.1.

Figure 4.1   Return to exports and China's trade balance (1978–2005)

After 1993 the trade balance was never in deficit and the return to exports did not relate to the balance of trade in the same way as when the balance of trade was in deficit. International attention was focused on China's unification of the official and swap exchange rates in 1994, which led to a 33 per cent devaluation of the official rate. Some commentators blamed the

1994 unification for the loss in the relative competitiveness of China's trading partners. But as shown in Table 4.1 and Figure 4.1, the renminbi rate of return to exports in 1994 actually fell due to a greater than 50 per cent decline in the rate of fiscal subsidization to exports. The devaluation of the official exchange rate in 1994 was overshadowed by the depreciation of the swap market rate in 1993. The swap rate depreciated by 24 per cent in 1993 and caused a depreciation of the weighted exchange rate of 22 per cent. In 1994, the weighted rate depreciated by only 7 per cent, despite devaluation of the official rate by 33 per cent.

During the Asian financial crisis from 1997, Chinese authorities held the renminbi exchange rate steady, but as the crisis deepened they raised the rate of subsidy to exports three years in a row (1999–2001). Return to exports increased to above that of 1997, but was below the returns of 1993 and 1994 when the balance of trade was in deficit or close to deficit. After the crisis ended for China and until 2004, there was little variation in the rate of return to exports. In 2004 inflation reduced significantly the rate of return to exports. Budgetary pressures had threatened the payment of export rebates and fiscal subsidies, but the rate of return to exports would have fallen further had these payments not increased. Between 2003 and 2004, rates of export tax rebates and fiscal subsidies more or less doubled (Figure 3.6, Table 4.1).

In 2005 export rebates and fiscal subsidies fell. They combined with revaluation of the renminbi that accompanied the end of the renminbi–US dollar peg in July that year to produce a negative rate of return to exports. The absence of a serious attempt to keep the rate of return positive that year was most likely due to the explosion in China's balance of trade surplus. China's balance of trade in 2005 more than doubled compared to the previous year (Figure 4.1). Throughout 2005 there was immense pressure on China, principally from the US, to rein in China's booming trade surplus. This surplus also made it difficult for Chinese planners to control the nation's money supply without resorting to sterilization, which would increase the Chinese government's future fiscal liabilities.

WHAT DETERMINES CHINA'S EXPORTS?

This section investigates the major determinants of China's export performance. First, following the discussion in the previous section, the weighted nominal exchange rate of renminbi (indirect quote) (Table 4.1) is adopted as one of the exogenous variables instead of the official exchange rate in our export function. It should vary positively with China's exports. Second, we use the IPPI to capture the impact of the costs of production on exports. We expect China's exports to respond negatively to the IPPI. Third, the value of imports is an explanatory variable in the export function. Imports are key inputs in the production of goods exported from China. Ever since Deng Xiaoping's open-door policy was introduced at the end of the 1970s, imported machinery and equipment have been used to improve the competitiveness of the export sector, and imported materials have been processed or assembled for exports. The growth in processing trade has been phenomenal. According to a 2004 report by the Ministry of Commerce (MOFCOM,[6] formerly MOFERT and MOFTEC), the value of processing trade accounted for 55 per cent of China's exports and 40 per cent of China's imports. Without time series data on the value of processing trade we use the value of imports as a proxy.

Our import variable captures the effect of foreign direct investment (FDI) on exports. China has seen a huge influx of FDI and FDI-induced imports. Chinese producers in processing trade are subcontractors and do not pay for their components and materials that are processed for exports; their customers who subcontract out the processing work are responsible for providing the inputs. However, to confirm whether imports or exports are endogenous, we ran the Granger Causality Test. Both the one-lag and two-lag pairwise Granger Causality Tests significantly rejected the null hypothesis that imports do not cause exports, which means that the causality runs one way from imports to exports.

Chinese governments at different administrative levels provide direct and indirect financial support to promote exports.[7] Since no detailed statistics are available we use the ratio of the value of export tax rebates from the central budget to total exports as a proxy for the rate of government financial support granted to exports. When rebates are neutral, they equal value-added taxes and they neither discriminate against nor favour exports. We assume that local and national subsidies correlate positively with central tax rebates. For example, central tax rebates would increase with other forms of financial support from the central government when there is rising pressure for the central government to promote exports and local officials should be motivated for career reasons to move in the same direction by increasing local financial support for exports. Rebates actually paid out are not the same as announced rebate rates since rebates are often issued as IOUs to manipulate fiscal expenditures, which are paid only when there is an urgent need to increase exports.

Our general regression model for China's exports is:

$$\ln EX_t = \beta_0 + \beta_1 \ln IM_t + \beta_2 \ln WNER_{t-1} + \beta_3 IPPI_t \quad (4.1)$$
$$+ \beta_4 REB_{t-1} + \beta_5 \ln WGDP + e_t$$

where *EX* is value of exports, *IM* is value of imports, *WNER* is weighted nominal exchange rate of renminbi per unit of foreign currency, *IPPI* is the industrial producer price index (Table 4.1), *REB* is the ratio of value of central rebates to total exports, *WGDP* is the world GDP, a proxy for the world demand for Chinese exports, and *e* is the classic error term.

There are two models of (4.1) (Model 1, $\beta_5 = 0$; Model 2, $\beta_5 \neq 0$) and two measurements of *WNER* (a, b). The first measurement is renminbi per US dollar, as presented in Table 4.1, assuming all exports are priced in US dollars. The second measurement is the trade-weighted *WNER* of four foreign currencies: US dollar, British pound sterling, Japanese yen and Hong Kong dollar, assuming exports to Europe are priced in sterling, to Japan in yen, to Hong Kong in Hong Kong dollars and to the rest of the world in US dollars, with variant weights over time based on Chinese official statistics (NBS 2004, Table 18.7 and similar tables from other years). The rebate variable is lagged one year to account for the delayed action of exporters responding to changes in fiscal incentives on exports.

The regression results from both models are presented in Table 4.2. They are robust with the expected sign for each variable. As the results show, China's exports respond to the nominal weighted exchange rate (*WNER*), depreciation of the renminbi – an increase in renminbi price of exports – will increase exports. Devaluation of the renminbi against the US dollar by 1 per cent will increase exports by 0.3 per cent, but devaluation of the renminbi by 1 per cent against a basket of currencies of China's main trading partners will increase exports by between 2.7 and 2.9 per cent. The regression results support our hypothesis that an increase in production costs, captured by the IPPI, would cause China's exports to decline, although to a rather smaller extent when compared with the impact of the exchange rate.

Export rebates are found to have a significant influence on exports, with a 1 per cent absolute increase in the export rebate rate producing about a 5 per cent increase in exports. Because of the correlation of export rebates and export subsidies,[8] this result suggests that countries concerned with China's trade surplus should focus more on China's export subsidies and rebates than on the US dollar–renminbi exchange rate. This view is consistent with the research of Coudert and Couharde (2005), who found that a revaluation of the renminbi would have only a minor effect on the US trade deficit, the single source of China's trade surplus.[9] However, an upward movement of the renminbi, if it lowers the resistance of other countries against allowing their currencies to appreciate against the US dollar because of their concerns over loss of competitiveness *vis-à-vis* China, can improve the US trade surplus (IMF 2006, p. 36).

A 1 per cent increase in imports results in about a 0.5 per cent increase in exports. A significant portion of China's imports are inputs into foreign-invested manufacturing production for exports and this result highlights FDI flows as an important determinant of China's exports. World GDP has the correct sign but is not significant. This indicates that the rapid growth in China's exports in the 1990s and 2000s has more to do with the relocation of global production to China than with the growth in world demand.

Table 4.2 China's export function

	Model 1a	Model 1b	Model 2a	Model 2b
Constant	1.3793***	1.6708***	1.3221***	1.5882***
	(0.4350)	(0.5645)	(0.4348)	(0.5936)
ln*IM*	0.4938**	0.4773**	0.5133***	0.4973**
	(0.1827)	(0.2025)	(0.1822)	(0.2098)
ln*WNER* (−1)	0.3218***	2.8579***	0.3119***	2.7307***
	(0.0798)	(0.8332)	(0.0797)	(0.8782)
IPPI	−0.0148***	−0.0178***	−0.0151***	−0.0175***
	(0.0045)	(0.0059)	(0.0045)	(0.0061)
REB (−1)	4.6112***	4.9714***	4.7289**	4.9663**
	(1.6374)	(1.8418)	(1.6285)	(1.8849)
ln*WGDP*			0.0246	0.0155
			(0.0223)	(0.0255)
Adjusted R-squared	0.70	0.65	0.71	0.63
Durbin–Watson statistic	1.925	1.884	2.016	1.883
F-statistic	11.5761	9.3413	9.6462	7.2085
Sample period (adjusted)	1986–2004	1986–2004	1986–2004	1986–2004

Note: Standard errors in parentheses with *** and ** indicate significance at the 1 per cent and 5 per cent levels, respectively.

PURCHASING POWER PARITY AND THE EXCHANGE RATE

As we have seen, China's foreign exchange system has been changed significantly since the beginning of reform. The system was a highly controlled multi-exchange rate regime in the late 1970s to the mid-1980s. It was then made a double-track plan-swap market exchange rate regime from the mid-1980s to 1993. The renminbi–US dollar peg was introduced after the 1994 unification of the official and swap markets, and was kept until July 2005 when the peg was discontinued and a managed float system introduced. From 2003 China has been the target of growing international criticism that its policymakers have deliberately undervalued the renminbi to maintain an unfair advantage for China in international trade. Various studies of the changes in China's exchange rate present different assessments, ranging from small overvaluation of the renminbi to undervaluation of about 50 per cent.[10] Empirical modelling of exchange rates is difficult and the diverse conclusions that the various studies reach are the result of their authors' different methodologies and assumptions (Dunaway and Li 2005). Higgins and Humpage (2005) regard it as 'next to impossible' to determine the equilibrium exchange rate for a developing country like China that is undergoing substantial structural change.

In this section we apply the theory of purchasing power parity to examine whether the weighted renminbi nominal exchange rate deviated from the PPP-implied renminbi exchange rate in the course of China's first 27 years of reform. There is no consensus in the economics literature on the equilibrium value of the renminbi. Hence, our objective in this exercise is to provide another perspective on the renminbi that will allow us in a simple way to compare exchange rates of the renminbi (against currencies of China's major trading partners). Our aim is to compare the values of different currencies against the renminbi. It is not to conduct a rigorous modelling exercise to determine the equilibrium renminbi exchange rate.

The law of one price (LOOP) is the lynchpin behind the PPP condition. In its absolute version, the LOOP assumes frictionless goods arbitrage and predicts that a given commodity should have the same price in any location so that the purchasing power of the two currencies is at parity in both countries when expressed in terms of the same currency of denomination. The PPP-implied exchange rate of the two currencies is then simply the ratio of the prices of the two countries (Cassel 1918). A common criticism of the absolute version of the PPP theory of exchange rate is that this theory does not take into account non-tradable goods and as a result tends to undervalue the exchange rate of low-wage countries (Balassa 1964; Samuelson 1964).

Most empirical studies applying the absolute version of PPP (Cassellian formulation) used the consumer price index (CPI) as a proxy for the aggregate price level. However, this formulation introduces a range of index number problems. For example, the basket of goods used to calculate the CPI differs across countries and tends to change over time. Moreover, countries like China publish only a limited range of price indices and offer scant information on how these indices are constructed. Some researchers try to moderate this criticism by converting absolute prices to rates of change in prices and using the relative version of PPP. Relative PPP postulates that the change in the nominal exchange rate of one currency *vis-à-vis* another over a given period of time should be proportional to the relative change in the price levels in the two countries issuing those currencies in this period. Problems remain in using the relative PPP approach to determine the equilibrium exchange rate because of the difficulty of choosing an appropriate 'base period' where the balance of payments is in equilibrium.

Table 4.3 Consumer price indices and ratios (1980–2005)

	CPI (1994 = 100)					CPI ratio (1994 = 100)			
	China	US	UK	Japan	HK	China/ US	China/ UK	China/ Japan	China/ HK
1980	32.7	55.6	46.3	76.2	31.9	58.9	70.6	42.9	102.4
1981	33.5	61.3	51.8	80.0	36.5	54.6	64.7	41.9	91.8
1982	34.1	65.1	56.4	82.1	40.3	52.5	60.6	41.6	84.7
1983	34.7	67.2	59.0	83.7	44.3	51.6	58.8	41.4	78.2
1984	35.6	70.1	61.9	85.6	48.1	50.8	57.5	41.6	74.1
1985	38.9	72.6	65.8	87.3	49.5	53.7	59.2	44.6	78.6
1986	41.3	73.9	68.1	87.9	51.0	55.8	60.6	47.0	81.0
1987	44.3	76.7	70.7	88.0	53.8	57.8	62.7	50.4	82.3
1988	52.5	79.8	74.1	88.6	57.8	65.8	70.8	59.3	90.8
1989	61.9	83.6	79.9	90.6	63.7	74.1	77.5	68.4	97.3
1990	63.9	88.1	87.5	93.4	69.9	72.4	73.0	68.4	91.4
1991	66.0	91.9	92.6	96.4	78.0	71.9	71.3	68.5	84.7
1992	70.3	94.7	96.1	98.0	85.3	74.2	73.1	71.7	82.4
1993	80.6	97.5	97.6	99.3	92.5	82.7	82.6	81.1	87.1
1994	100.0	100.0	100.0	100.0	100.0	100.0	100.0	100.0	100.0
1995	117.1	102.8	103.4	99.9	108.4	113.9	113.2	117.2	108.0
1996	126.8	105.8	105.9	100.0	114.9	119.8	119.7	126.8	110.4
1997	130.4	108.3	109.2	101.7	121.5	120.4	119.3	128.1	107.3
1998	129.3	110.0	113.0	102.4	124.7	117.6	114.5	126.3	103.7
1999	127.5	112.4	114.7	102.1	120.7	113.5	111.1	124.9	105.7
2000	128.0	116.2	118.1	101.4	117.1	110.2	108.4	126.3	109.4
2001	128.9	119.5	120.3	100.6	115.1	107.9	107.2	128.1	112.0
2002	127.9	121.4	122.2	99.7	111.4	105.4	104.6	128.3	114.8
2003	129.4	124.1	125.8	99.5	109.0	104.3	102.9	130.1	118.7
2004	134.4	127.4	129.5	99.5	109.0	105.5	103.8	135.1	123.3
2005	136.9	127.7	133.2	99.2	110.3	107.2	102.8	138.0	124.1
% p.a.	5.9	3.4	4.3	1.1	5.1	2.4	1.5	4.8	0.8

Sources: The Chinese data since 1985 are from *China Statistical Yearbook* (NBS 1986–2006), while CPI data for the period prior to 1985 are estimated using the NBS price index for retail sales. The US data are from the US Bureau of Labor Statistics available at http://www.bls.gov/data/home.htm; the UK, Japanese and Hong Kong data are from the following official statistics websites respectively available at http://www.statistics.gov.uk, http://www.censtatd.gov.hk/hong_kong_statistics, and http://www.stat.go.jp.

Table 4.3 presents the CPI series for China and its major trading partners and ratios of China's CPI to the CPI of these countries. Clearly, China experienced higher inflation than its trading partners in the early 1990s when Deng Xiaoping's southern tour of China reignited reform and set off an economic boom, after reform had come to a virtual stop in June 1989. The China–foreign CPI ratios show that China's lower price ratios first converged to the price ratios of its trading partners and then overtook them. In the exercise below we have used these CPI data to derive the PPP-implied nominal and real renminbi exchange rate.

The weighted renminbi nominal exchange rate (for the US dollar–renminbi WNER see Table 4.1) is specified as the nominal exchange rate, e, which is defined simply as the renminbi price of one unit of foreign currency. The real exchange rate, R is defined as:

$$R_t = \frac{e_t}{P_{C,t}} P_{F,t}$$
(4.2)

where P_C is the price level in China and P_F the price level in the foreign country.

Let us assume that PPP held in 1994, the year when the dual exchange rates were unified, so that:

$$\frac{P_{C,94}}{P_{F,94}} = e_{94}$$
(4.3)

$$R_{94} = \frac{e_{94}}{P_{C,94}} P_{F,94} = 1$$
(4.4)

To obtain ratio of prices of the two countries at a given time, we multiply the 1994 exchange rate, that is, e_{94} by the price indices of the two countries, denoted as X_C and X_F (1994 = 100) to obtain:

$$\frac{P_{C,t}}{P_{F,t}} = e_{94} \frac{X_{C,t}}{X_{F,t}}$$
(4.5)

No information is available on the quantity of major foreign currencies other than the US dollar – the British pound, the Hong Kong dollar and the Japanese yen – that were traded under the multiple and dual exchange regimes. We use rates of the US dollar in terms of these other major currencies and the US dollar–renminbi WNER rate to calculate the renminbi WNER in terms of these currencies (Table 4.4). Substituting the 1994 values of these WNERs ($t = 1994$) and relevant 1994 CPI ratios (Table 4.3) into equation (4.5) we can calculate the PPP-implied renminbi exchange rate for each foreign currency (Table 4.4). The calculated WNERs and PPP-implied renminbi exchange rates for the foreign currencies between 1980 and 2005 are plotted in Figure 4.2.

Now, by substituting equation (4.5) into (4.2), we can calculate the real exchange rate R by the following equation:

$$R_t = \frac{e_t}{P_{C,t}} \frac{P_{F,t}}{e_{94}} = \frac{e_t}{e_{94}} \frac{X_{F,t}}{X_{C,t}} \tag{4.6}$$

It is clear from Table 4.4 and Figure 4.2 that the actual renminbi exchange rate (WNER) valued against all the foreign currencies examined does not reflect the price changes in China relative to the price changes in the foreign countries. Using the 1994 unification as benchmark, the actual renminbi exchange rate converged to the price-ratio implied renminbi exchange rate during 1992–94, but the two exchange rates diverged soon after unification. An exception is the pound–renminbi exchange rate, where the actual and price-ratio implied exchange rates of the pound–renminbi converged on four occasions after 1987: in 1988, 1990, 1994 and 2003. Divergences between the price-implied renminbi exchange rate and actual renminbi exchange rate (WNER) indicate deviations from PPP. We use equation (4.7) to obtain estimates of the real exchange rate. These estimates are presented in Table 4.5. However, to compare these with the actual renminbi exchange rate e_t, we have to convert the latter into a 1994-based exchange rate index. The two indices for all four currencies are depicted in Figure 4.3.

The real exchange rate equals 1 when PPP holds. We define the exchange rate e as renminbi per unit of foreign currency, and equation (4.6) indicates the renminbi real exchange rate is overvalued if it is less than 1 and undervalued if it is greater than 1. Clearly, when comparing the renminbi against all four currencies, the 1994 unification separated two different periods in terms of the position and movements of the real and nominal exchange rates (WNERs).

First, prior to the 1994 unification, based on PPP, the renminbi was overvalued against all four foreign currencies. Second, the 1994 unification was obviously an effort to minimize or eliminate the overvaluation of the renminbi, and the nominal exchange rate (renminbi per unit of foreign currency) remained higher than the real exchange rate against all foreign currencies after unification. Third, after unification, movements of the real US dollar–renminbi and Hong Kong dollar–renminbi exchange rate are no longer proportional to each other due to the pegging of the renminbi and Hong Kong dollar to the US dollar. While the nominal rate remains unchanged, the gap between the two US dollar–renminbi rates narrowed continuously between 1997 and 2003, reducing the undervaluation of the nominal US dollar–renminbi rate; but this trend seems to have reversed since 2004 (Panel 1 of Figure 4.3). However, the gap for the Hong Kong dollar–renminbi has been increasing since 1999 after a short but significant narrowing in 1997–98 (Panel 4 in Figure 4.3). This may explain the significant amounts of 'hot money' flows through Hong Kong speculating on the appreciation of the renminbi in the first five years of the 2000s.

Table 4.4 Actual (WNER) versus PPP-implied renminbi exchange rate (indirect quote)

	US$/RMB		£/RMB		100¥/RMB		HK$/RMB	
	WNER	PPP-implied	WNER	PPP-implied	WNER	PPP-implied	WNER	PPP-implied
1980	2.7000	5.0731	6.2791	9.3247	1.1939	3.6243	0.5428	1.1427
1981	2.8000	4.7083	5.6202	8.5373	1.2701	3.5375	0.5007	1.0245
1982	2.8000	4.5206	4.8874	7.9987	1.1233	3.5087	0.4609	0.9444
1983	2.8000	4.4456	4.2411	7.7563	1.1793	3.4955	0.3851	0.8718
1984	2.8000	4.3816	3.7249	7.5969	1.1787	3.5136	0.3582	0.8268
1985	3.2376	4.6251	4.1593	7.8103	1.3586	3.7642	0.4156	0.8766
1986	3.7520	4.8113	5.5006	7.9967	2.2289	3.9655	0.4808	0.9030
1987	4.5133	4.9800	7.3770	8.2734	3.1198	4.2496	0.5788	0.9184
1988	4.9533	5.6701	8.8027	9.3454	3.8625	5.0022	0.6346	1.0122
1989	5.0726	6.3827	8.2925	10.2284	3.6746	5.7710	0.6503	1.0851
1990	5.2916	6.2435	9.4039	9.6322	3.6581	5.7733	0.6794	1.0194
1991	5.6273	6.1935	9.9195	9.4096	4.1851	5.7822	0.7242	0.9446
1992	6.2184	6.3962	10.9190	9.6539	4.9119	6.0478	0.8035	0.9186
1993	8.0244	7.1260	12.0414	10.8999	7.2248	6.8489	1.0374	0.9716
1994	8.6187	8.6187	13.2006	13.2006	8.4399	8.4399	1.1154	1.1154
1995	8.3510	9.8171	13.1782	14.9473	8.8764	9.8957	1.0796	1.2049
1996	8.3142	10.3291	12.9727	15.8036	7.6437	10.7025	1.0750	1.2310
1997	8.2898	10.3758	13.5765	15.7535	6.8546	10.8149	1.0709	1.1968
1998	8.2791	10.1355	13.7185	15.1093	6.3281	10.6585	1.0688	1.1571
1999	8.2783	9.7796	13.3910	14.6704	7.2791	10.5449	1.0669	1.1787
2000	8.2672	9.4980	12.3441	14.3095	7.2344	10.6586	1.0616	1.2199
2001	8.2683	9.3016	11.9899	14.1499	6.2980	10.8125	1.0604	1.2493
2002	8.2519	9.0831	13.2392	13.8136	6.9550	10.8250	1.0584	1.2803
2003	8.2805	8.9854	14.7525	13.5789	7.7461	10.9796	1.0589	1.3235
2004	8.2701	9.0924	15.9524	13.7023	8.0637	11.4030	1.0625	1.3755
2005	8.0751	9.2385	13.9175	13.5651	6.8611	11.6483	1.0516	1.3838

Note: For WNERs, differences exist between spot rates and average rate of a year. For inconsistent quotes by different authorities, especially since 2002, we calculate cross-rates for the renminbi using the data from Hong Kong Monetary Authorities available at http://www.info.gov.hk/hkma/index.htm, so they may not be the same as those given in Tables 3A.1 and 3A.2. As for the PPP-implied exchange rates, refer to the text for the methodology and Table 4.3 for price data used.

Sources: Individual country data are from the following official or bank websites, available at http://www.pbc.gov.cn/diaochatongji; http://www.federalreserve.gov/releases/h15/data.htm; http://www.bankofengland.co.uk/statistics/index.htm; http://www.boj.or.jp/en/stat/stat_f.htm; http://www.info.gov.hk/hkma/chi/statistics/msb/index.htm.

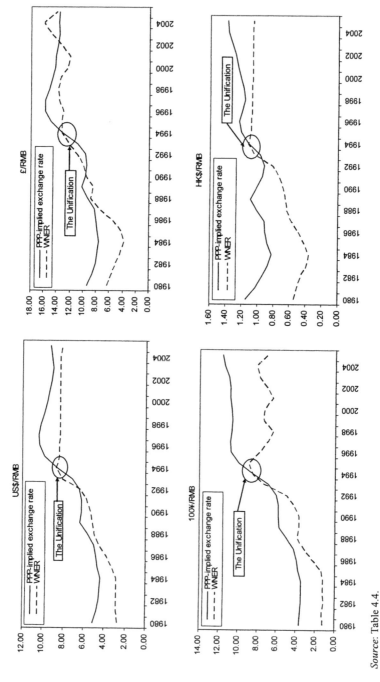

Source: Table 4.4.

Figure 4.2 PPP-implied versus nominal exchange rate of renminbi (indirect quote) (1980–2005) (1994 = PPP)

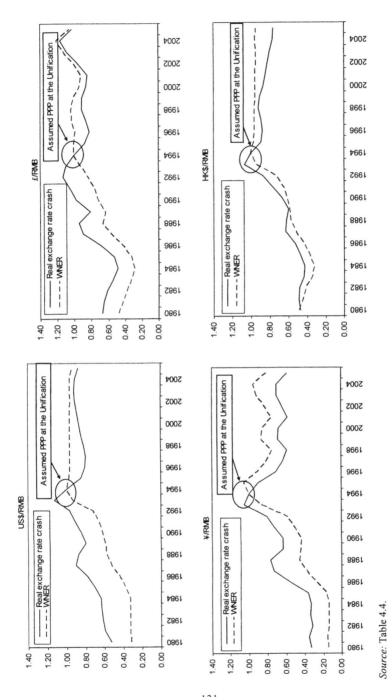

Source: Table 4.4.

Figure 4.3   Real and nominal exchange rate indices of renminbi (indirect quote) (1980–2005) (1994 = PPP)

Table 4.5   *Real exchange rate index of renminbi (indirect quote) (1994 =*
               PPP)

	US$/RMB	£/RMB	¥/RMB	HK$/RMB
1980	0.532	0.673	0.329	0.475
1981	0.595	0.658	0.359	0.489
1982	0.619	0.611	0.320	0.488
1983	0.630	0.547	0.337	0.442
1984	0.639	0.490	0.335	0.433
1985	0.700	0.533	0.361	0.474
1986	0.780	0.688	0.562	0.532
1987	0.906	0.892	0.734	0.630
1988	0.874	0.942	0.772	0.627
1989	0.795	0.811	0.637	0.599
1990	0.848	0.976	0.634	0.666
1991	0.909	1.054	0.724	0.767
1992	0.972	1.131	0.812	0.875
1993	1.126	1.105	1.055	1.068
1994	1.000	1.000	1.000	1.000
1995	0.851	0.882	0.897	0.896
1996	0.805	0.821	0.714	0.873
1997	0.799	0.862	0.634	0.895
1998	0.817	0.908	0.594	0.924
1999	0.846	0.913	0.690	0.905
2000	0.870	0.863	0.679	0.870
2001	0.889	0.847	0.582	0.849
2002	0.908	0.958	0.642	0.827
2003	0.922	1.086	0.706	0.800
2004	0.910	1.164	0.707	0.772
2005	0.874	1.026	0.589	0.760

Finally, the pound–renminbi real and nominal rates have converged significantly since 1997 after a short divergence in 1995–96. The nominal yen–renminbi rate tracks the real exchange rate since unification. Japanese officials alleged at the meeting of G7 finance ministers in early 2003 that China kept the renminbi undervalued in order to maintain its export competitiveness, but Figure 4.2 shows that based on PPP, renminbi overvaluation against the yen was the largest among the four currencies. In sum, our PPP-based analysis shows that the renminbi nominal exchange rate was significantly overvalued before unification in 1994 and remained overvalued afterwards, but only marginally. The British pound sterling was the one currency that the renminbi was undervalued against in 2004. Our analysis assumes that the PPP condition held in 1994, but even if PPP did not hold, our analysis indicates there is a far greater likelihood that the renminbi was undervalued against the US dollar than against the yen in the early to mid-2000s.

INTEREST RATE DIFFERENTIALS AND THE EXCHANGE RATE

The Chinese government has a long history of using differential interest rates to influence resource allocation to projects and sectors without paying careful consideration to the risks and economic returns of investments. The Chinese authorities have partially lifted controls on interest rates following economic reform, but progress has been slow. Throughout the 1980s, the state set and controlled over 200 interest rates (including interest rates on foreign currencies held in Chinese bank accounts). In some instances, interest rates were set around a reference rate, with bandwidths varying according to the type of financial intermediary and creditworthiness of the borrower (World Bank 1996, p. 29). By 1996, despite several interest rate reforms, the number of interest rates under control was still 148. Nevertheless, the pace of reform in interest policy picked up in 1996. In January 1996, China's inter-bank money market began operations and by June 1996 the PBC had abandoned all restrictions on inter-bank offer rates – CHIBOR (China Inter-Bank Offer Rate) – and liberalized further the money and bond markets. The auction method was adopted in the sale of Treasury bills and from October 1998, the band within which the interest rate could vary was widened (Gong and Dai 2000, pp. 270–71).

By the end of 2003, according to the governor of the PBC, Zhou Xiaochuan, 114 of the 148 interest rate categories had been eliminated, simplified by combining different interest rate categories, or 'liberalized' with greater flexibility. This left 34 interest rates still under tight state control, including, as the PBC governor admitted, the most sensitive interest rate – that on personal savings accounts.[11] However, there has been little progress on interest rate reform since the governor's statement in 2003. China's interest rate structure remains unduly complex, continuing to distort the allocation of scarce capital. In June 2006 there were still official controls over 29 interest rate categories (PBC 2006a).

With state control on interest rates, interest rate movements in China have deviated from those of its major trading partners. Table 4.6 lists the annual average of one-month inter-bank offer rates in China and its four major trading partners from 1980 to 2005. China opened its inter-bank money market in 1996, allowing the interest rate to float around the central bank's base rate. For 1980–95, we use the series of (short-term) working capital

The making of China's exchange rate policy

lending rates to industrial enterprises to link with the post-1995 CHIBOR rates to provide a continuous series of interest rates. Although the working capital lending rate is different from the CHIBOR, it is the interest rate most comparable to the CHIBOR.

Table 4.6   Inter-bank offer rates in China and its major trading partners (annual %)

	Inter-bank offer rate (1 month)				Interest rate differential			
	China*	US	UK	Japan	HK	China/ US	China/ UK	China/ Japan	China/ HK
1980	5.040	13.356	16.872	10.930	n.a.	−8.316	−11.832	−5.890	n.a.
1981	5.280	16.378	13.811	7.436	n.a.	−11.098	−8.531	−2.156	n.a.
1982	5.400	12.258	12.373	6.937	n.a.	−6.858	−6.973	−1.537	n.a.
1983	5.400	9.087	10.181	6.393	n.a.	−3.687	−4.781	−0.993	n.a.
1984	5.760	10.225	9.909	6.099	10.747	−4.465	−4.149	−0.339	−4.987
1985	5.760	8.101	12.421	6.538	6.557	−2.341	−6.661	−0.778	−0.797
1986	7.920	6.805	10.998	4.963	6.162	1.115	−3.078	2.957	1.758
1987	7.920	6.658	9.663	3.670	5.060	1.263	−1.743	4.250	2.860
1988	9.000	7.568	9.982	3.833	6.497	1.432	−0.982	5.167	2.503
1989	11.108	9.217	13.772	5.335	9.784	1.892	−2.663	5.773	1.324
1990	8.202	8.099	14.794	7.621	8.697	0.103	−6.593	0.581	−0.495
1991	9.000	5.688	11.734	7.544	6.362	3.313	−2.734	1.456	2.638
1992	8.370	3.522	9.674	4.633	3.999	4.848	−1.304	3.738	4.371
1993	9.540	3.023	6.004	3.071	3.454	6.518	3.536	6.469	6.086
1994	9.990	4.202	5.275	2.261	4.467	5.788	4.715	7.729	5.523
1995	10.530	5.837	6.499	1.244	6.074	4.693	4.031	9.286	4.456
1996	12.098	5.298	5.987	0.541	5.340	6.799	6.111	11.557	6.758
1997	10.600	5.460	6.672	0.623	6.969	5.140	3.928	9.977	3.631
1998	6.754	5.353	7.321	0.655	8.030	1.401	−0.567	6.099	−1.276
1999	4.143	4.970	5.348	0.251	5.835	−0.828	−1.205	3.892	−1.693
2000	2.582	6.273	5.973	0.366	6.151	−3.692	−3.391	2.216	−3.570
2001	2.954	3.787	5.003	0.141	3.638	−0.833	−2.049	2.813	−0.684
2002	2.378	1.678	3.933	0.093	1.819	0.700	−1.554	2.285	0.559
2003	2.458	1.126	3.638	0.044	0.969	1.333	−1.179	2.415	1.489
2004	2.925	1.401	4.448	0.026	0.313	1.524	−1.523	2.899	2.612
2005	2.140	3.274	4.673	0.035	2.908	−1.134	−2.533	2.106	−0.768

Note: Annual average of one-month inter-bank offer rate. *China's inter-bank offer rate (CHIBOR) began in 1996. The pre-1996 data are the banks' (short-term) lending rates for working capital of enterprises.

Sources: Individual country data are from the following official or bank websites, respectively, available at http://www.pbc.gov.cn/diaochatongji; http://www.federalreserve.gov/releases/h15/data.htm; http://www.bankofengland.co.uk/statistics/index.htm; http://www.boj.or.jp/en/stat/stat_f.htm; http://www.info.gov.hk/hkma/chi/statistics/msb/index.htm.

Figure 4.4 traces interest rate movements in the renminbi and other major currencies. It shows that between 1980 and 2004, changes in the renminbi interest rate almost never followed changes in the interest rate of the other major currencies. A simple correlation matrix shown in Table 4.7 indicates that while movements in the four foreign currency interest rates are highly correlated to each other, the renminbi interest rate exhibits almost no correlation with any of the foreign rates. However, Figure 4.4 shows that from the early 2000s, the renminbi interest rate appears to begin moving more in tandem with the interest rates of some of the major foreign currencies. This signals that after a decade of very rapid marketization of China's economy after Deng Xiaoping's famous journey to southern China, China's financial markets are beginning to integrate with other financial markets in the global economy. However, the correlation of China's interest rates with international rates is also a sign that economic integration as a result of globalization is creating difficult-to-control capital flows that are diminishing China's monetary independence in the presence of a pegged exchange rate.

Table 4.7 Correlation matrix of interest rates (1980–2004)

	RMB	HK$	¥	US$	£
RMB	1.0000	0.1074	0.1364	0.0609	0.2077
HK$	0.1074	1.0000	0.7260	0.9714	0.7837
¥	0.1364	0.7260	1.0000	0.7718	0.9402
US$	0.0609	0.9714	0.7718	1.0000	0.8203
£	0.2077	0.7837	0.9402	0.8203	1.0000

Source: Calculated using data from Table 4.6.

The interest rate parity (IRP) condition stipulates that in the absence of barriers across international financial markets, interest arbitrage should ensure that the rates of return of two financial assets with identical risks should be equal. For example, the interest rate differential of two perfectly substitutable domestic and foreign bonds should cover the forward premium or discount of the currencies of denomination of the underlying assets or the expected change in the exchange rate of these currencies at maturity, so that the incentive to engage in interest arbitrage is zero. Capital controls are a typical barrier to arbitrage, thus deviations from IRP can be used as an indirect indicator of the presence and effectiveness of capital controls.

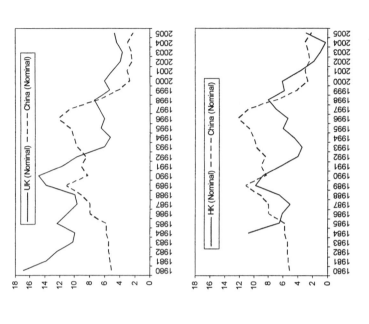

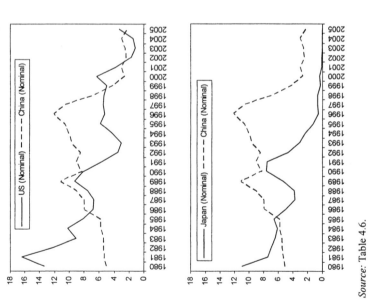

136

Source: Table 4.6.

Figure 4.4 Interest rate differentials (average annual percentage of one-month inter-bank offer rate) (1980–2005)

According to the IRP condition, a higher renminbi interest rate relative to the foreign currency interest rate indicates an expected depreciation of the renminbi *vis-à-vis* the foreign currency, causing the renminbi to trade at a forward discount. A lower renminbi interest rate relative to the interest rate of the foreign currency should indicate an expected appreciation of the renminbi, causing the renminbi to trade at a forward premium, equalizing the rates of return from holding the two currencies. That is:

$$(i - i^*)/(1 + i^*) = ER \qquad (4.7)$$

where $i - i^*$ is the renminbi and foreign currency (denoted by the superscript *) nominal interest rate differential with the same maturity term and ER is the forward premium or discount of the foreign currency at the end of the term with respect to the renminbi ($ER > 0$ denotes forward premium (discount) of foreign currency (renminbi)).

In 1997 the Bank of China became the first bank allowed to trade the renminbi forward. Development in the forward market has been slow. In 2004 forward trading volumes in renminbi were still insignificant; they were less than US$20 billion, which was only 1.7 per cent of China's total foreign trade in goods. As long as the renminbi was pegged to the US dollar, there was reluctance among China's corporations to hedge against foreign exchange risk. Most of them considered potential fluctuations in the renminbi to be very small and not worth the cost of hedging.

Only seven banks were licensed to offer forward foreign exchange contracts to their customers. They included China's big four state-owned commercial banks – the Agricultural Bank of China, Bank of China, China Construction Bank, and the Industrial and Commercial Bank of China – and the Bank of Communications, CITIC Industrial Bank and China Merchants Bank. These banks did not trade forward contracts with one another; they traded these contracts only with their customers. It was not until about a month after the end of the renminbi–US dollar peg on 15 August 2005 that China opened its inter-bank foreign exchange forward market for trade in US dollars and yen (GSFX 2006, p. 34). More deregulation of trading in foreign exchange accompanied the opening of the inter-bank foreign exchange forward market. Deregulation included increasing the number of players allowed to trade in foreign exchange and allowing banks to set the forward rate at their discretion.[12]

Before the establishment of the inter-bank foreign exchange forward market, China's monetary authorities had set the forward rates of the renminbi against other currencies on the basis of the spot rate and differences in the renminbi interest rate and the London inter-bank offer rates (LIBORs) of other currencies. The forward rates were not necessarily market-determined rates and they differed from the non-deliverable forward (NDF) contract rates set outside China. For example, there was a 2 per cent gap between the six-month renminbi forward rate and the NDF rate of RMB7.828 per US dollar on 1 August 2005 (Xu 2005).

NDF contracts were created in the 1990s primarily for currencies in emerging economies with no liquid money markets or euro currency interest rates. Two major renminbi NDF markets are Hong Kong and Singapore. Global average daily NDF renminbi–US dollar contracts had amounted to about US$150–200 million, but increased to about US$600 million in early 2004 in anticipation of a renminbi revaluation (Fung et al. 2004, p. 349). NDF contracts do not result in an actual exchange of currencies at maturity. The contract is settled at maturity in US dollars on the basis of the difference between the spot rate at maturity and the contracted forward rate. Renminbi NDF contracts are available to corporations that wish to hedge against fluctuations in the value of the renminbi but cannot do so because the renminbi is not tradable freely outside China because of capital controls.

Renminbi NDF rates, unlike renminbi forward rates in China, are market-determined rates and US dollar–renminbi NDF rates indicate violation of IRP. Since November 2002, despite higher interest rates for the renminbi relative to the US dollar (Table 4.6), NDF US dollar–renminbi rates were trading at a forward discount (Table 4.8), signalling market expectations of a renminbi revaluation rather than devaluation as suggested by IRP. In the presence of capital controls it is not surprising that IRP does not hold with respect to the renminbi. What is surprising, however, is that the post-November 2002 mean NDF US dollar–renminbi discount is rather small. We recalculate Table 4.8 to derive equivalent NDF renminbi–US dollar rates (Table 4.9) to obtain NDF premiums of the renminbi (direct quote) of not much more than 1.5 per cent at most, when many respectable economists cited in Dunaway and Li (2005) were suggesting that the renminbi was undervalued by as much as 25 per cent or more. A likely reason is that many of these economists were stating what they considered to be the required change in the exchange rate to balance China's international payments, without giving much weight to the fact that for financial markets much of China's capital inflows were speculative and could flow out as easily as they had flowed in.[13] As we noted in Chapter 3, capital controls have discouraged but not entirely prevented speculative flows, even though they are subjected to higher transaction costs than would be the case in the absence of capital controls.

Table 4.8 US$/RMB non-deliverable forward premium/discount

Maturity	Mean forward premium/discount (%)	
	Before 13 November 2002*	On or after 13 November 2002**
1 week	0.46	
1 month	1.88	−0.81
2 months	1.99	−0.85
3 months	2.21	−0.95
4 months	2.57	
5 months	2.81	
6 months	2.93	−1.17
9 months	3.33	−1.35
1 year	3.58	−1.45
2 years	3.67	−1.09
3 years	3.47	−1.09
4 years	3.56	−0.89
5 years	3.60	−0.91
9 years	3.75	
10 years	4.01	

Note: * From 19 January 1999. ** Until 4 November 2003.

Source: Fung et al. (2004, p. 350).

Table 4.9 RMB/US$ non-deliverable forward premium/discount

Maturity	Mean forward premium/discount (%)	
	Before 13 November 2002*	On or after 13 November 2002**
1 week	0.46	
1 month	−1.88	0.81
2 months	−1.98	0.85
3 months	−2.20	0.95
4 months	−2.55	
5 months	−2.78	
6 months	−2.89	1.18
9 months	−3.25	1.36
1 year	−3.45	1.47
2 years	−3.42	1.11
3 years	−3.15	1.13
4 years	−3.12	0.92
5 years	−3.05	0.95
9 years	−2.80	
10 years	−2.86	

Note: * From 19 January 1999. ** Until 4 November 2003.

Source: Calculated using data from Fung et al. (2004, p. 350).

CONCLUSION

The renminbi rate of return per US dollar of exports is a crucial economic indicator that influences exchange rate policy in China. In this chapter we have shown how the exchange rate and subsidies were used to vary the renminbi rate of return per US dollar of exports to influence exports when there was a serious imbalance in China's balance of trade, especially when it posted large deficits. Among the factors that explain China's exports, we find two that were more important than the renminbi exchange rate. These were the relocation of global production to China that was reflected in large FDI flows and machinery and material imports into China, and subsidies and export rebates.

In this chapter, we also demonstrated that the exchange rate was not undervalued significantly, if at all, in relation to the currencies of some of China's major trading partners in terms of simple PPP. This result finds support in the relatively small forward premiums for the renminbi in the non-deliverable forward markets between November 2002 and November 2003. But if indeed the renminbi was undervalued, its undervaluation in terms of the US dollar was likely to be larger compared to its undervaluation in terms of the yen. Finally, NDF rates did not adjust according to US dollar and renminbi interest rates, which indicates that capital controls in China, however imperfect, are still sufficiently effective to prevent interest rate parity.

NOTES

1. For example, Yang's Series 1 was defined by Yang as 'fiscal adjusted nominal renminbi exchange rate' (*caizheng yinsu de renminbi mingyi huilü*), but his analysis in Chapter 2 suggests that the series can be interpreted as renminbi unit cost of US dollar exports plus fiscal subsidies.
2. By the end of 1992, according to Ba (1999, p. 116), the swap centres handled 80 per cent of foreign exchange transactions. Accordingly, we set a ratio of 80 to 20 as the weights of the swap and official rates, respectively, for 1993. Based on this and the growth of foreign exchange turnovers in the swap centres since 1985 (Table 3A.1), we set the ratio as 30:70 for 1985–86, 40:60 for 1987–88, 50:50 for 1989–90, 60:40 for 1991 and 70:30 for 1992.
3. This figure differs from the RMB4.78 per US dollar reported in the first column of Table 4.1.
4. Calculated as the difference between the official and the swap market rates (RMB1.08) multiplied by the foreign exchange retention rate (80 per cent) of total export earnings (Yang 1993, p. 5).
5. Note that fiscal subsidies are technically not the same as export tax rebates. Only export tax rebates at rates above the VAT rate are fiscal subsidies. But enterprises often receive export subsidies on top of export rebates.
6. It was renamed in March 2003.

7. In the previous chapter, we pointed out that some sub-national governments are protesting that they are finding it difficult to refund export rebates, but the same sub-national governments are also often subsidizing local exports. Complaints from sub-national governments of their inabilities to refund export rebates are also often a ploy by sub-national governments to seek a larger share of tax revenues.

8. See pp. 93–5 of this book for an explanation.

9. We also pointed out in Chapter 1 that low labour costs in China are more important than the exchange rate in determining China's competitiveness in exports. Moreover, China's exports have a very high import content, so a revaluation of the renminbi will also lower the cost of China's exports.

10. For a survey of these studies, see Dunaway and Li (2005).

11. Zhou made the statement at the Euromoney, BOC and HSBC-sponsored China Conference on 3 December 2003. See the report by Sun (2003b) in the *21 shiji jingji baodao* (21st Century Economic Herald).

12. In August 2005, the PBC relaxed rules to increase the number of banks allowed to conduct forward sales and purchases of foreign exchange (PBC Document 201 and 202). The rules allow foreign banks as well as non-financial enterprises to trade foreign exchange forward. Interestingly, banks are given the freedom to set the forward rate at their discretion *(huilü you yinhang zixing queding)* (PBC, Document 201, Article 4, 2005). Document 201 was issued on 2 August and it did not mention non-financial enterprises. A few days later on 8 August, the PBC announced that non-financial enterprises satisfying certain criteria can apply for membership of the China Foreign Exchange Trading Centre (*Zhongguo waihui jiaoyi zhongxin*), which grants them the right to engage in spot trading of foreign exchange. However, non-financial enterprises require further approval from SAFE before they can deal in forward foreign exchange transactions (PBC Document 202, Article 3-3, 2005). Available at http://pbc.gov.cn/detail.asp?col=340&ID=574> and <http://pbc.gov.cn/detail.asp?col=340&ID=575, accessed 26 January 2006.

13. We discuss this point in greater detail in Chapter 6.

5. Institutions and exchange rate policy: China and the Asian financial crisis

During the late 1990s in a climate of concern about the Asian financial crisis (AFC), fears were expressed that China would devalue the renminbi. This was seen as a move that would further destabilize the other economies of East Asia. Many Asia-Pacific leaders, including US President Bill Clinton, praised China for not devaluing the renminbi at this crucial time. In his speech to the World Economic Forum in Beijing in 1998, Singapore's minister for information, George Yeo, contrasted the Asian region's views of Japan and views of China. Had Japan exercised global leadership, according to Yeo, 'the Asian financial crisis would have been quickly stabilized'. Yeo claimed the 'determination of the Chinese government not to devalue the renminbi, in order not to destabilize Asia further, will long be remembered' (Kelley 1998). The Thai prime minister, Chuan Leekpai, also publicly thanked China for maintaining the value of the renminbi. China's leaders lost no time in talking up China's promise to maintain the value of the renminbi. The cover story of the Chinese government's weekly international mouthpiece, *Beijing Review*, 9–15 March 1998, declared 'Renminbi won't devalue'. The same weekly in its coverage of the Second Asian European Meeting (ASEM) in 1998 reported on the compliments China received from Dutch prime minister, Wim Kok and European Commission president, Jacques Santer for China's conduct in the Asian crisis (Feng 1998).

Why did China not devalue its currency during the Asian financial crisis? Was it for strategic reasons, because the Chinese government wished to gain regional and perhaps broader goodwill, international prestige and/or favourable entry conditions into the World Trade Organization (WTO)? Was it also, or perhaps primarily, a question of economics? Some scholars, among them Huang and Yang (1998), Song (1998) and Yang (2000), argued that the Chinese government had no economic reason to devalue. In their view, China's economic fundamentals were solid and with the renminbi not fully convertible, there was little fear of massive capital flight from China. However, other scholars like Naughton (1999) argued that while China could not be forced to devalue because its currency is not fully convertible, the Chinese government did have reasons to devalue because China had lost its competitive market position following devaluation of the currencies of its major Asian trading partners. Moreover, although formal controls on capital flows were tight, massive amounts of capital could still flee China during the crisis, in anticipation of renminbi devaluation. This can be gauged from the average annual unexplained capital outflows of about US$15.4 billion between 1998 and 2000 indicated by the 'errors and omissions' item in China's balance of payments (Prasad and Wei 2005, Table 7).

POLICYMAKING IN POST-MAO CHINA

Economic policymaking has continued to change in the post-Mao era. The early post-Mao trend towards institutionalization has formalized further in the post-Deng era. The intense political struggles of the Mao period have also given way to increasing pluralization of Chinese policymaking (Bachman 2001; Shambaugh 2001). Moves toward pluralism and institutionalization in economic policymaking result from the massive expansion of the market and administrative decentralization, which are products of both economic and political reform, and the passing of the old revolutionary leaders who exercised immense personal authority.

Greater reliance on domestic and overseas markets and the increased autonomy that the centre has granted to localities have opened the policy arena to more voices and interests and expanded the capacity of these new voices and interests to influence policy. The ensuing politicization has made both the policies and the responses of stakeholders in them less predictable than before. Administrative decentralization has widened the reach of bureaucratic power, thus creating the need for more comprehensive policy coordination. For example, changes in the exchange rate affect different sectors of the domestic economy in different ways and have implications for managing foreign relations, so they impact unevenly on the work of different parts of the bureaucracy. The new complexity of market and political administration demands a more professional approach to economic policy formulation and implementation. Input into policymaking is therefore drawn from specialists within and outside the bureaucracy. Many of these sources were largely excluded from the policy arena in the Maoist period, when it was more important to be 'red than expert'.

Past revolutionary leaders like Deng Xiaoping and Chen Yun relied on their revolutionary reputations and extensive networks of supporters and clients. Post-Deng senior leaders, including former Chinese Communist Party (CCP) general secretary Jiang Zemin and former premier Zhu Rongji did not enjoy similar reputations, following and influence, and had to rely more on institutional than personal authority. Zhu Rongji, who as premier was nominally the senior leader in charge of the economy during the AFC, was responsible for economic policy. Yet he had to work hard to convince other senior leaders of the merits of his policy recommendations. The policy preference of senior leaders is likely to be based on personal or institutional ties, their perception of the national interest and how best to achieve it, or some mix of these. Regardless of what motivates individual leaders' preferences, the style of deciding policy is today more collective than autocratic. When a senior leader has a strong policy preference based on personal or institutional ties, analyses and other policy inputs from actors within the bureaucracy are unlikely to have a strong influence on the leader's final vote. Nevertheless, these analyses and policy inputs from institutional actors can be highly influential in the decision-making process and can swing the vote one way or another when there is deadlock between differently minded senior leaders who have strong policy preferences or when senior leaders do not have prior policy preferences to pursue.

Numerous studies have reported on Chinese economic policymaking, particularly in the reform period, but none has specifically examined exchange rate policy.[1] Moore and Yang (2001) considered aspects of China's exchange rate policy during the AFC in their examination of the impact on foreign policy of China's growing economic interdependence. However, their study did not examine China's exchange rate policymaking structure and the influence and role of key organs in policy formulation. The several studies of China's foreign exchange rate regime (for example Liu et al. 1997; Wu 1998) mainly concern the economic mechanics of the regime and are not concerned with the structure, processes or politics that produced specific policies.

Our research findings lead us to conclude that while institutional actors in exchange rate policymaking have no capacity to determine directly either the policy or its implementation, they nevertheless play a critical role in policy development. Because decisions on exchange rates affect the environment in which institutional actors function, these actors have a vested interest in policy development. But unlike energy policies, which Lieberthal and Oksenberg (1988) examined, for exchange rate policies institutional actors have less space in which to influence policy. Taking a decision on currency devaluation and then implementing this decision does not involve a drawn-out bargaining process requiring the cooperation of ministries and regions that could obstruct or delay policy implementation by deliberate foot-dragging and other resistance or by mere inaction or inertia.

The critical role of institutional actors in exchange rate policymaking instead lies in their analyses of exchange rate policy issues and their policy recommendations often based on these analyses – policy preparation rather than policy implementation. Thus, when the powerful Central Leading Group on Finance and Economics (CLGFE) (*Zhongyang caijing lingdao xiaozu*) made the decision not to devalue the renminbi during the AFC, that decision was informed by research and analysis carried out by CLGFE and other key policymaking organs, with inputs from key economic ministries. Importantly, officials close to the then premier, Zhu Rongji, who were in key institutional positions in the policymaking structure inside and outside the CLGFE, were able to shape policy by influencing the direction of the research, who conducted it, the style of analysis, and the type of research output that reached other top leaders.

To better understand the process of exchange rate policymaking in China, we present this process in a three-stage diagram in Figure 5.1. This diagram distinguishes clearly between policymaking and policy decision making, with the latter a part of the former. The first stage is where policy inputs are gathered from both formal and informal sources. The inputs include not only information and analyses, but also policy recommendations. The sources of these inputs include relevant ministries and research institutes and informal consultants. In recent years State Council ministries have increasingly extended their involvement in policy development from simply implementing externally determined policy to taking the initiative and providing input into policymaking, as the policymaking process becomes more institutionalized (Shambaugh 2001, p. 105).

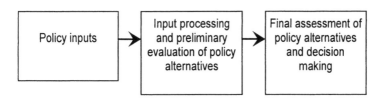

Figure 5.1 Exchange rate policymaking and decision making

The second stage is where key policy organs process and evaluate these inputs in preparation for the last stage, where those who make the final decision on policy undertake final evaluation of the received inputs before making their determination. In other arenas of economic policymaking where bargaining is an important part of policy implementation, the policymaking process will have an additional stage for policy implementation, where post-decision bargaining takes place between decision makers and decision implementers, as well as among decision makers and among decision implementers. With exchange rate policy, the final decision is definitive and does not offer ground for bargaining through implementation. Research on Chinese economic policymaking has focused on decision making and implementation, and tended to ignore the two stages that precede them. But changes in the functions of key economic ministries due to the systemic changes in administration forced by marketization, pluralization of actors, and institutionalization of economic policymaking mean that these ministries are involved at earlier stages of policymaking in inputs that can affect the final policy decision. Hence, comprehending the workings of the first two stages is ever more important for understanding how certain policies are produced.

ELITES IN ECONOMIC POLICYMAKING

According to the CCP constitution, the Central Committee is the party's supreme decision-making body. In practice, however, the supreme decision-making body is the Politburo and its standing committee, with a significantly smaller number of members.[2] Despite efforts to separate the functions of party and government, high-level policymaking and policy implementation in China is still under a unified command structure of party and government. Top party leaders are also top government leaders and they sit on joint party–government policymaking organs. Some purely government policymaking organs exist, but the most important and influential organs in policymaking are either joint party–government or solely party organs. The CCP Military Commission is a party organ but the CLGFE is a joint organ of the State Council and Politburo (Wang and Fewsmith 1995, p. 54). There is a rough division of labour among these organs, but their responsibilities sometimes overlap. Agricultural industry, for example, is a sub-group under the CLGFE, but rural affairs are managed by the CCP Central Leading Working Group on Rural Affairs (*Zhongyang nongcun gongzuo lingdao xiaozu*). The latter organ has wider responsibilities for rural affairs than the CLGFE and pays more attention to the social and political impacts of rural policy, which are often a direct result of agricultural policies that the CLGFE has determined. A top party leader heads each policymaking organ and top party leaders often head several policymaking organs. For example, Jiang Zemin as CCP general secretary chaired several key policymaking organs, among which were the CCP Military Commission, the Central Leading Group on Taiwan Affairs and the Central Leading Group on National Security (*Zhongyang guojia anquan lingdao xiaozu*).

Figure 5.2 shows the key actors in the policymaking structure for China's money and finance (which include the exchange rate) immediately after the Ninth National People's Congress (NPC) in March 1998.[3] The People's Bank of China (PBC), the State Development and Planning Commission (SDPC), the Ministry of Finance (MOF) and Ministry of Foreign Trade and

Economic Cooperation (MOFTEC) were the key ministries providing input into exchange rate policymaking. These State Council ministries in particular, with their individual institutional interests, have become initiators as well as implementers of policies. Overall, however, the key policy decision makers were the CLGFE and the CCP Politburo and its standing committee. The Politburo and its standing committee were the ultimate decision makers, but the Politburo normally rubber-stamped the decisions of the CLGFE because, with senior members of the Politburo standing committee as members of the CLGFE, the Politburo's imprint was already registered in CLGFE decisions. The remaining boxes in Figure 5.2 show the key assessors of policy inputs and those organs coordinating policy input, policy analysis and decision making.

The most important economic policymaking organ in China during the AFC was the CLGFE. The NPC had an Economic and Finance Committee, but this committee exerted no influence on exchange rate policy at this time. The CLGFE was established in 1954 and was the highest-level economic policy organ at that time. With a small staff, the CLGFE depended on State Planning Commission (SPC) staff to undertake policy work on its behalf. It had been relieved of most of its staff after the 1987 administrative reform (Gao 2004, p. 254) and hardly functioned at all in the two years immediately after the fall from power of party general secretary Zhao Ziyang in 1989. It operated as purely an advisory organ until 1993 when as party general secretary, Jiang Zemin converted it into the supreme organ of the party and state for economic policy decision making and, in many cases, policy implementation and supervision (Lam 1999). Chairing an organ, however, does not always mandate control over its workings and decisions. As party general secretary, Jiang Zemin chaired the CLGFE from 1991 until, according to some sources, his retirement from that position, but Zhu Rongji as vice-premier and later premier directed most of its work (Lam 1999, p. 78).

Zhu owed his meritorious rise in the party to Deng Xiaoping, who transferred him in 1991 from his positions as party secretary and mayor of Shanghai to a vice-premiership in Beijing to take a senior role in managing the economy. [4] Deng wanted to replace Yao Yilin, the then senior vice-premier, as chairperson of the CLGFE, preferably with Zhu. Deng did not prefer premier Li Peng for the position because he was considered too economically conservative. But not only was Zhu not the senior vice-premier, he was also only an alternate member of the Party Central Committee – he became a Politburo member only at the Fourteenth Party Congress in 1992 and senior vice-premier at the Eighth National People's Congress in 1993. In 1991, therefore, Zhu did not have the required seniority in the formal party hierarchy to head the CLGFE.

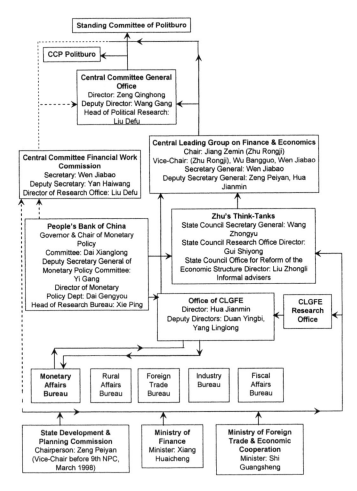

Note: -------- signifies that the CCFWC did not exist before June 1998. Lines of communication for non-monetary affairs CLGFE sub-groups are not shown.

Figure 5.2 China's monetary and financial policymaking structure (AFC)

Zhu's major economic task a year after his arrival in Beijing was to institute an austerity programme and reform China's banking system to combat inflation, which took off after Deng Xiaoping's 'southern tour' set off forces that led the party to continue market reform. For this task, Zhu was appointed governor of the PBC in 1993 and stayed in this position until 1995. Gao (2004, p. 251) in his biography of Wen Jiabao stated that Zhu took over from Jiang as chairperson of the CLGFE in 1994 but according to Lam

(1999, p. 78), Jiang never relinquished his position as head of the CLGFE. Zhu, however, did become premier in 1998 and was the key decision maker in China's policy not to devalue. He was serving as premier when the Chinese leadership announced to the world in March 1998 that China would not devalue. Zhu's tenure as economic supremo overlapped his positions first as senior vice-premier and later as premier. Li Peng's illness in 1997 and later his retirement as premier left Zhu as undisputed vice-chief to Jiang, even though Li was formally the number two in the party hierarchy.

In 1997 Zhu and three vice-premiers cum Politburo members were responsible for the five sub-groups under the CLGFE: agriculture, industry, foreign trade, monetary affairs and fiscal affairs, each of which was supported by a department that had bureau status. Formally, Jiang Chunyun looked after agriculture; Wu Bangguo, industry; Li Lanqing, foreign trades and Zhu, fiscal and monetary affairs, which include exchange rate policy. After Zhu became premier at the Ninth NPC in 1998, Wen Jiabao formally took over fiscal and monetary affairs. In practice, however, until the middle of 1999, Zhu took charge of the major issues in all the portfolios except agriculture. He pushed hard for reform of state-owned enterprises (SOEs) and financial and fiscal reforms, and played the key role in China's bid for WTO membership.[5]

A number of leading figures were involved in the CLGFE besides Jiang Zemin and Zhu Rongji. One was Wen Jiabao, the current premier. Wen was an alternate member of the Politburo and one of the secretaries in the Secretariat of the Central Committee (SCC) (*Zhongyang shujichu*) when Jiang replaced him as director of the influential Central Committee General Office (CCGO) (*Zhongyang bangongting*) with Jiang's chief political adviser, Zeng Qinghong, after the CCP's Fourteenth Party Congress in 1992. Zeng had not even made it into the Central Committee at the CCP's Fourteenth Party Congress in 1992, and his appointment as director of such a key party organ as the CCGO, without being in the Central Committee, was unprecedented. Many observers in China expected that Wen would be rewarded later for his 'sacrifice' (Gao and He 1999, p. 520). Wen was moved first to the less influential position of deputy to then vice-premier Zhu Rongji in the Central Leading Group on Agriculture,[6] but he was soon promoted to full member of the Politburo and was appointed as vice-chairperson and secretary general of the CLGFE in 1997 (Gao 2004, p. 256).[7]

Even though serving as the responsible leader for monetary affairs and secretary general of the CLGFE during the AFC, Wen did not exert great influence on monetary and exchange rate policy at this time. One person who did was Zeng Peiyan, Jiang's principal economic adviser. Lam (1999, p. 20) claimed that Zeng had a good command of the English language and was knowledgeable in world affairs. Zeng's first job as a fresh graduate of

Qinghua University in the early 1960s was to work under Jiang in the Shanghai Scientific Electric Equipment Research Institute (*Dianqi kexue yanjiusuo*) of the No. 1 Ministry of Machinery Building (*Diyi jixie gongye bu*) (Xiao Chong 1998, p. 105). In 1992, Jiang transferred Zeng to Beijing to be deputy secretary general of the CLGFE (with ministerial rank) and deputy chairperson and deputy party secretary of the SPC. In 1994, Zeng was given an additional role as director of the CLGFE administrative office (*bangongshi*) (Anon. 1994, p. 832; Shen 1999, p. 342; Xiao Chong 1998, p. 107; Xinhua 2003).[8] In 1982–84, he had been second and then first secretary of the Commercial Counsellor's Office at the Chinese embassy in Washington (Bartke 1991, p. 779). Zeng was made chairperson of the SDPC after the SPC's name was changed to the SDPC at the Ninth NPC in March 1998.

The *bangongshi*, which has ministry rank, performs various tasks for the CLGFE, coordinating its various sub-groups, supervising its research office (*yanjiushi*) and commissioning its outside research. It also produces reports and policy position papers for the members of the CLGFE and the Politburo and its standing committee to assist them in their policy deliberations, and it supervises policy implementation. Its director and his or her immediate superior – deputy secretary general of the CLGFE – are therefore highly influential in the policy process. In economic policymaking they can even be more influential than non-standing committee members of the Politburo. They may in some policy deliberations, under orders from top leaders of the CLGFE, report directly to the standing committee and bypass other members of the Politburo. For example, when the decision was taken in 1994 to devalue the renminbi, it was made by the standing committee and then announced to other members of the State Council, China's cabinet. The rest of the Politburo was unaware that devaluation was even being seriously considered until the decision to devalue was announced to the State Council.

Beside Zeng Peiyan, Jiang had Hua Jianmin to bolster his influence in national economic policymaking. In 1996 Jiang had transferred Hua from his position as Shanghai's vice-mayor to Beijing to be Zeng's deputy director in the CLGFE administrative office (Lam 1999, p. 22). Two years later Hua was appointed a deputy secretary general of the CLGFE and replaced Zeng as director of the CLGFE administrative office (*Fazhi ribao* 2003; Xinhua 2003), when Zeng was made chairperson of the SDPC while remaining a deputy secretary general of the CLGFE alongside Hua. Significantly, appointing Hua, who like Zeng was a member of Jiang's Shanghai faction, as director of the administrative office of the CLGFE reflects the importance of this position.[9]

With Zeng and Hua holding key positions at the CLGFE, Jiang was able to influence economic policy whether he was chairperson of the CLGFE or not.[10] Yet he was happy to let first Li Peng and later Zhu Rongji be responsible for the economy. He was, according to long-time China watcher Willy Lam, applying the lesson he learned from former party leader and premier Zhao Ziyang's disastrous overseeing of a hyper-inflationary economy in 1988: a poorly performing economy is fatal for one's political career; let someone else be the scapegoat (Lam 1999, p. 78).[11]

With Jiang willing to have Zhu as the chief economic manager, Zhu was undisputed boss of the CLGFE. But if necessary, Zhu had the PBC Monetary Policy Department (*Huobi zhengce si*) to counterbalance the influence of the CLGFE administrative office. Dai Gengyou was director of the PBC Monetary Policy Department during and for some time after the AFC and reported directly to Zhu. This department was then, and still is, at the core of monetary (and exchange rate) policy formulation. Its responsibilities include monetary policy research; drafting and implementing broad monetary policy and its policy targets; research into and recommending appropriate monetary tools to maintain the value of the renminbi; and research, drafting and implementing credit policy to promote national and regional economic development. While director of the Monetary Policy Department in the PBC, Dai Gengyou was also, according to an interviewee,[12] the head of the research office in the CLGFE. Dai Gengyou thus provided the vital link between the CLGFE and the PBC, which was Zhu's power base.

Zhu Rongji also had a valuable source of influence through his right-hand man, Dai Xianglong, who was a key figure in exchange rate policymaking during the AFC. Dai Xianglong succeeded Zhu Rongji as governor of the PBC in 1995 after serving as its deputy governor since 1993. Dai Xianglong spent almost his entire career in the banking sector until he was appointed mayor of the important city of Tianjin in December 2002.[13] Before his appointment to the PBC, he was deputy president of the Agriculture Bank of China (Li Baijing 1998, p. 15).

While serving as PBC governor, Dai Xianglong chaired the PBC Monetary Policy Committee, which was established in 1997 as an advisory body on monetary policy.[14] This committee is served by the PBC Monetary Policy Department that acts as its secretariat (ZJX 1999, p. 10). Although it has potential to influence monetary policy, the committee during the AFC did not exercise any real power and acted in a purely advisory capacity. Its influence over exchange rate policy during the AFC was considered minimal, with its views on policy largely dictated by Dai Xianglong.[15] The committee's deputy secretary general was a Western-trained economist – Yi Gang. Yi Gang obtained his PhD in economics from Illinois University in the US in 1986 and was an associate professor at Indiana University before returning to China to become professor and deputy director of Beijing University's China Economic Research Centre in 1993. In 1997 he was appointed deputy secretary general of the PBC's Monetary Policy Committee. He was later promoted to secretary general and became deputy director of the PBC's Monetary Policy Department under Dai Gengyou (Sun 2003a). He later took over from Dai Gengyou and was also made an assistant governor of the PBC[16] when Zhou Xiaochuan succeeded Dai Xianglong as governor in the post-Jiang Zemin policy structure (PBC 2006b).

Another important PBC department that influences monetary policy is its research bureau (*yanjiuju*), also known as the Finance Research Institute (*Jinrong yanjiusuo*) under Xie Ping, who headed it when Dai Xianglong ran the PBC. Its designated scope of research is wider than and overlaps that of the PBC's Monetary Policy Department. While the Monetary Policy Department's research focuses on short-run macroeconomic monetary policy (including the exchange rate), the research bureau's research includes short-term monetary policy as well as longer-term financial policies covering financial markets, financial risk and micro-effects of monetary and financial policies (ZJX 1999, p. 11). In the late 1990s, the PBC's research bureau was less influential than its Monetary Policy Department in monetary and exchange rate policy.

It is unclear whether the CCGO serves as intermediary between the CLGFE administrative office and Politburo or if the CLGFE administrative office sends reports and policy position papers directly to Politburo members. Between the fifth plenum of the Eleventh Central Committee in 1980 and the Thirteenth Party Congress in 1987, the Secretariat of the Central Committee, directly under the leadership of the standing committee of the Politburo, was the highest level policymaking and implementation organ of the Central Committee (Wu 1995, p. 26). When Zhao Ziyang became general secretary of the CCP in 1987, he downgraded the Secretariat into an advisory body and shifted many of its functions to the CCGO, which until then had functioned purely as a coordinating office among various top-level policymaking bodies (Ruan 1995, p. 17).

The CCGO became even more important under Jiang Zemin. Jiang had brought Zeng Qinghong from Shanghai to Beijing to manage his office of CCP general secretary and the CCGO.[17] The CCGO staff size under Zeng was expanded from 100 to 300. The CCGO makes policies, issues top-level party documents and controls the paper flow between the standing committee of the Politburo and central leadership groups and other lower-level CCP organs (Lam 1999, p. 34). It is also responsible for the personnel files and personal security of top leaders (Gao and He 1999, p. 517). Zeng's background was in neither economics nor finance and Jiang Zemin's support for Zhu Rongji's no-devaluation policy meant that the CCGO under Zeng was happy to follow the CLGFE's lead during the AFC. However, it is almost certain that the CCGO played an important role during the summer of 1998 to promote the no-devaluation policy among senior party officials gathered for the annual high-level leadership central work conference in Beidaihe, since the CCGO controls the flow of discussion papers for these conferences. During the 1998 Beidaihe conference, senior party officials who were worried about falling export growth applied heavy pressure to devalue the renminbi, and the control that the CCGO exercised over the discussion papers circulated among the conference participants would have been critical in cushioning the pressure applied. Wen Jiabao as secretary general of the CLGFE was given the responsibility of vetting the discussion papers (Lam 1998).

On 16 June 1998, the CCP Central Committee Financial Work Commission (CCFWC) (*Zhongyang jinrong gongzuo weiyuanhui*) was established, with Wen Jiabao as its secretary (ZJX 1999, p. 9).[18] Since Jiang Zemin favoured a no-devaluation policy, the establishment of the CCFWC was not due to disagreements between Jiang and Zhu Rongji over exchange rate policy.[19] Zhu and the CLGFE definitely played the leading role in the no-devaluation policy. The establishment of the CCFWC was a move designed primarily to give the CCP greater dominance over the state apparatus in formulating long-term policies for the finance sector. This move was partly in response to dissatisfaction within sections of the party over the state of the financial sector, especially over non-performing loans and corruption in that sector (Li Baijing 1998, pp. 15–17), which took on a sense of urgency with the looming AFC.[20]

The key responsibilities of the CCFWC were listed as ensuring adherence to financial policies and directives of the Central Committee and State Council, strengthening ideological work, regulating the cadre institutional structure in the finance area, integrating financial-system reform, combating corruption and undertaking field investigation and research (ZJX 1999, pp. 9, 614). There was no specific mention of the CCFWC regulating monetary policy and it certainly did not have anything to do with exchange rate policy. A reading of reports of the work of the CCFWC gives the impression that the CCFWC was mainly involved in formulating long-term financial policies rather than short-term monetary policies. The CCFWC was, for example, responsible for expanding the size and functions of stock markets in 1999 and 2000.[21] Despite the fanfare that surrounded its establishment, it did not seem to have much of an impact on policy after 2000. Wen Jiabao disbanded the CCFWC soon after the Sixteenth Party Congress (Naughton 2003, p. 43), when he was appointed a member of the standing committee of the Politburo and ranked third in the party hierarchy after Hu Jintao and Wang Bangguo. According to Naughton, Wen was shifting the focus in the finance area to the banking system away from the stock market and replaced the CCFWC with the Central Leading Group on Finance Safety (CLGFS) (*Zhongyang jinrong anquan lingdao xiaozu*).[22]

The CLGFE is a joint party–state organ whereas CCFWC was a party organ and was therefore not answerable to the CLGFE. Besides Wen Jiabao as secretary and Yan Haiwang as his deputy, commissioners of the CCFWC included deputy party secretaries of the PBC, China's Securities Supervision and Regulation Commission (*Zhongguo zhengquan jiandu guanli weiyuanhui*) and other major state-owned financial institutions, as well as the secretary of the CCFWC's disciplinary committee (ZJX 1999, pp. 9, 614). Legal scholar Liu Defu, with a PhD in law,[23] headed political research in the CCGO's research office (Zhong 1997) and it was no coincidence that he was appointed the first director of the research office of the CCFWC in 1998. Liu's appointment to this position allowed CCGO to have greater influence than otherwise over financial policy and Zeng Qinghong as Jiang's chief political adviser meant political considerations featured more prominently in financial policy deliberations.

An important part of China's economic decision-making structure during the AFC were the three think-tanks of Zhu Rongji: two formal and one informal.[24] The two formal think-tanks were the State Council Research Office (SCRO) (*Guowuyuan yanjiushi*) and the State Council Office for Reform of the Economic Structure (SCORES) (*Guowuyuan jingji tizhi gaige bangongshi*). The informal think-tank consisted of officials and academics holding full-time positions at government and party bureaucracies and at the academic institutions that Zhu consulted on an informal basis. These think-tanks provided Zhu with independent advice and arguments, which he could use to push his policy preferences at policy deliberation meetings of the CLGFE, especially if he disagreed with the policy evaluations generated by officials of the CLGFE. If Zhu acquiesced, the key economic ministries could also get their views heard by the CLGFE through Zhu's formal think-tanks if their views failed to reach the CLGFE's members through internal CLGFE channels. The key ministries are formally under the State Council and Zhu's formal think-tanks had State Council status that the CLGFE could not simply dismiss. Moreover, Liu Zhongli, the head of the SCORES, was a member of the CLGFE.[25] However, this was not an issue during the AFC since Jiang and Zhu were in agreement over exchange rate policy and Zhu had effective control over the CLGFE.

The SCRO has six research departments, an administrative office and a party committee office. The research departments deal with macroeconomics; rural economics; industry and transport; fiscal and financial issues; technology and science; and public security, religious affairs, civil associations and related areas. The SCRO's responsibilities include drafting the annual Government Work Report (*Zhengfu gongzuo baogao*), writing key speeches and undertaking research for the premier and vice-premiers. Before its restructure in 1998, the SCRO had 70 staff, managed by one director and two to four deputy directors. In 1999 it had a staff of 40, managed by one director and two deputy directors. Although the SCRO is a state organ rather than a party organ, its research staff must be CCP members. They must have extensive work experience and a strong academic record, which means at minimum an undergraduate degree from a well-recognized university. Many have masters degrees and some have PhDs. In 1999 Gui Shiyong headed the SCRO (ZN 1999, p. 123). Although Gui spent most of his career in the former SPC, Hong Kong political analyst Xiao Zhengqin considered him one of the most important of Zhu's 22 advisers.[26] The SCRO did not undertake significant research into the renminbi exchange rate and played no major role in making exchange rate policy during the AFC.

The second of the formal think-tanks, the SCORES, serviced Zhu's informal think-tank and provided whatever research and administrative support was required by Zhu's advisers (Chan 1998b). According to Xiao Zhengqin, Zhu had about ten administrative staff in his think-tank office (*zhinang bangongshi*). They performed other administrative duties for Zhu and administered his coterie of advisers. The SCORES originates from the former State Commission for Reform of the Economic Structure (*Guojia jingji tizhi gaige weiyuanhui*) (SCRES). Zhao Ziyang set up the SCRES to spearhead China's economic reform and was its first head. But with Zhao's fall from power in 1989, the SCRES slowly lost its influence. It was downgraded from a commission as part of a government restructure after the Ninth NPC in March 1998.[27]

During the AFC, the SCORES was headed by Liu Zhongli, a former finance minister (1992–98) and at that time a Central Committee member and one of Zhu's advisers (ZN 1999, p. 124). His appointment was to replace another adviser, Wang Mengkui, who was transferred to head a less prestigious and less important institution, the State Council Development Research Centre (SCDRC) (*Guowuyuan fazhan yanjiu zhongxin*).[28] According to some sources, Wang was also a key adviser to Jiang Zemin (Baum 1994, p. 469, fn 55; Chan 1998a), which could explain why Zhu replaced Wang with Liu Zhongli, who was closer to Zhu, to look after his think-tank office (Chan 1998a). During the AFC, Zhu commissioned several studies on the crisis through the SCORES, including one concerning the impact on China of fluctuation of the US dollar–yen exchange rate. Liu Zhongli, a fiscal centralist, was credited with successfully implementing the 1994 tax reform that sought to redress the problem of 'poor centre, rich localities' (*qiong zhongyang fu difang*) by giving the centre a larger portion of tax revenues (Li Xiaozhuang 1998, pp. 312–21). He was seen to represent the MOF in the exchange rate policy debate among Zhu's closest advisers and in the CLGFE.

Xiao's list of Zhu's 22 most important advisers comprised six academics and 16 party and state officials (Xiao Zhengqin 1999, p. 35). The six academics are economists Wu Jinglian, Liu Guoguang, Wang Jue, Lin Yifu, Wang Luolin and scientist Lu Juexiang. The academic adviser closest to Zhu during the AFC was Wu Jinglian, who in 1994 persuaded Zhu to merge the two foreign exchange markets and devalue the official exchange rate (Lam 1999, p. 372). Wu was also one of Zhao Ziyang's most trusted economic advisers. He is generally cautious and considers high inflation as economically and politically destabilizing. He does not believe that the price of high rates of inflation is worth paying to achieve rapid economic growth (Xiao Zhengqin 1999b, p. 35).[29] Because of his views on inflation, it is highly probable that Wu was against devaluation.

Beside Yi Gang, the economist who was in a position to put forcefully to Zhu the dominant Western economic approach to analysing the AFC and China's exchange rate during that period is the University of Chicago trained Lin Yifu, who runs the China Economic Research Centre at Beijing University. Basing his arguments purely on positive economics, he openly advocated a no-devaluation policy. Instead of devaluing the renminbi to overcome China's deflationary pressures, Lin advocated stimulating domestic, especially rural demand, the potential of which he thought had not been fully exploited (Lin 2000).

Many of the officials in Zhu's informal think-tank were then, or formerly, attached to economic and financial organs of the State Council.[30] The past employment histories of these officials suggest that their views on the renminbi would have been influenced strongly by views dominant within the PBC and the MOF. It appears that none of these officials had spent substantial time in foreign trade or any other portfolio. Foreign affairs were an important but not critical consideration determining exchange rate policy during the AFC. China's application to join the WTO was not the key factor determining China's no-devaluation policy. The major concern of China's leaders during the AFC was the national economy.[31] As we explain later in this chapter, key economic ministries in general supported no devaluation, which was also the preferred policy of China's foreign affairs policymaking community. Jiang and Zhu as the two most senior members of the CLGFE were also the two most senior members of the Central Leading Group on Foreign Affairs (CLGFA), the key foreign affairs decision-making body. While the CLGFA might have discussed exchange rate policy, determination of this policy was by the CLGFE.

Having considered elites in economic policymaking who were influential in shaping the no-devaluation decision, let us turn to examine the positions of the nation's key economic ministries – the SDPC, MOFTEC, MOF and PBC – on exchange rate policy through the reform period until the AFC. We see how the relative influence of these ministries over exchange rate policy changed, with the SPC – the forerunner of the SDPC – being the most influential at the beginning of reform, and the PBC being the most influential by the end of the 1990s.

MINISTRIES AND THE EXCHANGE RATE

State Development Planning Commission

In March 1998, the SPC was recast as the State Development Planning Commission.[32] Its role has been gradually reduced with economic reform. Under central planning, the SPC was the most influential economic ministry. In the early years of economic reform with the reintroduction of the market as a system of distribution, the market was seen only as supplementing the economic plan (*jihua wei zhu, shichang wei bu*). State-owned enterprises had to meet production targets in the plan, but they could sell any production beyond that in the free market. In similar spirit, SOEs were guaranteed quantities of supplies specified in the plan but they were free to purchase any additional quantities in the free market. The existence of this dual system (*shuanggui zhi*) was a major factor behind the SPC's objection to devaluing the renminbi in 1988.

The state's loss of control over the money supply in the second half of the 1980s led to high inflation, which at one point in 1988 hit an annual rate of 30 per cent.[33] The difference between plan prices and market prices, which were much higher, led to massive rent-seeking by officials as they diverted goods from the plan to the market. Inflation and official corruption were major factors behind massive demonstrations in Beijing in 1989. The political turmoil made a deep impression on the SPC, which at this time was headed by Zou Jiahua.[34] Diversion of goods from the plan was adversely affecting SOEs because this made it difficult for them to obtain subsidized inputs from the plan, and SOEs were unable to compete in the open market for those inputs. The SPC was concerned that devaluation of the renminbi would increase market prices, further widening the difference between market and plan prices and thereby worsening official corruption by encouraging the diversion of even more inputs away from SOEs and putting more financial pressure on them. The prevailing orthodoxy then was that state ownership and predominant use of the plan (not market) to allocate resources is a *sine qua non* of a socialist economy, and inflation and rent-seeking were putting this system at risk.

Continuation of the dual-track system was obviously untenable for political, economic and social reasons. But the return to central planning was not only a retreat from reform, it was also infeasible. After much debate and personal intervention by Deng Xiaoping to kick-start the stalled economic reform, the CCP Fourteenth Central Committee at its third plenum in 1993 officially announced the end of central planning with the formal adoption of the 'socialist market economy' (*shehuizhuyi shichang jingji*). Since then, central planning has not been a *sine qua non* of a socialist economy. The SDPC no longer drew up a production plan and was responsible for drawing up and implementing investment plans only for major policy development projects. Nevertheless, because state investment in China was still substantial, the SDPC's influence on the economy was still considerable at the time of the AFC.

In this 'socialist market economy', use of the market means that the old administrative tools of central planning are no longer relevant for managing the short-term macroeconomic performance of the economy. Indirect economic levers of monetary and fiscal policies are now the standard tools of short-term macroeconomic management. By the time of the AFC, the SDPC had lost its dominant role in short-term macroeconomic management. Nevertheless, it still had an interest in this area. A major influence on the SDPC in its consideration of exchange rate policy was the impact of devaluation on the cost of development projects. The SDPC not only drew up plans for major state development projects, but it also had to ensure their successful completion within budget. This means that although it did not have to be concerned with leakages of supplies from the plan to the market, unlike in 1988, it had to consider seriously the impact of exchange rate changes on project costs since projects use imports. Any devaluation of the renminbi would therefore increase the domestic currency cost of planned and existing projects such that projects would have to be scaled down. Under central planning, the SPC was guaranteed that the MOF would provide the required fiscal subsidies. However, the MOF could no longer guarantee these required subsidies because economic and fiscal decentralization had reduced the capacity of the state to raise tax revenue. Budgetary revenue fell from 35 per cent of gross domestic product (GDP) in 1978 to only 11 per cent in 1995. The tax reform of 1994 helped to improve revenue collection but budgetary revenue in 1997, the figure on which economic policy in 1998 was based, still reached only 11.6 per cent of GDP (NBS 2001, p. 246).[35] For this reason, the SDPC did not favour a lower-value renminbi.

The inevitable increase in project costs from renminbi devaluation was a key factor in the SPC opposing devaluation in 1988. At that time key investment projects in the state budget were underfunded as a consequence of inflation. As manager of these projects, the SPC delayed payment, refused to pay, or underpaid for the equipment and materials purchased from SOEs for these projects (Ou 1995, p. 69). Thus, while the SPC was trying to protect SOEs from the adverse effects of rent-seeking, the SPC was also making it difficult for SOEs financially by its delayed or non-payment of bills that it owed them. The SPC acquiesced to devaluation of the renminbi at the end of 1989 only after inflation was brought under control. In 1998 inflation was not a problem. But now the economic environment had changed considerably, causing the SDPC to continue to favour no devaluation, but for a very different reason, as we discuss below.

Ministry of Foreign Trade and Economic Cooperation

When the Chinese authorities began to implement economic reform in 1978, foreign investment in China was virtually non-existent and foreign trade was only 9.8 per cent of GDP.[36] Early in the twenty-first century, foreign trade and investment are extremely important for China. Foreign trade by 1998 was 34 per cent of GDP, and foreign investment 5.3 per cent of GDP. The influence of the MOFTEC (formerly MOFERT)[37] in exchange rate and trade policy has increased correspondingly in the reform period. As detailed in Chapter 3, domestic and international trade procedures have been reformed gradually and, as we shall see, reform has had a significant impact on the political economy of exchange rate policy.

Foreign trade under central planning was conducted strictly within the foreign trade plan. Only foreign trade corporations (FTCs) were allowed to trade internationally. They were not allowed to keep the foreign exchange that they earned and foreign exchange for imports was strictly rationed. The exchange rate at this time was overvalued, resulting in losses to FTCs that the MOF had to subsidize. In 1984, the scope of the state trade plan was reduced and control over foreign exchange relaxed, making more foreign exchange available for imports. Mandatory exports in the plan were set at 60 per cent of plan exports and another 20 per cent were assigned to provinces as export targets. The renminbi was devalued 15.1 per cent against the US dollar to reduce the losses of the FTCs.[38] The FTCs' monopoly position on international trade was abolished, the number of FTCs was increased and their many branches were made independent. While mandatory exports and imports continued to be channelled through designated FTCs, enterprises could appoint FTCs of their choice to act as their agents in non-mandatory trade (Cerra and Dayal-Gulati 1999, p. 5).

Further trade reforms were carried out in 1988. Export targets were relaxed in exchange for smaller export subsidies. Export subsidies were reduced to 4 per cent of export value, but this was insufficient to keep FTCs in the black. High rates of domestic inflation in 1987 and

1988 had increased the domestic costs of exports but price reform did not lead to commensurate adjustments to planned prices or to the nominal exchange rate (Ou 1995, p. 71). Furthermore, enterprise reforms concurrent with the trade reforms in 1988 made enterprises responsible for their profits and losses. No longer were losses of FTCs automatically covered fully by the state budget. Rising domestic prices and an overvalued exchange rate made it increasingly unattractive for producers to help the MOFERT meet the compulsory export targets in the mandatory-export plan. Until this time the MOFERT did not hold a view on an appropriate exchange rate. But as the ministry responsible for fulfilling the foreign exchange earnings plan and for the performance of FTCs under these changed circumstances, the MOFERT now clearly had a vested interest in the exchange rate. The MOFERT therefore pressed for a devaluation of the official exchange rate. It also advocated increasing the proportion of exchange earnings that exporters could retain under the retention quota scheme, which could be swapped for renminbi at a higher rate in the swap market with other enterprises that were short of retained foreign exchange.

The MOFERT had another related reason for advocating these proposals. As described in Chapter 3, China opened its first foreign exchange market for domestic enterprises in 1988 in Shanghai and later opened several more, which subsequently linked together to form a national market, in China's coastal cities. The swap rate in this market, which was higher than the official exchange rate, coexisted alongside the official rate. Enterprises inevitably sought import projects that could be funded at the official rate but these enterprises were reluctant to turn in their export earnings at the official rate, which would yield them less renminbi than if exchanged at the swap rate (Wu 1998, p. 84). The MOFERT therefore found it difficult to meet the export earnings target in the mandatory-export plan. For reasons explained in the next section, the then SPC, MOF and PBC opposed devaluation of the official rate in 1988 and most of 1989. Nevertheless, the massive fall in inflation following a monetary squeeze and economic retrenchment after the June 1989 army crackdown allowed the MOFERT to carry the debate and the exchange rate was devalued by about 21.5 per cent in December 1989 (Yang 2000, p. 16).[39]

The liberalization of foreign trade was conducted *pari passu* with liberalization of the domestic economy in the 1990s. The mandatory-export plan was abolished in 1991 and replaced with a 'negotiated' export plan to encourage exports, and more domestic enterprises were allowed to conduct foreign trade directly.[40] The CCP's 1993 plenum formalized the separation of SOEs from state administration, and the MOFTEC was therefore no longer responsible for the losses of the FTCs. Nevertheless, it was still responsible for the overall foreign trade performance of the economy.

Exporters and importers began to respond to price in response to liberalization of foreign trade and foreign exchange administration (Cerra and Dayal-Gulati 1999, pp. 13–15). The MOFTEC has a vested interest in a low renminbi exchange rate but its influence over exchange rate policy began to wane after 1994. The tax reform of 1994 introduced tax rebates to compensate exporters for the value-added tax (VAT) of 17 per cent. In the same year, the exchange rate was unified with a devaluation of the official rate to bring it into line with the swap-market rate. These two policies reduced the MOFTEC's influence over exchange rate policy. The MOFTEC's advocacy for a lower renminbi carries less weight now that the official rate has been unified at the swap-market rate, and the MOFTEC can also seek higher tax rebates for exporters as an alternative to a lower renminbi exchange rate. Furthermore, in 1995 the authorities formally made the exchange rate an instrument for conducting monetary policy and not an instrument to promote international trade. This shift in function relocated the primary influence over exchange rate policy from the MOFTEC to the PBC.[41]

Ministry of Finance

Until the high inflation of the late 1980s, the MOF favoured a lower exchange rate because overvaluation of the exchange rate had resulted in FTCs incurring losses that required massive subsidies from the MOF. In the late 1980s, however, the MOF supported the SPC against devaluation of the renminbi. Chinese imports had low price elasticities and the MOF believed that devaluation would increase the cost of material inputs to producers, worsening the losses of SOEs.[42] The then influential National Price Bureau (NPB) (*Guojia wujia ju*) supported the MOF and the SPC against a lower renminbi. Between 1978 and 1993, the NPB was responsible for estimating the impact of the cost of key imported materials on domestic prices and had calculated that a 1 per cent devaluation of the renminbi would increase domestic inflation by 1.55 per cent (Yang 2000, p. 14).

The non-state sector, especially non-SOEs in the eastern and southern coastal provinces, was a significant exporter and benefited from devaluation of the renminbi. However, devaluation did not advantage most large SOEs since most of these SOEs were not export oriented. As pointed out before, many SOEs were already suffering from official rent-seeking in the late 1980s due to inflation, and renminbi devaluation would have put further pressure on the state budget for SOE relief. Furthermore, the MOF was concerned with tax deliveries from SOEs and sub-national governments. The tax system then operating was based on a fixed-contract delivery system, which disadvantaged the central government during times of high inflation. This was because the amounts to be delivered by the SOEs and sub-national governments were fixed for the full contract period, so that in real terms the value of taxes delivered to the centre actually declined in a booming and inflationary economy (Liew 1994, pp. 182–3). Thus, the MOF was faced with a significant rise in the demand for public expenditure just when its real income from taxes adjusted for inflation declined. It was no wonder that the MOF lobbied strongly against devaluation in the late 1980s.

People's Bank of China

The influence of the PBC over monetary policy, especially the exchange rate, has grown substantially over the reform period. The PBC has been transformed from subservience to the MOF in the late 1970s, to dominant force in economic policy formulation in the late 1990s. Before 1983, the PBC acted as both a central and a commercial bank. It was made China's central bank officially only in 1983, gaining ministry-level status. In the late 1980s, the PBC opposed devaluation of the renminbi on the grounds that such a move would exacerbate the already serious inflationary situation with little effect on exports and imports, which had low price elasticities. It also argued that the financial losses of the FTCs were the responsibility of the MOFERT or MOF, and not the PBC (Ou 1995, p. 71). Although the PBC used inflation as an excuse to oppose renminbi devaluation in 1988, price stability was formally the responsibility of the NPB.[43] Ou Jiawa used this understanding to support his argument that the PBC cared less for price stability than for the stability of banking operations. In this view, the PBC's opposition to renminbi devaluation was motivated more by concern for the impact of devaluation on the amount of bad loans in the banking system than concern for its impact on inflation per se.

Loss-making SOEs, suffering from the combined effects of poor management, inflation and rent-seeking, were bailed out in the late 1980s with bank loans from state-owned banks and with fiscal subsidies. There was little expectation that these loans would be paid back and the PBC was therefore anxious that non-performing loans in the financial system would be kept to a minimum. As it turned out, serious attempts to resolve the problem of non-performing loans were made only with the CCP's adoption of the 'socialist market economy' agenda in 1993 and especially in the wake of the AFC. The remedial measures implemented included bankrupting loss-making SOEs or partially or fully privatizing them. In 1989 in the aftermath of the Tiananmen crackdown, however, the focus of China's leaders was political stability rather than SOE reform. Therefore, the PBC was concerned by any policy that it perceived could exacerbate the financial difficulties of SOEs, since such a policy would increase the amount of bad debts in the banking system.

In 1995 the National People's Congress formally enshrined in law the PBC's position as China's central bank by passing the PBC Act (*Zhongguo renmin yinhang fa*). The passing of the Act was significant. This Act (Articles 1–3) makes it clear that the responsibilities of the PBC extend beyond regulating the country's financial system to responsibility for short-term macroeconomic management, including maintaining the stability of the value of the renminbi. For example, the PBC is now responsible for controlling inflation, whereas in the past this was the responsibility of the NPB, which has been abolished (Mao 1995, p. 2).[44] The Act explicitly specified monetary policy as the appropriate tool for the PBC to use in macroeconomic management.

Monetary policy as defined in the Act includes management of the renminbi exchange rate. Article 5 of the Act gives the PBC the right to recommend and implement exchange rate policy, but exchange rate policy has to be approved by the State Council. Hence, although Article 7 states that the PBC under the leadership of the State Council is 'independent of interference from sub-national governments, levels of all government ministries, social groups and individuals' (Mao 1995, p. 3), the PBC is not an independent central bank as is commonly understood, but is guided by decisions of the State Council.[45] This underling status is made clear in notes published by the Legal Department of the PBC that explain Article 5: 'The State Council as China's [supreme] organization in charge of regulating the national macroeconomy' examines and approves all major financial policies (Mao 1995, p. 33). Nevertheless, despite the wording of the PBC Act, as previous analysis in this chapter has pointed out, real power over the macro-economy rests with the Politburo standing committee.

The 1995 Act and subsequent passing of the State Council's 1996 PRC Regulations on Foreign Exchange Management (*Waihui guanli tiaoli*) converted the renminbi exchange rate from an instrument of trade promotion to an instrument of monetary policy. The 1996 regulations replaced the 1980 Regulations on Foreign Exchange Management, which stated that the aim of foreign exchange management was to increase foreign exchange earnings and economize on foreign exchange expenditures (Gao and Huang 2000, p. 355). The 1996 regulations are significant. Article 33 of these regulations stipulates that the PBC has the exclusive right to determine both the reference exchange rates and the band within which market exchange rates are allowed to deviate from the reference rates (Long 1997, p. 84). On 1 December 1996, the State Council announced that the renminbi had become convertible in the current account and from 1998, the PBC began to pay attention to the link between interest rate and exchange rate, taking note of the influence of foreign exchange on the volume of basic money (ZRYY 1999, p. 11).

It is inevitable that a country's central bank becomes more influential in short-term macroeconomic policymaking as the country's economy becomes increasingly marketized. In China the end of central planning has inevitably weakened the SPC, the ministry that drew up and implemented the central plan. Money dominates modern market economies and as China's financial markets are opened further, monetary policy will progressively dominate short-term macroeconomic management. Commentators and analysts of short-term macroeconomic conditions right across the industrial world tend to pay relatively more attention to the actions of central banks than the actions of finance ministries, and as China integrates more and more with the world economy, influence over macroeconomic policy will shift from the MOF to the PBC.[46] Nevertheless, as this chapter's earlier section on elite economic policymaking points out, the CLGFE and ultimately the standing committee of the Politburo were the key decision makers on financial matters during the AFC. The PBC is best regarded as a very influential source of monetary and financial policy input, and also as a key assessor of exchange rate policy inputs from other sources because of its close relationship with the CLGFE through Zhu Rongji, who controlled the workings of the CLGFE and whose protégé, Dai Xianglong, held the pivotal position of PBC governor at that time.

1989 DEVALUATION AND 1998–89 NO DEVALUATION COMPARED

All key ministries except the MOFERT opposed devaluation in 1988 and during most of 1989. Yet the MOFERT had its way in achieving devaluation. China's trade deficits were not the reason. Trade deficits in 1988 and 1989 were only 1 and 1.1 per cent of GDP respectively (NBS 2000, p. 65). Devaluation was implemented more than six months after the June 1989 military crackdown. This was in the middle of the economic retrenchment programme that enforced implementation of the economic plan, shifting the balance away from the market to the plan in resource allocation. Inflation was reduced dramatically in the second half of 1989. By 1990 it had fallen to an annual rate of 3 per cent from a high of 30 per cent in 1988. The incidence of rent-seeking fell in response to the political and economic crackdown and the fall in inflation. By the end of 1989 when devaluation was actually carried out, the concerns of the SPC, MOF and PBC over the negative political, economic and social effects of renminbi devaluation had subsided.

Instead, the MOF saw devaluation as a way of tackling the losses of FTCs, which had faced an overvalued exchange rate, so devaluation would reduce the need for the MOF to provide fiscal subsidies.

In explaining why China did not devalue during the AFC, some observers placed great emphasis on the influence of China's foreign policy objectives and the symbolic value of the no-devaluation stance.[47] Some observers argued that in stabilizing the value of the renminbi, China sought to win kudos from its Asian neighbours who were depending on China to maintain the value of its currency so it would not further destabilize their economies. In this view, China's Asian neighbours would have regarded devaluation of the renminbi most unfavourably as a 'beggar-thy-neighbour' policy. China would gain prestige by not devaluing. Moreover, devaluation is a zero-sum strategy and a Chinese devaluation would most likely induce similar currency devaluations by other Asian countries in response. At this time China wanted to be seen as behaving 'responsibly' to improve its standing in Asia. There was a strong undercurrent of resentment in Asia towards the United States, fuelled by a perception that instead of assisting Asian countries to overcome the crisis, the United States was opportunistically buying Asian assets on the cheap and gaining access to Asian markets as a result of the crisis. Some observers also noted China's imperative to demonstrate to Europe and the United States a more responsible international posture in an attempt to garner support for its entry into the WTO.

There is no doubt that China's relations with the rest of the world were taken into account in the decision not to devalue. The then deputy governor of the PBC, Liu Mingkang, acknowledged at a press conference in 1998 that devaluation would improve China's export performance and stimulate the national economy. But he was firm that this was not the best means to achieve these ends; China's exports have high import content and devaluation would increase input costs, making devaluation less effective (Anon. 1998). And as Liu made clear, there were more than domestic considerations: 'The Chinese government is a responsible member of the big family that is the international community' (*Guoji shehui dajiating zhong yige fuzeren chengyuan*) and devaluation would make it more difficult for China's Asian neighbours to recover from the crisis. Liu's opinions expressed to a press conference no doubt echoed those of his immediate bosses, Dai Xianglong and Zhu Rongji. Yet it is doubtful that foreign policy considerations were sufficient on their own, without strong domestic bureaucratic support or at least bureaucratic acquiescence from key economic ministries for a no-devaluation policy. Table 5.1 shows the schema of exchange rate policy preferences of these ministries during the AFC.

The MOFTEC favoured devaluation on the basis of its long-term support to exporters. But its case for devaluation was muted by increases in VAT rebates to exporters, further relaxation of export controls and financial loans to exporting enterprises experiencing difficulties.[48] The MOF estimated that it could not reimburse the whole 17 per cent of VAT to exporters to encourage exports without severely affecting central finances. Hence, from 1995 onwards, the central government reimbursed only 9 per cent of VAT to exporters, leaving a tax on exports of 8 per cent (Long 1999, p. 412). Research by the Development Research Centre of the State Council estimated that every 1 per cent increase in the VAT reimbursement rate increased GDP by 0.6 per cent and increased tax revenues by 0.9 per cent. However, the increase in tax revenues would flow mainly to provincial governments and not to the central government because of the way revenues from different taxes are distributed between provincial and central governments (Long 1999, pp. 413–14).[49] The MOF therefore preferred promoting exports via a lower exchange rate than through higher VAT reimbursements. The MOF's preference for devaluation was reinforced by the large projected increases in government investment required to boost GDP growth. However, provincial governments with a large concentration of export industries, for example Guangdong, preferred higher VAT reimbursements to devaluation. Besides being able to collect more taxes from the increase in GDP that resulted from an increase in VAT reimbursements, the central government, as we noted in Chapter 3, was responsible for refunding all the rebates even though local governments collected a share of the VAT taxes.

Table 5.1 Exchange rate policy preferences of China's key economic ministries during the AFC

		Preferred degree of long-term exchange rate flexibility	
		Moderate	Fixed
Preferred short-term exchange rate decision	No devaluation	PBC	SDPC
	Devaluation		MOFTEC, MOF

Estimates of the contribution to GDP growth from different expenditure components of GDP for 1992–98 are shown in Table 5.2. These estimates were revised in the 2000s in the light of revised data, but for understanding policymaking during the AFC the data used to inform policymaking, that is, the data available when policy was formulated, and not post-crisis data are relevant. The estimates based on data available during the crisis clearly show a significant decline in the growth of household consumption in 1997 and 1998 compared to 1996, which policymakers would have taken note of. The fall in the growth in domestic demand was exacerbated by deterioration in foreign markets for Chinese goods. During 1998, falls in the value of the yen and other Asian currencies worsened China's trade position, contributing to a further slowing of China's economic growth. Most of this fall in growth was attributed to the reduction of exports to the Association of South East Asian Nations (ASEAN) (10.5 per cent), Japan (4.3 per cent) and South Korea (30.2 per cent) (HKTDC 1998). Nevertheless, the contribution of net exports to GDP in 1997 was unusually high and net exports could not be expected to continue to grow at the 1997 rate in 1998. In 1999, China's foreign trade deteriorated further. The contribution of net exports to GDP growth was negative for the first time since 1993. Economic policy would have to focus on expenditure-changing (increasing overall domestic demand) instead of expenditure-switching (switching demand from traded to non-traded goods through devaluation) to achieve the targeted growth rates in 1998 and 1999.[50]

Table 5.2 Contributions to China's GDP growth (%)

	HC	GC	GFCF	INV	Net X	GDP growth
1992	6.6	2.0	7.3	−0.8	−1.1	14.1
1993	4.9	1.5	7.1	1.1	−1.5	13.1
1994	5.5	1.5	3.9	0.4	1.3	12.6
1995	4.8	0.5	2.5	0.9	0.3	9.0
1996	5.1	1.0	3.2	0.0	0.5	9.7
1997	3.5	1.1	2.4	−0.3	1.8	8.6
1998	3.9	1.4	4.7	−2.6	0.4	7.8
1999	5.1	1.7	3.8	−1.9	−1.7	7.1

Notes:
HC = household consumption, GC = government consumption, GFCF = gross fixed-capital formation, INV = change in inventories, Net X = net exports.

 GFCF is likely to be overestimated and INV underestimated because capital goods that state sector units, including SOEs, ordered from SOEs, but were not delivered, were normally recorded as GFCF rather than INV.

Source: Estimates by the authors from data in NBS (2000).

 Regardless of their stances on devaluation during the AFC, the MOFTEC and MOF would generally prefer a fixed exchange rate. The MOFTEC saw benefit in a low renminbi exchange rate because this makes China's enterprises internationally competitive and it also saw benefit in a stable exchange rate because this minimizes exchange rate risk for China's enterprises engaged in foreign trade. The MOF would generally prefer a stable exchange rate since this enhances the MOF's influence. As a competitor with the PBC for policy influence, the MOF favours continuation of the renminbi–US dollar peg, which makes the MOF more influential *vis-à-vis* the PBC in determining macroeconomic policy since fiscal policy is more effective than monetary policy under a stable exchange rate in the presence of international capital mobility (Fleming 1962; Mundell 1963). Although China has capital controls, between 1992 and 1996 China's informal capital outflow was 43 per cent of formal capital inflow (Li Yang 1998 cited in Huang and Yang 1998, p. 5), and between 1998 and 2000 non-FDI (foreign direct investment) capital outflows averaged US$53.6 billion, of which US$15.4 billion were unrecorded (Prasad and Wei 2005, Table 7). These circumstances suggest that the MOF's preference for a stable exchange rate has strengthened now that China has joined the WTO, since capital mobility is expected to increase significantly in response to further relaxation of capital controls.

Monetary policy was relatively ineffective during the AFC and responsibility for stimulating domestic demand was put largely on the shoulders of fiscal policy. Non-government investment remained sluggish even though the PBC lowered interest rates five times in 1998, because the crisis had lowered business confidence. Businesses were apprehensive about new projects while commercial banks became more cautious of bad loans and were reluctant to lend (Zhang 1999, p. 181). Moreover, significant amounts of capital were flowing out of China in anticipation of renminbi devaluation. Furthermore, increased marketization resulting from economic reform had increased competition in China's economy. This, combined with the low level of business confidence in 1998, created deflationary pressures. Consumer prices fell by 0.8 per cent and retail prices by 2.6 per cent in 1998 compared to a year earlier. In 1999 consumer prices fell a further 1.4 per cent and retail prices a further 3 per cent (NBS 2000, p. 289) and many enterprises and consumers postponed their spending in anticipation of a further fall in prices. Deflation also kept real interest rates high and was an additional disincentive to increase private sector spending.

Responsibility for achieving the targeted 8 per cent growth rate therefore was centred largely on fiscal policy. China's leadership was becoming desperate in the middle of 1998. It was concerned that a growth rate below 8 per cent would not be enough to absorb rising unemployment from enterprise reform to prevent political and social instability. Preliminary figures showed that annual economic growth in the first half of 1998 was only 6.6 per cent, well short of the targeted 8 per cent.[51] Compounding the government's problem were natural disasters, which affected 14 provinces. Some senior party leaders such as Li Peng, Xie Fei and Tian Jiyun supported calls from other party leaders like Li Lanqing and Luo Gan, and state bureaucracies like the MOF, the State General Bureau of Taxation (SGBT) (*Guojia shuiwu zongju*) and the Ministry of Agriculture to lower the targeted growth rate (Luo 1998, p. 7). Yet the government did not lower the growth target. Instead, it dramatically increased infrastructure spending in the second half of 1998 in a last-ditch effort to achieve the target. State budgetary appropriations to capital construction were increased 78 per cent from RMB57.5 billion in 1997 to RMB102.1 billion in 1998 and a further 45 per cent to RMB147.9 billion in 1999 (NBS 2000, p. 174). In 1998 fixed-capital investment spending contributed 5.2 per cent to the 7.8 per cent growth in GDP, the highest rate since 1993, when this spending contributed 7.1 per cent to the 13.1 per cent GDP growth. But, as a share of GDP growth, this spending's 1998 contribution of 67 per cent was greater than the 63 per cent share in 1993.

It is understandable that the MOF and the SGBT were in favour of a lower growth target. Since fiscal policy was to carry the burden of achieving the 8 per cent target growth rate, a lower growth rate required lower government spending, which would make a smaller demand on the state budget. The SDPC, on the other hand, benefited from large government spending on infrastructure projects and therefore supported the growth target. In 1988, the SPC was concerned with curbing inflation and the resulting rent-seeking that was diverting supplies in the plan away from SOEs, and it acquiesced to devaluation in 1989 only after inflation was brought under control. By 1998 the plan no longer existed and China's main economic problem in 1998 and 1999 was deflation rather than inflation. Consumer prices fell by 0.8 per cent and retail prices by 2.6 per cent in 1998 compared to 1997 prices.[52] The SDPC's major responsibility was drawing up and implementing large state investment projects, and under deflationary conditions devaluation increasing project costs was not an issue. Nevertheless the SDPC strongly advocated no devaluation. It did so because without devaluation, China's leadership would have to opt for increased infrastructure spending to meet its economic growth target, which would give the SDPC control over more resources. The SDPC was also concerned about exchange rate fluctuations since these introduce uncertainty to large-project management, which involves significant foreign inputs. China's finance industry was still relatively undeveloped with limited opportunities for hedging foreign exchange risks and this strengthened the SDPC's preference for exchange rate stability.

Although the MOF preferred to lower the growth target and devalue the renminbi, in 1998 the situation of central finances was not as bleak as in 1988 and 1989, when the centre received respectively only 33 per cent and 31 per cent of total budgetary revenue (NBS 2000, p. 267). Budgetary revenue as a percentage of GDP had increased from 10.9 per cent in 1996 to 11.6 per cent in 1997 and to 12.6 per cent in 1998 (NBS 2000, p. 256). During that period the central government slightly increased its share of total budgetary revenue from 48.9 per cent in 1997 to 49.5 per cent in 1998 to 51.1 per cent in 1999 (NBS 2000, p. 267). The budget deficit was 0.8 per cent of GDP in 1996 and 1997 and even after the substantial increases in government spending in 1998 the deficit was still a modest 1.2 per cent of GDP (NBS 2000, pp. 53, 255).[53] Hence, although the MOF preferred to lower the growth target, the MOF was not against relying on increases in government spending rather than devaluation to boost the growth rate.[54]

The role of the PBC was critical. Using fiscal stimulus in lieu of devaluation was feasible because the fiscal position of the government could accommodate it. But had the PBC argued strongly against this policy, the outcome could have been quite different. The PBC's responsibilities had changed since 1989. Under central planning, prices were set centrally and the NPB was responsible for controlling prices. Market deregulation as part of economic reform made administrative price control no longer feasible, and monetary policy was now regarded as the major policy tool to maintain overall price stability in the economy. Inflationary experiences of the late 1980s and during the years immediately after Deng Xiaoping's southern tour in 1992, which set off a speculative boom, highlighted the importance to price stability of centralizing the management of monetary policy. This recognition inclined the Chinese authorities to give the PBC the responsibility for price stability in the economy. In 1998, despite facing a deflationary economy, the PBC was concerned with the inflationary effects of renminbi devaluation because only recently had it been able to bring inflation under control.[55] As economist He Liping saw it, the PBC was targeting the renminbi–US dollar rate as an anchor to stabilize China's inflation rate (He 2000, p. 19).

Besides inflation, the PBC was concerned with the effect of renminbi devaluation on the Hong Kong dollar. Many financial analysts predicted that devaluation of the renminbi would make it difficult for the Hong Kong Monetary Authority (HKMA) to maintain the Hong Kong dollar–US dollar peg, forcing a devaluation of the Hong Kong dollar. This would undermine confidence and cause instability in Hong Kong, causing China to lose face since not long before, in July 1997, China had regained sovereignty over Hong Kong. Although Hong Kong is responsible for managing its own economy under the Basic Law, the PBC is indirectly responsible for maintaining the stability of Hong Kong's financial system. Basic Law or no Basic Law, Hong Kong is part of China and the Chinese authorities have pledged to maintain the stability of Hong Kong's economy. At a seminar sponsored by the HKMA in 1993, then deputy governor of the PBC, Chen Yuan, pledged to cooperate with the HKMA to maintain both the financial stability of Hong Kong and Hong Kong's position as a major international financial centre (Chen 1993/94, pp. 64–5). Zhu Rongji at a conference on financial reform and prevention of financial risk in 1998 reportedly nominated wanting not to place additional pressure on the Hong Kong dollar as one of three reasons for not devaluing the renminbi.[56] Many journal and newspaper articles published in Hong Kong and mainland China also gave this justification, including several in journals published by the PBC.[57]

Nevertheless, debate within the PBC over whether to devalue the renminbi continued until the second half of 1998. The PBC as the ministry largely responsible for short-term macroeconomic management had to work towards achieving the targeted growth rate and there was disagreement among officials within the PBC on whether the growth target could be achieved without devaluation. Yi Gang, the deputy secretary general of the PBC's Monetary Committee, caused a stir in international financial markets when he expressed the view in a joint paper at a conference in Canberra in 1998 that many analysts believed China's exports would be hit badly in the second half of that year, which would 'certainly [create a] need [for] real exchange rate adjustment'.[58] Yi was later forced to deny publicly that he was predicting devaluation of the renminbi and the paper was later published without his name (Song 1998). Dai Xianglong was governor of the PBC and close to Zhu Rongji and there is no doubt that he worked hard to swing the PBC behind the no-devaluation decision.

As mentioned earlier, the renminbi–US dollar peg reduces the effectiveness of monetary policy relative to fiscal policy in the presence of international capital mobility. Capital controls are likely to be relaxed further now that China has joined the WTO. Thus, while the PBC might have continued to favour maintaining the renminbi–US dollar peg for a period after the AFC, the PBC under Dai Xianglong favoured progressively enlarging the band within which the renminbi–US dollar rate was allowed to divert from the fixed renminbi–US dollar peg. Dai Xianglong as the PBC's governor voiced this position in an interview published in the US business magazine, *Business Week* (Sito 2001). The position is no doubt driven by concern to increase the effectiveness of monetary policy as capital controls are relaxed, lest the PBC loses out to the MOF in capacity to influence macroeconomic policymaking.

In sum, of the four key economic ministries involved in exchange rate policy, the two most influential – the PBC and the SDPC – supported a no-devaluation policy in 1998. To stimulate exports, the MOF preferred devaluation to higher VAT rebates, but it could live with a higher budget deficit to support the no-devaluation policy. The MOFTEC, also seeking to stimulate exports since it was under pressure from exporters, also preferred devaluation, but increased VAT rebates moderated that pressure, so it too did not push hard for devaluation. All four ministries except for the SDPC were under the control of ministers close to Zhu; Zeng Peiyan, the minister in charge of the SDPC, was Jiang Zemin's principal economic adviser and Jiang was in favour of no devaluation. Thus, the key ministries with input into exchange rate policy broadly supported, or acquiesced to the no-devaluation decision. More importantly, we see here the overriding influence of Zhu, who held effective control over exchange rate policy inputs and analyses into the CLGFE. Zhu controlled his State Council think-tanks and the research office of the CLGFE, which were the two formal sources of policy inputs and analyses to the CLGFE.

The initial decision not to devalue was made some time at the end of 1997. On 16 January 1998 PBC governor Dai Xianglong told journalists at a press conference in Beijing that the value of the renminbi would be maintained (ZB 1998, p. 2092). One month later on 16 February 1998, PBC deputy governor and chief of the State Administration of Foreign Exchange (SAFE) (*Waihui guanliju*), Zhou Xiaochuan, reiterated this position at a meeting of SAFE regional bureau chiefs in Beijing. He advised that China would not suffer the same fate as other Asian countries and the renminbi would not be devalued (ZB 1998, p. 2096). Further assurance came from Zhu Rongji, who affirmed at the press conference during the Ninth National People's Congress first plenum on 19 March 1998 that the renminbi would not be devalued (ZB 1998, p. 2098).

The initial decision not to devalue was not remarkable because, as Table 5.2 shows, China's economy in 1997 was in good shape. China's foreign trade in 1997 was in a very healthy position and GDP growth was still very strong. By the end of 1997 the full impact of the AFC had not hit China. The key topic discussed at the important joint party and State National Financial Work Meeting (*Quanguo jinrong gongzuo huiyi*) in mid-November 1997 was financial reform. The meeting's focus was on regulating bank credit to forestall the type of banking crisis that appeared to be behind much of the AFC. The rate of the renminbi was not an issue (Cao 1998).[59]

There are lags between export orders and actual shipment of these orders and between shipment and exports being actually received by importers and recorded by customs and statistical authorities. The severity of the AFC became apparent only towards the end of the first quarter of 1998 and the exchange rate became a major policy decision in June when the falling value of the yen put additional pressure on China's already beleaguered foreign trade sector. Pressure on China's leadership to devalue the renminbi was strongest during the summer of 1998 at the annual Central Work Conference in Beidaihe and, as mentioned earlier in this chapter, the CCGO played an important role in moderating this pressure. Further criticisms over handling the effects of the AFC were raised in November at the joint Party–State Central Economic Work Conference, which brought together top Chinese leaders in charge of the economy and representatives from the provinces. The provincial representatives focused their criticisms on Zhu Rongji for what they perceived to be the centre's overly ambitious economic growth target and its inadequate response to the AFC. The PBC was also criticized, with delegates proposing to the centre a personnel reshuffle at the PBC (Li 1999). However, as pointed out earlier, provincial representatives preferred increased VAT reimbursements on export products to devaluation because VAT reimbursements increase provincial tax revenues. Thus, the series of VAT reimbursements in 1998 and 1999 would have softened the provinces' push for devaluation.

Since the key ministries that provided input into exchange rate policy broadly supported or acquiesced to the policy position of no devaluation, it is not surprising that Zhu Rongji was willing and able to maintain this position despite coming under increasing pressure to accept currency devaluation. Moreover, all four key ministries except the SDPC were under the control of ministers close to Zhu, and Zhu had effective control over exchange rate policy inputs and analyses flowing into the CLGFE. Regardless of whether Jiang Zemin or Zhu was nominally head of the CLGFE, Zhu was the acknowledged economic czar and he would have been expected to place the economy ahead of foreign relations. Zhu's view on devaluation was heavily influenced by the institutional position he held as the person with overall responsibility for the Chinese economy. Zhu was accountable to the NPC[60] and it would have been difficult for him to push for a policy that clearly contradicted the consensus among the key economic ministries and his think-tanks. Zhu needed to muster sound reasons within the ministries and think-tanks to argue for his policy position. Had key ministries and Zhu's think-tanks favoured devaluation, it would have been difficult for Zhu to muster a convincing counter-argument to present to his peers in the Politburo and its standing committee.

According to interviewees in our fieldwork, Zhu consulted widely on exchange rate policy. The individual views of Zhu's advisers are not widely known. Lin Yifu was the only one of Zhu's advisers outside the party and state bureaucracy who had publicly expressed his views on the exchange rate. Virtually all articles in official internal publications [61] argued for no devaluation, but there were exceptions. An article in the journal *Gaige neican* (Inside Information on Economic Reform), which used to be published by SCRES,[62] complained that the culture of the 'two whenever(s)' (*liange fanshi*) was stifling debate over exchange rate policy.[63] According to the author, Jia Baohua, whenever researchers and officials discuss exports, 'they avoid discussing the link between exports and the exchange rate and whenever they discuss the exchange rate, they avoid discussing the possibility of devaluation' (Jia 1999, p. 29). 'It cannot be denied that the current exchange rate policy is imposing a huge cost to China in terms of lost exports' (Jia 1999, p. 30). He asked rhetorically whether the no-devaluation promise was unconditional, regardless of economic circumstances (Jia 1999, p. 32). A year before, an article by Jia was published in the same journal putting the case for devaluation. He argued that devaluation serves as an engine of growth (*huochetou*) (Jia 1998, p. 14). In his view, there is no contradiction between looking after China's self-interest (*minzu liyi*) and internationalism (*guojizhuyi*). China was qualified (*you zige*) to help other Asian economies recover only if China's economy was not itself in crisis. Thus China's greatest contribution to the Asian and world economies would be to maintain its own economic growth rate, requiring China to maintain export growth and therefore devalue the renminbi (Jia 1998, p. 16).

Others in the bureaucracy shared Jia's criticism of the no-devaluation policy, but Zhu Rongji was careful to ensure that discussion of exchange rate policy was managed and dissenting views kept strictly within the bureaucracy to prevent the rise of populist pressures for devaluation. The CCP's public relations machine promoted the no-devaluation policy nationwide and prevented the expression of any pro-devaluation views in the media.[64] Fan Gang was one of the few mainland economists who spoke publicly in favour of devaluation. His talk to a small audience in Shenzhen was reported in *Ta Kung Pao*, a pro-Beijing daily in Hong Kong, but his talk was not reported in the media on the mainland (Lam 1999, pp. 375, 430). How debate over exchange rate policy was managed during the AFC shows that while there was growing pluralization in economic policymaking in China, the ability to influence policy by those outside the bureaucracy – especially its inner circles – was very much limited.

CONCLUSION

Economic reform has brought growing institutionalization and pluralization in China's economic policymaking. This has enhanced the role of institutional actors in economic policymaking. Therefore, research into those who provide and analyse policy inputs has become as important as research on those who decide policy, since their views are informed by these analyses and inputs. During the AFC, the CLGFE was the key exchange rate policy decision maker. Zhu Rongji was effectively in charge of the CLGFE, but he was only able to sustain the no-devaluation policy throughout the AFC because he had the support of Jiang Zemin and other leaders in the Politburo standing committee. Their support was not granted in a disinterested void but was based on support provided by key economic ministries in the policymaking structure, buttressed by Zhu Rongji's control of the key organs controlling and evaluating exchange rate policy inputs – the research office of the CLGFE and the Monetary Policy Department of the PBC.

The individual functions, vested interests and degrees of influence on exchange rate policy of the key economic ministries – the SDPC, PBC, MOF and MOFTEC – have been transformed as China's economy is marketized in line with economic reform. At the beginning of economic reform in the late 1970s, the SPC, the SDPC's predecessor, was the most influential economic ministry, followed by the MOF. But continuing economic decentralization has reduced the role of the SPC in the economy, and the greater importance of monetary policy as the economy is marketized has increased the influence of the PBC. By the second half of the 1990s, the PBC had become the most influential ministry in macroeconomic policy.

In this chapter we have seen how economic conditions and the functions and responsibilities of the key ministries help to determine the ministries' views on exchange rate policy. For most of the late 1980s, fear of inflation dominated discussions on exchange rate policy. Inflation had played a major role in subverting the economic plan and undermining SOEs, which required subsidies to stay afloat, imposing demands on the national budget. This concern led the key economic ministries except the MOFTEC to object to currency devaluation. The renminbi was devalued in late 1989 only when the concerns of the objecting ministries were alleviated after inflation was brought under control.

Key economic ministries supported or acquiesced to the no-devaluation policy during the AFC. Among the ministries, the PBC and the SDPC were the policy's most enthusiastic supporters. The PBC worried about future inflation and the stability of the Hong Kong dollar and the SDPC hoped that additional demands placed on fiscal policy as a result of no devaluation would increase state investments in infrastructure projects. The MOFTEC favoured devaluation to promote export promotion but it did not push hard because its interest in this outcome was partially satisfied by the introduction of substitute measures to stimulate exports. The MOF did not have a firm position on devaluation because the state budgetary position had improved over the last few years, and with or without devaluation, fiscal policy had to play the dominant role in stimulating demand to achieve the GDP growth target.

Further liberalization of financial markets will definitely proceed now that China is a member of the WTO. China was insulated somewhat from the AFC because of capital controls. Although the complete lifting of capital controls is unlikely in the foreseeable future, continuous liberalization of foreign trade and of direct and portfolio investment will make it easier to evade capital controls. As mobility of capital across national borders increases, the starker the trade-off will be between the renminbi exchange rate and interest rates. It was therefore highly likely that the renminbi rate would be made more flexible, a move supported by the PBC. The more flexible the exchange rate in the presence of capital mobility, the more effective is monetary policy relative to fiscal policy. This development would not please the SDPC and the MOFTEC as the SDPC's operations and China's traded sector – the MOFTEC's main constituency – would face greater foreign exchange risks and therefore higher transaction costs in their operations with a more flexible exchange rate. However, the new party leadership after the Sixteenth Party Congress under Hu Jintao has restructured the SDPC and the MOFTEC – changing their identities and responsibilities – to realign their institutional interests and indirectly alter their relative influence in the bureaucracy.

The next chapter will examine changes in the CCP leadership and China's policymaking structure after the Sixteenth Party Congress at the end of 2002. The PBC continues to cement its place as the most influential ministry in short-term macroeconomic policymaking, a result of China's deepening integration with the global economy, and the CLGFE is likely to remain the key decision maker of macroeconomic policy. In Chapter 6 we argue that the seemingly supreme position of the PBC in macroeconomic policymaking at the beginning of the new millennium is not as unchallenged as it once was with the restructuring of the SDPC under the new party leadership. But regardless of what happens to where key economic ministries are situated in the bureaucratic hierarchy, globalization and WTO membership will impose constraints on policy. The CLGFE will have to depend increasingly on these ministries for policy inputs and key policy organs for expert advice on the set of feasible economic policies and the nature of the trade-offs inherent in them. We see in the next chapter how these ministries interacted with the economic environment in 2005 to produce the policy that brought an end to the renminbi–US dollar peg.

NOTES

1. These include Hamrin and Zhao (1995), Lieberthal and Oksenberg (1988), Lieberthal and Lampton (1992), MacFarquhar (1974, 1983, 1997) and Shirk (1993).
2. The Politburo elected at the Fifteenth Party Congress in 1997 consisted of seven members in the standing committee plus 15 other full members and two alternate members. The Politburo elected at the Sixteenth Party Congress in 2002 consisted of nine members in the standing committee plus 15 other full members and one alternate member.
3. We exclude from this figure two commissions: the China Securities Regulatory Commission, which the 1998 Securities Law defined as the regulator for China's capital markets, and the China Insurance Regulatory Commission, established in 1998 to supervise

China's insurance industry. The two together with the China Banking Regulatory Commission, created in 2003 to take over the supervisory functions of the PBC, are important official financial institutions, but their function is mainly to regulate rather than contribute to policymaking.

4. The account in this paragraph is informed by Gao (2004, pp. 253–4).

5. According to an unconfirmed report in Hong Kong, after the middle of 1999, many of his responsibilities were transferred to Li Lanqing, Wu Bangguo and Wen Jiabao, leaving him in charge of only the environment and economic development of northwest China. See Luo (1999, p. 11). According to interviews, Zhu was still in charge of the economy in 2000. He could focus more of his attention on the economy of western China since developing the poor western part of China became one of the major objectives of the CCP. A Central Leading Group on Development for the West was being established in 2000. See Lu (2000, p. 31).

6. This became the CCP Central Working Group on Rural Affairs in 1994. Jiang Chunyun headed this working group as well as the agriculture sub-group in the CLGFE. See Gao and He (1999, pp. 515, 519).

7. Wu Bangguo was the other vice-chairperson (*Chinaonline* 1999; Gao 2004, p. 256).

8. The Chinese word is *bangongshi* to differentiate it from a *bangongting*, which is of higher rank and is often translated as 'general office'.

9. He was also, like Zhu and Zeng, a Qinghua graduate, who majored in kinetics.

10. Moreover, with Zhu as chairperson of the CLGFE, Wu Bangguo, who belonged to Jiang's Shanghai faction, would be senior deputy chairperson.

11. Inflation was a major factor behind the political unrest in 1989 and ultimately ended Zhao's political career.

12. A former senior official in an economic ministry, who the authors interviewed in Beijing in 2001.

13. Tianjin is one of four cities in China that have provincial status in the administrative hierarchy. The others are Beijing, Chongqing and Shanghai.

14. Members of that committee appointed in June 1998 were Dai Xianglong, the governor of the PBC (chairperson) and ten other members: Dai's two deputy governors (Liu Mingkang and Shang Fulin); deputy head of the SDPC (Wang Chunzheng), representatives of the State Economic and Trade Commission (*Guojia jingji maoyi weiyuanhui*) (Zhang Zhigang) and China's Securities Supervisory and Regulatory Commission (*Zhongguo zhengquan jiandu guanli weiyuanhui*) (Chen Yaoxian); deputy minister of finance (Zhang Youcai), head of the State Administration of Foreign Exchange (*Waihui guanli ju*) (Wu Xiaoling); the presidents of China Industrial and Commercial Bank (Liu Tinghuan) and China Agricultural Bank (He Linxiang); and Huang Da, president of China Financial Studies Association and People's University professor (ZGG 1998, pp. 652–3; ZJX 2000, p. 629).

15. Separate interviews with two members of the Chinese Academy of Social Sciences who are acknowledged experts on China's exchange rate and have published in the area. One of them pointedly said that the Monetary Policy Committee was 'still not fully institutionalized' at the time of the Asian crisis.

16. This is a very senior position in the PBC that ranks just below that of deputy governor. Beside the governor, there are six deputy governors and three assistant governors (PBC 2006b).

17. Like Zeng Piyan and others mentioned above, Zeng Qinghong was a member of Jiang's Shanghai faction. He served as head of the CCGO from 1993 until 1999, when his deputy, Wang Gang, replaced him.

18. Wen's promotion to full Politburo membership and secretary general of the CLGFE and appointment as secretary of the CCFWC signalled he was likely to be made a member of the Politburo standing committee at the Sixteenth Party Congress in 2002 and succeed Zhu Rongji as premier at the Tenth National People's Congress in 2003.

19. There is no direct but strong circumstantial evidence to suggest Jiang favoured a no-devaluation policy. Jiang is known to be a strong supporter of China's WTO entry. See Pearson (1999, p. 183 and 2001, pp. 363–4). China's WTO entry is a sensitive issue in

China because of the massive economic restructuring that will accompany WTO entry. Furthermore, the bombing of the Chinese embassy in Belgrade complicated Sino–US negotiations over China's entry (Fewsmith 1999). In November 1999 the annual Central Economic Work Conference, which was held soon after the signing of the US–China WTO Agreement, only obliquely referred to the fact that the agreement was discussed at that conference. Jiang (but no other senior leader) was shown celebrating the signing of the agreement with Charlene Barshefsky, the chief US negotiator, on Chinese television. This showed that Jiang was willing to take a political risk to express support for China's WTO entry. Maintaining the value of the renminbi was a price that he was prepared to pay. In keeping his promise to President Clinton and other world leaders not to devalue, he (and China) gained prestige and hoped that this would facilitate China's entry into the WTO (Liew 2001, p. 48). During his visit to China, Clinton emphasized the contribution of China to Asia's economic stability by not devaluing and the Chinese press played this up. See Office of the Press Secretary, 'Press availability by President Clinton and President Jiang', The White House, Beijing, PRC, available at http://www.usembassy-china.gov/english/press/hotPresscon.html. (27 June 1998), p. 4; Xinhuashe (1998, p. 1) and Moore and Yang (2001, pp. 220–22) made a similar point about China using its no-devaluation policy to promote its WTO application.
20. Staff appointed to the CCFWC were mainly party organization specialists rather than financial professionals to make the CCFWC independent from the banking system and to insulate the CCFWC from the lobbying efforts of the latter (Heilmann 2005, p. 3).
21. Information supplied by Willy Wo-Lap Lam.
22. More on this in the next chapter.
23. He was a member of the Shandong Normal University Class of 1978 and obtained his PhD from the Central Party School in 1989. He passed away in 2004. He was the author of the two well-known books: *Sikao Zhongguo* (Thoughts on China) and *Zhongguo dashi* (Trends in China's history) (Zhong 1997; ZDX 2005).
24. Material in this and the next section is drawn largely from Xiao (1999c, p. 40). This changed after Zhu was no longer premier. See Chapter 6 for details.
25. Radio Press, China Directory, cited in Onishi (2003).
26. Xiao (1999a, p. 35). For a discussion on Jiang Zemin's advisers see Gao (1999).
27. A commission is higher in rank than a ministry while the office here (SCORES) denotes a rank that is equivalent to that of a ministry.
28. The SCDRC was originally named the Centre for Economic, Technological and Social Development Research (*Jishu jingji yu shehui fazhan yanjiu zhongxin*). It was established in 1985 by combining three State Council research centres: the Centre for Economic Research (*Jingji yanjiu zhongxin*), the Technical Economics Research Centre (*Jishu jingji yanjiu zhongxin*) and the Centre for Price Reform Research (*Jiage gaige yanjiu zhongxin*). Under Ma Hong it became an important think-tank providing research support to Zhao Ziyang and his reformers. It played an important role in drafting of the Seventh Five-Year Plan. Although less influential now, its reports and those of research institutes in the Academy of Social Sciences still have some influence on policymakers.
29. Wu's views on inflation are widely known. In the 1980s he argued strongly against the high-growth, high-inflation strategy favoured by some of Zhao's advisers.
30. They included secretary general of the State Council, Wang Zhongyu; the two directors of Zhu's think-tanks, Gui Shiyong and Liu Zhongli; a former deputy governor of the PBC and State Development Bank president, Chen Yuan; former president of the China Construction Bank, Wang Qishan; director of State General Administration of Taxation, Jin Renqing; president of China's Construction Bank and former director of the State Administration of Foreign Exchange, Zhou Xiaochuan; and chairperson of China's Securities Regulatory Commission, Zhou Zhengqing. See Xiao (1999a, p. 35) and ZN (1999). Zhou Xiaochun had worked under Chen Yizi at the China Economic System Reform Institute (*Tigaisuo*) during the 1980s. The institute was then a very influential economic think-tank, but was disbanded after being implicated in the Beijing demonstrations of 1989. Zhu Xiaohua, a former deputy governor of the PBC and former president of the China Everbright Bank, was also one of Zhu's closest advisers. He was removed as president of the bank in 1999

and later expelled from the CCP for corruption. He was put on trial in 2002 and sentenced to 15 years in prison (China Briefing 2002, p. 24).

31. Interviewees consistently said that foreign affairs were either not an important consideration or were overwhelmed by domestic economic considerations during exchange rate policy deliberations.

32. It became the National Development and Reform Commission (*Guojia fazhan he gaige weiyuanhui*) in 2003 and took over the policy research functions of the SDRC and the SCORES (Brahm 2003). Some foreign publications refer to the commission as the State Development and Reform Commission. The functions of the body are discussed in Chapter 6.

33. On this topic see Liew (1997, pp. 127–37).

34. He was close to Chen Yun, the doyen of central planning.

35. In 2000, budgetary revenue was still only 15 per cent of GDP (NBS 2001, p. 246).

36. Calculated using data on foreign capital actually used, with foreign loans excluded (GTS 2000, pp. 65, 587–8).

37. Before 1993 the MOFTEC was known as the Ministry of Foreign Economic Relations and Trade (MOFERT), which was established in March 1982. Thus, in the text the acronyms MOFTEC and MOFERT are used interchangeably depending on whether it is referring to events before or after 1993.

38. Calculated using indirect quote for renminbi and data in NBS (2000, p. 588).

39. See section on 'Reform in a plan–market system' in Chapter 3.

40. The import plan was abolished in 1994. See Li et al. (1998, pp. 336–46).

41. See the 'PBC' section below for more details.

42. See for example Ba (1999, p. 133) and Wu and Song (1991, pp. 117–18).

43. This explains why the NPB opposed devaluation of the renminbi. Any significant devaluation would make its job of maintaining price stability more difficult.

44. Reforms aimed at strengthening the capacity of the PBC to control credit through tightening its institutional structure were announced in 1994 but were completed only in 1998. The reforms ended up first with nine and later ten cross-provincial PBC branches instead of the six that were originally proposed (Liew 1997, pp. 137–40; ZRYY 1999, pp. 12–13). The ten branches are located in Chendu, Chongqing, Guangzhou, Jinan, Nanjing, Shanghai, Shenyang, Tianjin, Wuhan and Xian (PBC 2006c).

45. In the banking literature, central bank independence means that the central bank can vary interest and exchange rates without the need to refer the decision to the state Cabinet.

46. John Edwards in his biography of Paul Keating, a former Australian prime minister and before that, treasurer, recalled the conflict in 1983 between the Reserve Bank of Australia (RBA) and Treasury over whether to liberalize Australia's foreign exchange market. The former was in favour and the latter against. A crucial consideration in the conflict was that liberalizing the foreign exchange market would mean the RBA would replace the Treasury as Australia's most influential short-term macroeconomic policymaking body. See Edwards (1996, pp. 216–32).

47. This paragraph draws from Liew (1998). See also Zhou (1998), Huang (1998), Lu Jianren (1998) and Lu Yi (1998).

48. For example, export quotas for 26 products were abolished and the number of products subject to export licences was reduced from 115 in 1998 to 59 in 1999. Also in 1998, 15 per cent of the textile quota for export to the United States, which used to be totally controlled by the government, was allocated directly to exporting enterprises (Hai and Zhong 1999).

49. This point was discussed in some detail earlier in p.93.

50. See Corden (1979, pp. 19–20) for the theory underlying this assertion.

51. The published figure was 7 per cent. The figure of 6.6 per cent appeared in an internal document of the Office of the State Council (*Guowuweiyuan bangongting*). See Luo (1998, pp. 6–7).

52. In 1999 the corresponding figures were 1.4 per cent and 3 per cent (NVS 2000, p. 289).

53. Further fiscal expansion increased the budget deficit to 2.2 per cent of GDP in 1999, but by then economic recovery in the rest of Asia had removed the pressure for China to devalue the renminbi.
54. Support for a loose fiscal policy was made clear in a book published by several senior researchers from the SDPC, the MOF and other government ministries. See Bai et al. (1998).
55. Several interviewees expressed this view. See also Zhou (1998, p. 84). The PBC is not alone among central banks in being concerned with inflation in a deflationary environment. The Bank of Japan is another pre-eminent example.
56. The other two reported reasons for not devaluing were: desire not to exacerbate the financial crisis in Southeast Asia or to worsen US trade deficits with China, which would impact negatively on Sino–US relations (Xiao Ren 1998, p. 28).
57. See for example, Zhao (1998), Zhang and Xu (1998) and Li Fuyang (1998, pp. 6–7, 17).
58. Yi expressed the view in a joint paper presented with Song Ligang at the Australian National University in 1998. See Yi and Song (1998).
59. At that meeting, Zhu announced to the assembled provincial governors and city mayors that their powers to direct the activities of local bank branches had been abrogated. Some provincial leaders had abused these powers, resulting in funding of many economically unsound local projects that produced non-performing loans.
60. See Tanner (1999) for a discussion on the changing role of the NPC after Mao.
61. Among the publications examined were *Jinrong cankao* (Finance Reference) published by the PBC; *Jinrong yanjiu baogao* (Finance Research Report) published by the PBC and China's Finance Studies Association; *Gaige necan* (Inside Information on Economic Reform) published by the SCRES; and *Diaocha yanjiu baogao* (Investigation Research Report), published by the SCDRC.
62. *Zhongguo gaige zhazhishi* (China Reform Journal Press) now publishes the journal. The change in publisher is because the SCRES was downgraded and the journal's status has declined. The journal's lower status may explain why the two articles were allowed to be published there.
63. Critics of Hua Guofeng, Mao's chosen successor, accused him of subscribing to *liangge fanshi* – the belief that whatever Chairman Mao said and did was correct. Thus, Jia's criticisms were particularly sharp.
64. Close examination of the 1998 issues of *Jingji ribao, Renmin ribao, Shanghai jingji bao, Shenzhen shangbao, Tianjin ribao, Xiamen ribao* and *Zhejiang ribao* found extensive coverage of the Asian financial crisis and the renminbi, but all articles argued in favour of no devaluation.

6. The WTO and China's exchange rate

As we have seen through Chapter 5 of this book, party and powerful people link inextricably with policy in analysis of decision making about the renminbi. Not surprisingly, the changes in national leadership at the Sixteenth Party Congress in 2002 that heralded the election of Hu Jintao as president, Wen Jiabao as premier,[1] and a change in top personnel including members of the Central Leading Group in Finance and Economics (CLGFE), have influenced exchange rate policymaking. Whereas under Jiang Zemin and Zhu Rongji, China's engagement in the global economy was instrumental in national policymaking, priorities of the new leadership have shifted subtly to foremost concern on domestic stability. Change in people and priorities at the national helm has inevitably shifted the political-economy turf on which policy decisions about the renminbi are made.

In this chapter, then, we move beyond the leadership of Jiang Zemin and Zhu Rongji to survey the landscape of exchange rate policymaking under the new leadership and examine how this new landscape produced the 2005 decision to discontinue the renminbi–US dollar peg. The circumstances that produced the 1998 decision not to devalue after the Asian financial crisis (AFC) no longer prevail, and the change of leaders and consequently of national priorities has brought change in institutional arrangements. The new ministerial configuration merges segments whose sectoral interests do not necessarily align, and in some cases oppose each other. It means that because positions taken by ministries and other bodies are now informed by preferences considerably more divergent than before, they are less clear-cut and predictable than before. This presents a picture of developments in renminbi policy that is somewhat different from that presented in the previous chapter about decision making at the time of the AFC. Yet it also underscores a central argument of this book that renminbi policy is very much the product of human understandings of and responses to the political, economic and social circumstances on which renminbi policy decisions are made.

The key exchange rate policy question in 2005 was the direct opposite of that during the AFC: should China revalue its currency and by how much? Related to this key policy question was the choice of China's exchange rate regime: should China continue to peg its currency to the US dollar? This chapter will analyse China's decision in 2005 to discontinue the renminbi–US dollar peg, adopting an approach similar to one that we used to study China's no-devaluation policy during the AFC. Both approaches explain policy decisions on the basis of bureaucratic rank of major policy organs, their policy preferences, and influence of individual key policymakers who have to operate within given economic constraints.

THE WTO AS THE BIG BAD WOLF: WHO IS AFRAID OF IT NOW?

In Beijing in November 1999, foreign trade minister Shi Guangsheng on behalf of China, and United States trade representative Charlene Barshefsky on behalf of the US, signed the agreement on conditions of China's entry into the World Trade Organization (WTO) (Lawrence and Holland 1999, p. 81). The agreement was later formally approved by President Clinton and ratified by the US Congress after intense lobbying by the White House and US businesses. The US House of Representatives passed the bill granting China 'permanent normal trade relations' (PNTR) by a vote of 237 to 197 on 24 May 2000. The 'yes' vote in the House of Representatives was comfortable if not overwhelming, but the 'yes' vote in the US Senate on 19 September that year was surely overwhelming: 83 'yes' to 15 otherwise. The US had been the major stumbling block to China's membership of the WTO and in granting China PNTR, the US Congress paved the way for China's entry into the WTO on 11 December 2001.

China's leaders were sensitive about the US–China WTO Agreement. Many in China's bureaucracy at that time felt that Premier Zhu Rongji gave away too many concessions during his earlier trip to the US, especially since the concessions failed to secure US agreement at that time, and they were suspicious of the US–China WTO Agreement finally signed later in Beijing (Liew 2001, p. 53). The extreme sensitivity of China's leaders over the agreement was reflected in the report in the party newspaper, *Renmin ribao* (People's Daily), on the Central Economic Work Conference that was held immediately after the US–China WTO Agreement was signed. [2] The conference was an annual meeting of central and regional party and state leaders to map out the economic strategy for the next year. It was therefore surprising that the only part in the report that indicated even remotely that the WTO Agreement was discussed at that meeting was several sentences expressing the point that globalization is affecting all countries, including China. According to the report, the conference expressed the view that globalization offers China new opportunities and challenges, and China would have to increase its sense of urgency to work hard to develop the economy even faster. The term 'WTO' or its Chinese equivalent (*shimao*) did not appear at all in the text of the article.

It is ironic that fears inside China over China's WTO entry when the US–China WTO Agreement was signed have been largely overshadowed by concerns among sections of the international community, especially in the US, of China's rapid economic growth and growing influence in the world economy. Policymakers in many countries, especially in the US, were concerned about the value of the renminbi, believing that behind China's relentless economic march forward was an undervalued renminbi, which gave China an unfair competitive advantage in world trade and investment. China's entry into the WTO signals its commitment to engaging with the global economy, which has contributed significantly to national rebirth.

However, WTO entry is not a one-way street and WTO entry binds China to abide by WTO rules. A careful perusal of the WTO documents covering China's accession to the WTO (WTO 2005b) shows without doubt that WTO rules, which oblige China to deregulate its markets more than it would otherwise have done, will limit the autonomy of China's policymakers. For example, in its negotiations over accession to the WTO, China agreed to open its retail banking market to foreign banks by 2007. In August 2006, China made the first move toward fulfilling this promise by inviting foreign banks to discuss draft regulations that allow the entry of foreign banks into retail banking (Ryan 2006).[3] The entry of foreign players into China's retail banking market will make it easier for capital to move in and out of China and bind China's policymakers ever more tightly to constraints of participating in the global economy.

GENERAL ECONOMIC AND SOCIAL CONTEXTS

Fixed versus Flexible Exchange Rate

Since we are concerned with China's exchange rate policymaking, the obvious questions are: what do existing researchers have to say about the renminbi? and what currency policy would best serve China's economic interest? Should China have discontinued its currency peg and allowed the renminbi to appreciate, or kept the peg but revalued the currency? Or should it have done nothing? A consensus seemed to have emerged among international economists after the emerging markets' financial crises in the second half of the 1990s that in the presence of international capital flows, pegged but adjustable exchange rate regimes encourage speculation and are unstable. In response to this consensus, many economists recommend freely floating exchange rates or super-fixed regimes. However, a small but not insignificant number of economists, like Edwards (2003, p. 92) and Frankel (2003, p. 92), pointed out that this consensus has come about without much theoretical justification and may not be warranted if one takes a long historical perspective rather than focusing on experiences of the 1990s. China seems to have embraced this minority view and discontinued the renminbi–dollar peg. But it maintained some control over its exchange rate by adopting a managed float regime.

There are always interest groups wanting to influence monetary policy to fix domestic demand or the exchange rate to determine international competitiveness. If the People's Bank of China (PBC) is independent, policymakers can rely on a flexible exchange rate to target inflation. Without an independent PBC, a state commitment to low inflation is not credible with societal groups desiring low inflation. But PBC independence is only a necessary but not sufficient condition for credible official commitment to low inflation. Many economists, such as Guillermo Calvo, Barry Eichengreen and Larry Summers, have questioned the ability of institutions in an emerging country to target inflation, and have pointed out that central bank independence has to be complemented with transparent political institutions. In the absence of transparent political institutions, a fixed exchange rate regime has more credibility with these societal groups than central bank independence (Broz 2002).

However, many financial crises in emerging markets occurred under a fixed exchange rate regime that had open capital accounts. China has capital controls but they are becoming increasingly less effective as the nation becomes more integrated into the global economy. In Chapter 3 we cited a Chinese government study reported in Zhong (2004) that found evidence of significant investment flows into mainland China that originated from offshore financial centres. Gunter (2004, p. 82) estimated that during the AFC (1997–2000) when the renminbi was under pressure, there was capital flight of more than US$100 billion a year from China. Post-Asian crisis, with pressure on the renminbi to revalue, increases in foreign direct investment (FDI) from 1998–2000 to 2001–05 were dwarfed by increases in other capital flows. Of the total US$67.7 billion annual average increase in the capital and financial account in this period, increase in FDI accounted for only US$12.3 billion. Non-FDI capital flows (including errors and omissions) increased from an annual average of minus US$53.6 billion in 1998–2000 to US$23 billion in 2001–05, a change of US$77 billion per year. In 2004, non-FDI capital flows (including errors and omissions) actually exceeded FDI flows, but in 2005, sentiments appeared to have changed and non-FDI flows were minus US$21.6 billion. The turnaround of these flows between 2004 and 2005 is startling – from positive 4.9 per cent in 2004 to minus 1 per cent of GDP in 2005 (Table 6.1). Non-FDI, unlike FDI capital flows are highly liquid and short term, and managing these flows is a major challenge for officials in emerging markets that may have capital controls that are formally tight but in practice are weak; capital can flow out just as quickly as it can flow in. For example, some of the dramatic fall in non-FDI capital inflows in 2005 could simply be due to speculators changing their tactics: reducing capital inflows but increasing over-invoicing of exports and under-invoicing of imports. Another reason is the development of non-deliverable forward (NDF) markets outside China and relaxation of rules covering capital outflow.

Table 6.1 Balance of payments (US$ billion) (% GDP) (1998–2005)

Items	Annual average (1998–2000)	Annual average (2001–2005)	2001	2002	2003	2004	2005
Foreign reserve increase	8.5	139.6	47.3	75.5	117.0	206.4	207.0
(% GDP)	0.8	8.8	4.0	5.8	8.0	12.0	9.3
Current account balance	23.7	65.9	17.4	35.4	45.9	68.7	160.8
(% GDP)	2.3	4.2	1.5	2.7	3.1	4.0	7.2
Capital account balance	0.3	68.0	34.8	32.3	52.7	110.7	63.0
(% GDP)	0.0	4.3	2.9	2.5	3.6	6.4	2.8
Net FDI	38.5	50.8	37.4	46.8	47.2	53.1	67.8
(% GDP)	3.8	3.2	3.1	3.6	3.2	3.1	3.0
Net errors and omissions	−15.4	5.8	−4.9	7.8	18.4	27	−16.8
(% GDP)	−1.5	0.4	−0.4	0.6	1.3	1.6	−0.8
Non-FDI capital account balance (including errors and omissions)	−53.6	23.0	−7.4	−6.7	23.9	84.6	−21.6
(% GDP)	−5.3	1.5	−0.6	−0.5	1.6	4.9	−1.0

Note: US dollar–renminbi rates (2 decimal places) for converting renminbi GDP to US dollar GDP taken from Chapter 3, Appendix Table A3.2 in this book.

Source: GSFX (2006, pp. 8–9), NBS (2006), Prasad and Wei (2005, Table 7), and authors' calculations.

In 2004 the US one-month inter-bank offer rate was 1.524 per cent lower than the equivalent term inter-bank offer rate in China. In 2005 the US rate increased by 1.873 per cent and the China rate fell by 0.785 per cent so that the US rate became 1.134 per cent higher than the rate in China (Table 4.6). This means that between 2004 and 2005 there was a swing around in the US–China one-month inter-bank offer interest rate differential of 3.658 per cent. Moreover, China continues to control the renminbi deposit rate and since 2003 the spread between the renminbi and US dollar deposit rates has been about 1 per cent (IMF 2005b). Higher US dollar interest rates appear to be sufficient to cause significant non-FDI outflows from China in 2005, despite expectations of renminbi revaluation. Unrecorded capital outflows captured by the errors and omissions term in China's balance of payments show the highest unrecorded capital outflows since the AFC (Table 6.1).

The capital outflows may not be that surprising if we consider expectations on the timing of renminbi appreciation and China's asymmetric capital liberalization in an effort to lower its accumulation of foreign reserves that makes it easier for capital to flow out of China than into it. Figure 6.1 shows that the longer the maturity, the larger the expected appreciation of the renminbi, as indicated by the renminbi NDF rates of various lengths of maturity. China's government had held firm to its position of a stable renminbi and even though it discontinued pegging the renminbi to the US dollar and let it appreciate immediately by around 2 per cent when it discontinued the peg, the market obviously did not believe the currency would appreciate significantly in the near future. Thus higher US dollar deposit rates induced short-term capital flow out of China and hedging of this capital outflow helped to raise renminbi NDF rates. With development of NDF renminbi markets, there is no need for speculators once they manage to send capital out of China to resend it back into China in the future when they expect renminbi revaluation. Advertisements indicate banks are promoting NDFs as possible instruments for currency speculation.[4]

The case for a flexible renminbi rests on the fact that this allows China to have an independent monetary policy, and the exchange rate will adjust automatically in response to flows in the current and capital accounts and reduce opportunities for speculation against the renminbi. In Chapter 3 we directed attention to the domestic pressures on the Chinese authorities to discontinue the currency peg and let the renminbi appreciate because China's large and growing current account surpluses were compromising the authorities' ability to control domestic money supply and inflation. That the authorities had difficulty controlling inflation with a pegged exchange rate was evident in 2004, when prices as measured by the industrial producers' price index (IPPI) increased by 8.2 per cent compared to the year before. In 2005, the index increased by 3.1 per cent (Table 4.1). Property and land prices also rose; in some cities they rose by as much as 20 per cent in a year (NBS 2006, Table 9.18).

A currency peg involves the government making an implicit contract with the industrial sector. The government normally will find it very difficult to vary the exchange rate and any change to the existing rate, no matter how desirable, will inevitably be too late (Frenkel 2003, p. 87). This delay provides opportunities for profit to currency speculators. China tried to dampen appreciation pressures arising from its large and growing foreign reserves by relaxing capital controls, as described in Chapter 3, but this simply put pressure on its pegged exchange rate. The right approach, Prasad et al. (2005, p. 18) advised, is to make the exchange rate flexible before lowering barriers to capital mobility and not the reverse.

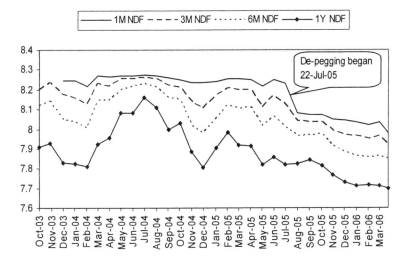

Note: Data shown is approximately the 15th day of each month.

Figure 6.1   US dollar–renminbi non-deliverable forward rates since August 2003

For all the above reasons, the International Monetary Fund (IMF) supported discontinuing the renminbi–US dollar peg and has argued for even greater flexibility in the exchange rate since the end of the peg.[5] It is true that opting for a flexible renminbi regime does not equate with wanting a renminbi revaluation.[6] However, given China's rapid accumulation of foreign reserves and US pressure on China to revalue, the wide market expectation in the middle 2000s was that the end of the peg and floating of the renminbi would lead to renminbi appreciation. The expected inevitability of renminbi appreciation following floating of the renminbi was a major factor behind the reluctance of China's policymakers to end the peg. One reason for this reluctance was the lack of consensus among economists on the equilibrium renminbi exchange rate, which we noted in Chapter 4, citing Dunaway and Li (2005) and Higgins and Humpage (2005).[7] Another reason was fear of deflation – a scenario whose major proponent is Ronald Mckinnon.

Mckinnon took a position opposite to that of the IMF and argued that the Chinese made a mistake in discontinuing the renminbi–US dollar peg. In a series of widely circulated papers that he authored (2005a, 2005b) and co-authored with Schnabl (2004a, 2004b), Mckinnon pointed out that the peg had served China well. He claimed that the period of the peg was a period of high export and economic growth and low inflation in China, and was concerned that China's economic growth would suffer without the peg. According to his analysis, appreciation reduces demand in the traded sectors, makes China a less attractive place for FDI and produces a negative wealth effect, which reduces domestic consumption and investment. The fall in domestic demand then reduces imports even though imports are cheaper and leaves China's trade surplus undiminished, which would induce even more US pressure on China to appreciate its currency further. The resulting deflation from currency appreciation would put downward pressure on interest rates and China might end up in a near-zero interest liquidity trap like Japan experienced from the late 1980s to the 1990s. Japan, according to Mckinnon, capitulated to US pressure to appreciate the yen, because of its large trade surplus with the US in the 1970s and 1980s, and ended up enduring more than a decade of deflation. Mckinnon pointed out that growth in money wages in the ten years since the mid-1990s in China had tracked growth in labour productivity in China's most open tradable sector – manufacturing – and made the rate of inflation in China converge with that of the US, keeping international competitiveness in balance. But if the exchange rate were not anchored and appreciation seemed likely, employers in China would have been more cautious when bidding for labour and wage growth would have fallen below the rate of productivity growth. Mckinnon was pointing out that renminbi appreciation would have been compensated for in China with lower wages, which would leave US trade deficits with China largely unaffected.

Mckinnon's and Schnabl's views on the renminbi–dollar peg are echoed in a book by Wang and Zeng (2004), where they present the case that China will not be able to maintain its position as 'factory of the world' (*shijie gongchang*) if China were to relax control over the exchange rate. According to Wang and Zeng, revaluing the renminbi will weaken China's international competitive position and lower its ability to create much-needed employment. Citing Mckinnon approvingly (Wang and Zeng 2004, p. 98), they blame Japan's recession in the 1990s on its decision to revalue the yen following the Plaza Agreement in 1985. A year earlier Wang, the deputy chief accountant at the *Renmin ribao* (People's Daily), and Zeng, an academic at the Shanghai Maritime University, had published a popular book with strong nationalist overtones – *Jingti Meiguo de dierci yinmou* (Be vigilant against America's second plot). Here they criticized US policies toward China. Before the Chinese authorities discontinued the currency peg, there was no shortage of writings in China supporting the peg and criticizing international pressure on China to end the peg. Wang's and Zeng's book is just one of many. In another well-known book, researchers at the Faculty of Finance and at the Contemporary Finance Research Centre, Shanghai Finance and Economics University, interpreted the US pressure on China to revalue the renminbi as part of US strategy to slow China's rise (SCD 2004, pp. 12–13).

Mckinnon's views on the peg are known to China's key policymakers but a majority of them were obviously not convinced sufficiently by this argument, as the peg was discontinued. Yu Yongding, a member of the PBC Monetary Policy Committee under Dai Xianglong's successor as PBC governor, Zhou Xiaochuan, argued that it was Japan's loose monetary policy rather than revaluation that was the source of Japan's macroeconomic problem. He argued that it was the forced repatriation of funds back to Japan in 1995 by Japanese financial institutions to reverse the deterioration in their capital–asset ratios as a result of large corporate bad debts after the bursting of Japan's 'bubble' economy that caused revaluation of the yen. He set out his arguments in a written piece that is significant, but little known outside China. Titled suggestively, 'Dispel the fear of renminbi revaluation', it appeared as a chapter in an edited volume (Yu 2004) published under the auspices of the International Finance Research Centre (IFRC) of the Chinese Academy of Social Sciences, where he is director.[8] This volume is a publication from the centre's research into the renminbi exchange rate and includes a translation of the article by Mckinnon and Schnabl (2004a).[9] Inclusion of this article is clearly an attempt by the IFRC to juxtapose the two contrasting views on the renminbi, allowing Yu to counter the views of Mckinnon and Schnabl, which are well known in China among those in the economic policy circle.

Yu has a solid grasp of Western research on exchange rate regimes, including China's, and he clearly wishes to offer an alternative view to that of Mckinnon's, since the latter's research provides ammunition for anti-US nationalists. Yu does not want China's exchange rate policy to be unduly influenced by populist nationalist sentiments that might draw intellectual support from the research of respected international scholars, lest official policy turns out to be opposite to what is expressed in nationalist sentiments. There are strong arguments from influential and respected economists for and against the renminbi peg, but what ultimately matters is how Chinese policymakers appraise these positive arguments in the context of their understanding of renminbi political economy. Yu (2004, p. 89) claims that China faces two difficult choices in slowing its accumulation of foreign exchange: continue to run a surplus in its capital account but allow its current account to be in balance or deficit, or maintain its current account surplus but restrict FDI flows into China and encourage capital outflows from China. The former requires revaluation of the renminbi but the latter brings on even more complex problems, which Yu did not specify.

Export Growth, Savings and the Terms of Trade

Mckinnon's explanation of why renminbi appreciation is unlikely to reduce US trade deficits with China is not among the most common reasons offered by analysts. The most common reasons analysts offer were those we discussed in Chapter 1: high import content of Chinese exports, low Chinese manufacturing wages, and inadequate US savings. The last reason is especially poignant. Analysts have often pointed out that the Bush administration has made large tax cuts to the wealthy while increasing military expenditure significantly to fight in particular the war in Iraq, which has shifted the US budget from a 2.4 per cent of gross domestic product (GDP) surplus at the end of the Clinton administration to a 2.6 per cent of GDP deficit in 2005 (Table 6.2), while the federal debt has ballooned to US$2.2 trillion as of January 2006 (Table 1.2). A change in the US dollar–renminbi exchange rate would produce largely a substitution effect, but the real requirement here is increased US savings. Without an increase in US savings, renminbi appreciation will only switch some US import demand away from China to demand from other countries. Between October 2000 and August 2006 the US dollar depreciated by 35 per cent against the euro, yet the US bilateral deficit with the euro zone doubled (FT Lex 2006).

Table 6.2   US fiscal budget (2000–2006)

Fiscal year	Budget surplus/deficit		% of GDP
	Current $	2000 $	
2000	236.2	236.2	2.4
2001	128.2	125.3	1.3
2002	−157.8	−151.3	−1.5
2003	−377.6	−353.1	−3.5
2004	−412.7	−375.9	−3.6
2005	−318.3	−280.6	−2.6
2006*	−432.2	−361.3	−3.2

Note: *US Government estimate.

Source: US Government (2006, Table 1.3).

Ben Bernanke (2005), successor to Alan Greenspan as governor of the US Federal Reserve Board, tried to turn this argument on its head by arguing it is not that the US is not saving enough, but that its trading partners, especially those in Asia, are saving too much and spending too little. While exports were a significant factor in China's phenomenal economic growth in the 1990s and 2000s, most of these exports involved processing imported components and their domestic value-added is therefore small. The share of domestic final demand in GDP is much larger than the share of net exports (Table 6.3).[10] Wasteful as much of the domestic investment expenditures were, it is nevertheless difficult to make the case that China was not spending enough. The problem was that, as discussed in Chapter 3, China's previous various highly centralized foreign exchange management systems had made it extremely difficult for Chinese enterprises and localities to obtain foreign exchange if they did not export. As a result, sub-national governments made great efforts to attract FDI and granted incentives to domestic enterprises to invest in production facilities to export, and as discussed in Chapter 4, FDI and export subsidies had a greater influence on China's exports than the exchange rate. But overinvestment in export production was at the cost of deterioration in China's terms of trade and underinvestment in public health and education.

Table 6.3 Expenditure composition of GDP (%) (1996–2004)

	Private consumption	Government consumption	Net investment	Change in inventories	Net exports
1996	47.1	11.5	34.2	5.2	2.1
1997	46.5	11.6	33.6	4.4	3.8
1998	46.7	12.0	35.0	2.4	3.9
1999	47.6	12.6	35.7	1.5	2.7
2000	48.0	13.1	36.5	−0.1	2.5
2001	46.6	13.2	37.3	0.7	2.2
2002	45.3	12.9	38.9	0.4	2.6
2003	43.3	12.2	42.1	0.2	2.2
2004	41.4	11.5	43.8	0.4	2.9

Source: NBS (2005), Tables 3.13, 3.14.

China's previous tightly controlled foreign exchange system, by encouraging overinvestment in export production, has contributed to the huge expansion in world productive capacity in manufacturing. This has pushed down China's export prices while its rising demand for imported inputs into export production has pushed up import prices. The sum of the two effects is deterioration in China's terms of trade. Figure 6.2 shows China's terms of trade have been falling since the late 1970s, when China embarked on its post-Mao opening up to the global economy and started promoting foreign trade and investment.

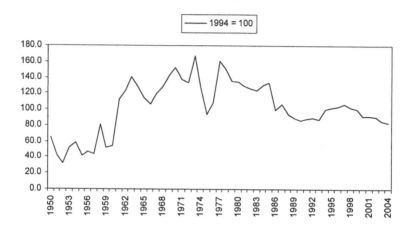

Note: Terms of trade are measured as average export price over average import price of commodities (1994 = 100). The measurement for 1950–81 is based on quantity of major trade commodities and for 1982–2004 on import and export prices recorded by Customs.

Source: Wu and Shea (2006, Figure 9).

Figure 6.2   Terms of trade (1950–2004)

From Investment for Export to Investment in Public Goods

The World Bank estimated that China's Gini coefficient increased from 0.29 in the 1980s to 0.39 in the 1990s, transforming China from one of the world's most equal countries (in terms of income) before reform to one in the middle of world rankings by the 1990s (World Bank 1997a, p. 2). In 2001 income inequality in China worsened further, with the Gini coefficient increasing to 0.45 (UNDP 2005, p. 271). China's Human Development Index (HDI) performs better than its GDP per capita in world rankings and China performs better in human poverty than in income poverty (UNDP 2005, pp. 220, 227), which indicate a state capacity to deliver public services. However inequality of access to public goods such as health (World Bank 1997b) and education (Solinger 1999, pp. 266–9) has nevertheless accompanied the increase in income inequality. This is the result of China's weakening of its pre-reform commitments to state-guaranteed social rights

(Wong 2004, p. 170), but it can be reversed with greater state spending on public goods such as health and education, instead of continuing direct and indirect public subsidies to investments for export (and upmarket real estate), which have low social rates of return.[11] China for far too long has been over-reliant on capital for its economic growth.[12] China's average annual GDP growth between 1998 and 2003 was 8 per cent. The contribution from employment to this growth, despite China's huge surplus labour, was a meagre 0.3 per cent. The contribution from capital on the other hand was a huge 4.9 per cent, with residual factors contributing the remaining 2.8 per cent. Among residual factors, multi-factor productivity and sectoral change contributed 1.3 per cent and 0.5 per cent, respectively; education contributed a modest 1.1 per cent (OECD 2005, p. 32).

Increased Government Social Commitments

China's leaders are aware that there is still much poverty in China's countryside and this poses long-term danger for the party. In 2004 a book published in China, written by a husband and wife team on poverty and the miserable living conditions of peasants in the Chinese countryside – *Zhongguo nongmin diaocha* (An investigation into China's peasants) (Chen and Wu 2005) – attracted widespread attention inside and outside China. It became a best-seller in China, with an estimated 8 million pirated copies sold (Yang 2006). Policymakers have been aware of problems in the countryside for a long time and have labelled these problems the '*san nong wenti*' – *nongye, nongcun, nongmin* (agriculture, village, peasant). Wen Jiabao in his 2005 Government Report delivered to the National People's Congress emphasized the need to strengthen work on the *san nong wenti* (Wen 2005). One of the countryside's major difficulties, which are described in great detail in the Chen and Wu book and are familiar to China's central policymakers, are the exorbitant formal and informal taxes levied on the countryside by local authorities.

In 2004 the central authorities introduced a new agricultural policy of abolishing the 'three types of agricultural taxes' (*nonye san shui*) and providing other forms of subsidies to agriculture. However, this new policy is making a huge dent in the national budget. According to the Chinese tax authorities, formal agricultural taxes in 2003 totalled about RMB60 billion (Ni 2005, p. 280), or according to our calculations, 2.8 per cent of government revenue and 20.4 per cent of budget deficit. In addition to formal agricultural taxes, sub-national governments had also levied their own informal agricultural taxes and levies to help fund much-needed local government expenditure in such areas as health and education. The central government has promised to stamp out these informal levies but alternate sources of government revenue have to be found to fund local public goods and services. The tax authorities estimated that in 2003 the total cost to all levels of government of abolishing the formal and extra-legal agricultural taxes and levies would be between RMB160 and RMB180 billion (Ni 2005, p. 281), or according to our calculations, 7.4–8.3 per cent of government revenue or 54.5–61.3 per cent of budget deficit. The 2004 policy also contains direct subsidies to farmers for grain, seeds and agricultural machinery, and increases in investment on rural infrastructure. But these increases in fiscal spending are relatively modest and have dwarfed the elimination of the agricultural taxes (Gale et al. 2005). China has been running a budget deficit for some years (Table 6.4) and will be careful to ensure, with additional state expenditure on the countryside, that any exchange rate policy that it implements will not exacerbate budget deficits.

Table 6.4 Government finance (1996–2004)

	100 mil. RMB revenue	Annual % growth	100 mil. RMB expenditure	Annual % growth	100 mil. RMB balance	% deficit/ GDP
1996	7 408.0	18.7	7 937.6	16.3	−529.6	−0.8
1997	8 651.1	16.8	9 233.6	16.3	−582.4	−0.8
1998	9 876.0	14.2	10 798.2	16.9	−922.2	−1.2
1999	11 444.1	15.9	13 187.7	22.1	−1 743.6	−2.1
2000	13 395.2	17.0	15 886.5	20.5	−2 491.3	−2.8
2001	16 386.0	22.3	18 902.6	19.0	−2 516.5	−2.6
2002	18 903.6	15.4	22 053.2	16.7	−3 149.5	−2.9
2003	21 715.3	14.9	24 650.0	11.8	−2 934.7	−2.4
2004	26 396.5	21.6	28 486.9	15.6	−2 090.4	−1.5

Note: Since 2000, government domestic and foreign debt interest payments have been counted in government expenditures.

Source: NBS (2005, Table 8.1) and authors' calculations.

POST-JIANG ZEMIN ECONOMIC POLICYMAKING ELITES

Before we can examine how China's post-2002 policymakers interpret the economic and social environments that we have considered above in the context of renminbi political economy, we need to track how China's economic policymaking structure has changed after the Sixteenth CCP Congress and Ninth National People's Congress (NPC). The congresses saw the retirement of both Jiang Zemin as general secretary of the party and country president, and Zhu Rongji as premier, to be replaced by Hu Jintao and Wen Jiabao, respectively as general secretary and president, and premier. The members of the Central Leading Group in Finance and Economics after the change in personnel at the Sixteenth Party Congress and the Tenth National People's Congress, as evident from documentary, internet and interview sources, are listed in Table 6.5.

Table 6.5 Post-Jiang CLGFE

Chairperson	Wen Jiabao
Vice-chairperson	Huang Ju
Members	Wu Yi, Zeng Peiyan, Hui Liangyu, Hua Jianmin, Ma Kai, Jin Renqing, Zhou Xiaochuan, Li Rongrong
Secretary general	Hua Jianmin
Deputy secretary general	Ma Kai, Wang Chunzheng
Office director	Wang Chunzheng
Office deputy director	Chen Xiwen, Yang Linglong, Liu He

Sources: Various documentary, internet and interview sources. See text for details.

The change in China's leadership has led to significant changes in the economic policymaking structure. The new policymaking structure is shown in Figure 6.3. The obvious difference between this structure and the former policymaking structure under Jiang Zemin (Figure 5.2) is the absence in this structure of the Chinese Communist Party Central Committee Financial Work Commission (CCFWC). This commission, as pointed out in Chapter 5, has been abolished and replaced with the Central Leading Group on Finance Safety (CLGFS), which is not concerned with exchange rate policy. As we discuss below, the function of the Ministry of Finance (MOF) remains unchanged, but functions of other key ministries in the monetary and exchange rate policy structure were restructured and as a result their relative influences in the policymaking structure have been altered. Hu Jintao, like Jiang Zemin before him, has left control of the economy to the nation's premier, Wen Jiabao, who now chairs the CLGFE. Wen is not as dominant in the bureaucracy as Zhu was; there is greater pluralization and institutionalization of economic policymaking under Wen. But this is to be expected given the gradual trend in China since the passing of Mao toward collective as opposed to autocratic decision making in the bureaucracy.

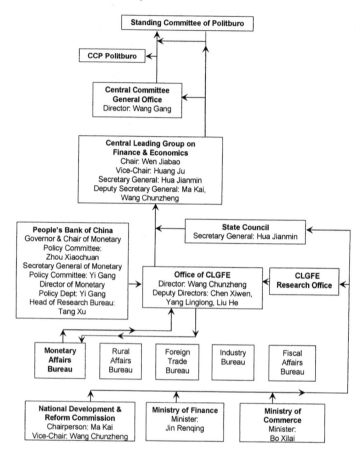

Figure 6.3   China's monetary and exchange rate policymaking structure (2003–)

Personnel Movements in the CLGFE

We are cognisant that people's perceptions are affected to some extent by their past experiences. Hence we describe the backgrounds of some of the human policy actors, which we will later incorporate in our analysis on how the new policymaking structure operates within China's post-WTO entry economic and social environment to produce the 2005 currency policy of discontinuing the renminbi–US dollar peg.

Zhou Xiaochuan took over from Dai Xianglong as PBC governor in December 2002 after the Sixteenth Party Congress. Zhou graduated from the Beijing Chemical Industry Institute (*Huagong xueyuan*) in 1975 and obtained his PhD from Qinghua University in 1985. In 1986 he joined the now defunct State Commission for Reform of the Economic Structure. Former party leader Zhao Ziyang established this influential commission, which attracted many reform-minded officials to work there. After the fall of Zhao from power, the commission lost influence and in 1991 Zhou moved to become deputy president of the Bank of China (BOC). After leaving the BOC in 1995, he held various senior positions in banking and finance – according to times of appointment: head of the State Administration of Foreign Exchange (SAFE), deputy governor of the People's Bank of China, president of China's Construction Bank and chairperson of the State Securities Regulatory Commission – before being appointed PBC governor (PBC 2006b).

One of the most significant promotions in the economic ministries that occurred under Wen Jiabao is the promotion of Yi Gang. In 2003, Yi Gang replaced Dai Gengyou as director of the PBC Monetary Policy Department and was promoted from deputy secretary general to secretary general of the PBC's Monetary Policy Committee. In July 2004 he was made a member of the PBC Party Committee and assistant PBC governor (PBC 2006b; Sun 2003a; Ye 2003). In the previous chapter we noted that Yi had to retract a statement that he made at a conference in Australia during the AFC that China might be forced to devalue the renminbi, but that indiscretion has obviously not impeded his career in the PBC. His career since returning to China from the US has been in either academia or at the PBC and he can therefore be relied upon to recommend monetary and exchange rate policies from a central bank perspective.

Hua Jianmin has taken over from Wen Jiabao as secretary general of the CLGFE and from Wang Zhongyu as State Council secretary general. Like Wen during the AFC, Hua does not seem to hold strong views on the renminbi. This may relate to him not having specific responsibility in an economic area compared to other members of the CLGFE. He is an engineer by training and most of his career before 1991 was spent in power generation research and administration. In 1991 he moved to economic planning, with his appointment as deputy director of Shanghai's Planning Commission. He was made vice-mayor of Shanghai in 1994, before appointment as deputy director of the CLGFE administrative office in 1996 and secretary general of the CLGFE in 1998 (Xinhua 2003). It seems that he has not spent time in any work unit that obviously had a consistent preference for a particular renminbi policy. In addition to his positions in the CLGFE and State Council, Hua is also president of the State Administration Institute (*Guojia xingzheng xueyuan*).

There were significant staff movements in the administrative office of the CLGFE after Wen Jiabao took over the chair's position. Of special significance were the appointments of Wang Chunzheng and Chen Xiwen. Wang replaced Hua Jianmin as director and Chen was made a deputy director together with Liu He. Wang Chunzheng was also made deputy secretary general of the CLGFE, filling one of the two deputy positions vacated by Zeng Peiyan and Hua Jianmin. Unlike Hua, Wang had spent his entire career, except for a stint as a researcher, in national planning – joining the State Planning Commission (SPC) in 1963 – and other economic policy work. He graduated in agriculture from the People's University and was made deputy chair of the SPC in 1990 and SPC's deputy party secretary in 1997.[13] He is deputy chair of the renamed National Development and Reform Commission (NDRC) and deputy director of the administrative office of the State Council's Leading Group for Development of the Western Region (*Guowuyuan xibu diqu kaifa lingdao xiaozu*) (LGDWR) (*Junzheng* 2005).

Ma Kai is Wang's superior in the NDRC and LGDWR, respectively as chairperson and director of the administrative office, and is the other new deputy secretary general of the CLGFE. As in the previous policy structure, the chairperson and deputy chairs of the national planning organ are the deputy secretary generals of the CLGFE. Ma's previous major appointments before being promoted to deputy chair of the SPC in 1995 were as deputy chair of the State Council Office for Reform of the Economic Structure (SCORES) between 1993 and 1995 and chief of Beijing's Price Bureau before then. He was appointed as a member of the CCP Central Committee in 1997 and as deputy secretary general of the State Council in 1998. He was re-elected to the Central Committee in 2002 and promoted to chairperson of the NDRC in 2003. He has a postgraduate degree in political economy from the China People's University (*Renda*), but has never worked in a finance organ in the bureaucracy (*China Vitae* 2004).

The deputy directors of the CLGFE administrative office in Wen Jiabao's administration have high profiles. The activities of Chen Xiwen in particular are widely reported. Chen is a member of the 'lost generation'.[14] He graduated from middle school in Shanghai in 1966 soon after the start of the Cultural Revolution. During the Cultural Revolution he was sent to the countryside in the remote northeast province of Heilongjiang. Chen gained entry into *Renda*'s Department of Agricultural Economics when university entrance examinations in China were restored in 1978. He graduated in 1982 and became a researcher at the Institute of Agricultural Economics of the Chinese Academy of Social Sciences. In 1990 he transferred to the State Council's Development Research Centre and in 1994 began work at the CLGFE administrative office (Sina 2005). Chen replaced Duan Yingbi, president of the Agricultural Economics Association, who was appointed president of the China Poverty Fund (*Zhongguo fupin jijinhui*) after he left the CLGFE. Chen has a reputation of being liberal minded and has a higher profile as a deputy director compared to Duan when he was occupying that position. Chen is also director of the administrative office of the Central Leading Working Group on Rural Affairs (*Zhangyang nongcun gongzuo lingdao xiaozu*).

Another deputy director, Yang Linglong, is a graduate of the Central Finance Institute, now the Central Finance and Economics University (*Zhongyang caijing daxue*). Like Chen, he is a member of the 'lost generation'. He was sent to a 'May 7' cadre school in the Henan countryside during the Cultural Revolution and later became a member of a rural propaganda team working in various counties in the poor province of Gansu. In 1971 he became an editor and journalist at *Gansu ribao* (Gansu Daily). From 1983 to 1987 he worked in various official positions in Gansu, before he was promoted to deputy director of the General Office at China's Construction Bank in 1987. The next year he was promoted again, this time to the CCP Central Committee General Office to be the head of its research office. Yang received his promotion to deputy office director of the CLGFE in 1998 (Junzheng 2005).

The last and youngest deputy director, Liu He, is a graduate of *Renda* and Harvard, where he received a Masters in Public Administration from the Kennedy School. After graduating from *Renda*, he taught at his alma mater before moving to the Development Research Centre of the State Council in 1986. A year later he transferred to the SPC, where he worked on the Eighth, Ninth and Tenth Five-Year Plans. In 1998 he was appointed deputy chair of the Standing Committee of the State IT Centre (*Guojia xinxi zhongxin*). Between 2001 and 2003 he was deputy director of the State Council Office for IT Development and Promotion (*Guowuyuan xinxihua gongzuo bangongshi*). In 2003 he joined the Office of the CLGFE (CDRF 2006).

Of particular relevance to our discussion on renminbi policy in this chapter of the members of the CLGFE that we have not yet covered are Wu Yi, Hui Liangyu and Li Rongrong. Wu Yi is the only woman in the CLGFE. She graduated and worked for many years as a petroleum engineer before becoming party secretary and deputy chief executive officer (CEO) of Beijing Yanshan Petrochemical Corporation in 1983. From 1988 to 1991 she was deputy mayor of Beijing. She was appointed as deputy minister of the MOFERT (later renamed MOFTEC – Ministry of Foreign Trade and Economic Cooperation) in 1991 and was promoted to minister of MOFTEC in 1997. Wu was elected to the CCP Central Committee at the Fourteenth, Fifteenth and Sixteenth Party Congresses and into the Politburo at the Sixteenth Party Congress (*Fazhi ribao* 2003). She is extremely competent and is entrusted to oversee all WTO-related work in the bureaucracy. She was the minister appointed to manage the central government's response to SARS (severe acute respiratory syndrome), when the government appeared to be floundering in the face of the crisis around 2003. Her performance during the SARS crisis has considerably enhanced her reputation and influence.

Hui Liangyu, a member of the Muslim Hui nationality, graduated from Jilin Agricultural College in 1966. Like Yang Linglong, he was sent to a 'May 7' cadre school – in his case to a school in Jilin Province – during the Cultural Revolution. He worked in Jilin on agricultural research and policy until promoted in 1987 to be deputy governor of Jilin and later was appointed as deputy party secretary. Hui was later promoted to party secretary of Anhui – one of the poorest provinces in China[15] – in 1998 and was made party secretary of Jiangsu in 2002. He was elected to the CCP Central Committee at the Fifteenth and Sixteenth Party Congresses and promoted to the Politburo in 2003. In 2003 he was also appointed as a vice-premier and deputy head of the Central Leading Group on Rural Affairs (*Fazhi ribao* 2003; Xinhua 2006a).

Li Rongrong, the most junior of the CLGFE members, is a graduate in chemical engineering from Tianjin University. He had hands-on experience in industry, including as a factory director, before being appointed as the deputy director, Planning and Economic Commission of Jiangsu Province in 1986. In 1992 he was appointed secretary general and deputy chair of the State Economic and Trade Commission and in 2003 was promoted to chairperson of the State Assets Supervision and Administration Commission (SASAC). He was elected to the CCP Central Committee at the Sixteenth Party Congress (Xinhua 2006b).

Key Institutional Policy Actors

National Development and Reform Commission

A notable difference between Figures 5.2 and 6.2 is the name change of the State Development Planning Commission (SDPC) to the National Development and Reform Commission (*Guojia fazhan he gaige weiyuanhui*). In Chapter 5 we expressed the view that the SDPC would lose influence with the end of central planning and adoption of the market. We did not anticipate that the nature of the SDPC would change under the post-Jiang party leadership, allowing it to retain a considerable level of influence in the bureaucracy. Post-Jiang the SDPC has been restructured and reinvented as the NDRC. The new body retains the traditional planning and policy research functions of the SDPC, but also incorporates the State Council Office for Reform of the Economic Structure, which was the think-tank of Zhu Rongji, and parts of the State Economic and

Trade Commission (SETC). The main functions of the NDRC include that it 'participate in the formulation of fiscal and monetary policies ... control and monitor the total size of China's foreign debts ... and maintain the balance of international payments' (NDRC 2006a). The NDRC also has an Office of Policy Studies that is to 'organize studies on issues concerning economic and social development, reform and opening-up, and the international economy' (NDRC 2006a). Soon after its creation, the NDRC produced a report that covered 13 critical issues facing China. Among the issues were Sino–US relations, Taiwan, globalization and poverty (Brahm 2003). The NDRC, by taking over the SCORES, has become more influential than when it was the SDPC, and judging by its list of main functions it certainly expects and is expected to play an important role in any exchange rate policymaking.

Beyond doubt there is less 'planning',[16] but with the SDPC's reinvention as the NDRC, and as its functions indicate, its influence in macroeconomic policymaking has not declined but in fact has increased under Hu Jintao and Wen Jiabao. One major reason is the official newly created emphasis on both poverty reduction and income inequality, especially in the countryside, in the face of widespread social unrest. While Zhu Rongji's (and Jiang Zemin's) focus was on WTO entry to integrate China into the global economy, with China now in the WTO, Hu and Wen have switched emphasis to addressing rural poverty. By incorporating the SCORES, the NDRC is able to stamp its influence on macroeconomic policymaking through its research into the social and political impacts of macroeconomic policy.

Any appreciation of the renminbi will disadvantage agriculture and undo some of the efforts since 2004 to provide support by reducing rural taxation and increasing rural subsidies. Expectation was that the renminbi would appreciate if the currency peg was discontinued and the renminbi was allowed to float freely. Hence the NDRC would not have favoured a free float of the renminbi. It would have preferred the peg to continue but it could live with a managed float exchange rate system that would prevent the renminbi from appreciating to a level that threatened the interests of the countryside.

In Chapter 5 we argued that the SDPC favoured a fixed exchange rate during the AFC because of its difficulty in hedging foreign exchange risks in its large infrastructure projects in the absence of developed foreign exchange forward markets. This was no longer an issue in 2005 because the expectation then was for renminbi revaluation not devaluation, so the immediate foreign exchange risk was minimal. And any official move to free the fixed exchange rate would surely be accompanied in the long term by official actions to develop meaningful foreign exchange forward markets.

Ministry of Commerce (MOC)
The Ministry of Foreign Trade and Economic Cooperation does not exist in the new policy structure. It has been merged with the former Ministry of Commerce and elements from the State Economic and Trade Commission to form the mega Ministry of Commerce. The new mega ministry has the mandate to promote and regulate domestic as well as foreign trade and investment. For foreign trade and investment, its responsibilities include ensuring that Chinese laws are in harmony with China's international treaties and agreements, representing China in dealings with the WTO and guiding and regulating foreign investment. On the domestic side of its work, one responsibility is to integrate the domestic market by overcoming regional protectionism (MOC 2006).

The national policy emphasis on China's international obligations and desire to remove regional protectionism insinuates de-emphasis of the MOFTEC's former role of promoting exports. Furthermore, with WTO membership opening up many previously closed industrial sectors to foreign ownership, there is the issue of whether China's assets are being sold too cheaply to foreigners because of a perceived undervaluation of the renminbi. Foreign investment is no longer seen exclusively as a vehicle to increase exports, and is now also very much perceived as a way that foreign corporations penetrate the Chinese market. Revaluing the renminbi makes Chinese assets more expensive to foreigners and raises the barrier to entry to potential foreign competitors into China's domestic market.

On the question of fixed versus flexible exchange rate, we concluded in Chapter 5 that producers of non-traded goods and import-competing producers favour a flexible rate, which guarantees monetary autonomy, while export-oriented producers favour a fixed rate to minimize transaction costs in foreign trade. The MOC thus incorporates a much more diverse and to some extent inherently contradictory set of interests in its responsibilities than the MOFTEC. Its position on the exchange rate is therefore not as predictable as the position held by the MOFTEC, which because it represented largely the interests of exporters, favoured a low and fixed renminbi.

People's Bank of China
Of all the institutional policymaking actors, the PBC would appear at first glance to have been the one most in favour of discontinuing the renminbi–US dollar peg and allowing the renminbi to appreciate. The PBC is aware that China's capital account is porous in practice. Xie Ping, general manager of the Central Huijin Investment Corporation, when he was chief of the PBC's research department said openly at a conference in the Netherlands in 2003 that it is 'almost impossible' to control capital flows and 'capital account liberalization is inevitable and will be fulfilled much more quickly than we

expect'. Xie Ping also emphasized what is known commonly among economists: China cannot have an independent monetary policy with a currency peg (Xie 2003, p. 286). This problem was highlighted in Chapter 3 where we showed how the PBC is experiencing difficulty in controlling China's money supply and inflation in the face of continuing growth in foreign reserves. We pointed out in Chapter 5 that with international capital mobility, a flexible exchange rate makes monetary policy more effective than fiscal policy in macroeconomic management and this makes the PBC more influential than the MOF in determining macroeconomic policy. During the AFC, the PBC was concerned with devaluation causing domestic inflation. In 2004–05 it was the difficulty of controlling domestic credit and therefore inflation with a pegged exchange rate that was the PBC's major concern.

Commercial banks were cash rich as a result of the huge increases in foreign exchange inflows, despite sterilization efforts of the PBC, as explained in Chapter 3. Deposit rates remained controlled and this maintained a wide spread between deposit and lending rates to help boost the profits of banks (Xie 2003, p. 286), most likely to make them ready for initial public offering (IPO) listings.[17] Official control over interest rates is also a means for the Chinese government to keep the cost of government borrowing low, and is reflected in the relatively flat yield curve for Chinese government bonds (Bottelier 2005, pp. 16–17). Hence, while government bonds with short maturities can be competitive because they are risk-free, those with long maturities are not so attractive and commercial banks prefer to lend their funds elsewhere and are often allocated quotas of government bonds that they have to purchase.[18] With official control over interest rates, commercial banks are therefore keen to continue to lend to enterprises and households and not purchase official bills and bonds, and have to be restrained with administrative measures during periods of monetary tightening.[19] But this has not always significantly reduced bank lending when required. New bank loans during boom times will initially lower the ratio of loans that are non-performing and make the banks look good, but are likely to increase the ratio in the future.

The PBC also has its own problems with regard to non-performing loans (NPLs). In 1998, the central government transferred about RMB1.4 trillion (US$170 billion) of non-performing loans of the Agricultural Bank of China (ABC), Bank of China, China Construction Bank (CCB) and Industrial and Commercial Bank of China (ICBC) to four newly created state-owned asset management corporations (AMCs).[20] The transfer of NPLs and the later injection of new capital to these banks were designed, certainly in the case of the BOC, CCB and ICBC, to clean up their balance sheets and increase their capital–asset ratios with the aim of preparing these banks for future IPO listings (Hope and Hu 2006; Yu Ni 2005).

The PBC had, by 27 June 2005, lent RMB1.2 trillion (US$150.9 billion) to the four AMCs to help them divest the NPLs of the 'big four' and other commercial banks, but the AMCs were able to dispose of only 27 per cent of NPLs from China's five largest commercial banks (PWC 2005, November). The recovery rate on NPLs was so low that the AMCs had trouble paying the interest owed to the PBC (Yu Ni 2005). The PBC does not normally favour administrative measures to control credit since they can be very blunt and arbitrary, but more importantly, they permit other policy organs to intrude into credit policy, which the PBC sees as its turf. But it was difficult for the authorities in 2005 to avoid using administrative measures to discourage lending when the PBC had difficulty controlling the money supply as a result of not only a fixed exchange rate, but also official decisions to keep the cost of government borrowings low and use AMCs to handle commercial banks' NPLs.

The PBC's interest is in having the AMCs successfully disinvest themselves of their NPLs. This inclines it to call for keeping interest rates low and the exchange rate stable so as not to make non-performing assets less attractive to potential domestic and foreign investors. The PBC is also keen not to see any further increase in NPLs. Excess investment in manufacturing in China has resulted in falling manufacturing prices and declining terms of trade. Renminbi revaluation will put further pressure on prices and raise the immediate likelihood of more NPLs. But failure to control bank lending will increase NPLs in the future. The PBC is therefore not against a short-term policy combination of low interest rates and a stable exchange rate, and reliance on administrative measures to ration credit. This conjecture is supported by comments on the disposal of NPLs that Xie Ping made at a conference, where he said that the PBC supports this policy combination (Yu Ning 2004).[21] The PBC was acting more like a policy bank than a central bank when it issued loans to the AMCs and this has influenced its policy outlook.

There is also the issue of how renminbi revaluation would affect the capitalization of banks. Reducing the share of NPLs improves capital–asset ratios of banks, but renminbi revaluation has the opposite effect. In 2004 the central government had injected US$60 billion of its foreign reserves into the Bank of China, China Construction Bank and Industrial and Commercial Bank of China. The injection of foreign reserves into these banks presents the advantage of reducing the stock of official foreign reserves, assuming of course that these banks had not sold their US$60 billion injection on to the PBC. If our assumption is correct, then any significant revaluation of the renminbi would reduce the value of the US$60 billion assets in the balance sheet of these banks and lower their capital–asset ratios. [22] While ensuring commercial banks have adequate capital–asset ratios is not the direct responsibility of the PBC – it is the responsibility of the China Banking Regulatory Commission (CBRC) – the ratios relate to finance safety, which is the concern of the CLGFS, and current and former PBC governors Zhou Xiaochuan and Dai Xianglong together with Wen Jiabao are its three most senior members (WL 2002). Thus the PBC is comfortable with a managed float exchange rate system, which will still grant it pre-eminence in macroeconomic policymaking but permits policy intervention to control the speed of any revaluation of the renminbi. It is not widely known, but Yu Yongding had proposed this system in his 2004 chapter.[23]

Ministry of Finance

In recent years the MOF has chalked up considerable outward loans. They include substantial loans to sub-national governments. By the middle of 2005 sub-national governments had borrowed RMB141 billion (US$17.4 billion) from the MOF, using their share of tax revenues as collateral. They have used these loans to settle the accounts of customers of underperforming local financial institutions that the PBC had shut down. Loans owed to the MOF by poor counties have exceeded 100 per cent of county revenue in many cases, driving these counties into deficit (Yu Ni 2005). This manifests the problem of poor corporate and state governance, which can be solved only in the long term. In the short term, the MOF seeks to recover as much as possible from these loans, but appreciation of the renminbi will very likely lower the chances of it being successful. Renminbi appreciation lowers prices and increases real interest rates, and most of the poor counties struggling to repay MOF loans rely on agriculture, which will be affected adversely by a higher renminbi.

The MOF has overseen a series of budgetary deficits since about 1996 and wants to reduce these deficits. It would therefore prefer that agriculture be supported through the exchange rate rather than through increased fiscal outlays, and so would support abolishing the export rebate and cutting fiscal subsidies to exports, in lieu of renminbi revaluation. Such a strategy would reduce the state's fiscal burden and lower the pressure for renminbi revaluation without disadvantaging agriculture.[24] Wu Yi, an influential member of the CLGFE as indicated above, led the charge in 2003 to reform the export rebate policy (HKTDC 2003) and, as we indicated in Chapters 3 and 4, export rebate rates were lowered in 2004 and both the actual amount of rebates paid and rate of export subsidy fell in 2005. But as we also pointed out in Chapter 3, protests from local governments prevented the central government from being able to pass on to local governments more responsibility for paying out the export rebates.

DISCONTINUATION OF THE CURRENCY PEG

China has discontinued the renminbi–US dollar peg and adopted a managed float exchange rate system, where the value of the renminbi is pegged against the value of a basket of currencies, allowing a movement of a maximum +/–3 per cent in any given day.[25] The US had applied immense pressure on China to discontinue the renminbi–US dollar peg and substantially revalue the renminbi. In the end, China had attended to the former but not the latter. While some observers speak of US achievement, others question whether the US had actually 'made' China do anything different from what it intended anyway.

There is without doubt a fundamental shift in emphasis between the Jiang Zemin–Zhu Rongji and the Hu Jintao–Wen Jiabao leadership.[26] While the former leadership was deeply concerned with engaging the global economy, the latter is more concerned with poverty and income inequality, especially in the countryside and western China. Jiang Zemin and Zhu Rongji were just as concerned as Hu Jintao and Wen Jiabao with social stability. But it is understandable why the former were focused more on integrating China into the global economy and obtaining WTO membership than on the destabilizing effects of globalization. Jiang became party leader in 1989 after the most serious public challenge to CCP rule since the establishment of the People's Republic and at about the same time as communism collapsed in Eastern Europe. These two events created a consensus among senior CCP leaders that the CCP could retain power in the long run and avoid the fate of the communist parties of Eastern Europe only through market reform and engagement with the global economy. Post-Jiang, China is a recognized global economic power and member of the WTO. In this new era, Hu and Wen are less concerned with rapid enlargement of the size of the economic pie than with a more equitable distribution of that pie.

China does not enjoy a comparative advantage in agriculture and as a result its countryside has been particularly hit hard by globalization. In 2002 the urban–rural income gap accounted for between 26 and 40 per cent of total income inequality in China. This is 10 per cent higher than the highest contributions of urban–rural income inequality to total income inequality for other countries (Sicular et al. 2007, p. 122). Post-WTO entry incomes of village residents were projected in a Chinese Academy of Social Sciences (CASS) study to fall by 2.1 per cent, and rental price of agricultural land by 18.4 per cent. In addition, agriculture was projected to lose 10 million jobs as a result of WTO entry (Li et al. 2000, p. 70).[27] According to a World Bank study, the contribution of primary sector (mainly agriculture) growth to poverty reduction between 1980 and 2001 was four times the contribution from secondary and tertiary sectors, despite the fall in the share of the primary sector in GDP (Ravallion and Chen 2004, cited in Ravallion 2004). Ravallion (2004, p. 11) in another World Bank study made the poignant observation that: 'Arguably the bulk of China's trade reform has been after the times of most rapid poverty reduction, and (indeed) in times of relatively stagnant poverty measures'. What these studies clearly demonstrate is that if poverty is to be successfully eliminated in China, the focus of policy has to be on agriculture. This discovery is not surprising when one realizes that the primary sector in 2005 provided 44.8 per cent of national employment despite accounting for only 12.6 per cent of GDP (NBS 2006, Tables 3.2 and 5.1). The benefits from globalization are insufficient to reduce poverty significantly.

Moreover, fiscal decentralization has made many local governments worse off, forcing them to impose informal levies to fund public goods. The plight of many rural communities is often further exacerbated by local official corruption. Rural unrests are growing and there is a subtle but perceptible shift in policy emphasis under Hu and Wen from China engaging with the global economy to China confronting the social costs of engaging with the global economy. Hu, Wen and other senior party leaders have recognized that globalization-generated economic growth alone will not keep the CCP in power.

This realization is reflected in the reconfiguration of China's exchange rate policymaking structure that is manifested in the renewed influence of the restructured and renamed NDRC and the appointment of a number of party leaders as members of the CLGFE and officials to important positions in the CLGFE administrative office who, from our brief descriptions of their backgrounds earlier, are clearly strong advocates for the rural sector and poor western regions. Hu Jintao himself was at one time party secretary of the poor autonomous region of Tibet and has been actively promoting many of his protégés with long periods of service in the poor northwestern regions – members of the so-called Northwestern Faction – to top party positions (Lam 2007). It is no coincidence that Wang Chunzheng, the director of the CLGFE office (ministerial level) and two of his deputies (vice-ministerial level) have backgrounds in agriculture. Chen Xiwen, who is credited with drafting a series of central government documents that reduce tax burdens on farmers and provide subsidies for agriculture, has a very high public profile. He has expressed sympathy for protestors in the countryside in media interviews, including with two Hong Kong-based newspapers where he praised *Zhongguo nongmin diaocha* and admitted that violent protests in the countryside have alerted central leaders to problems in the countryside.[28] He also emphasized that the 'san nong' problems must be solved (*fei jiejue buke*).

The three key ministries in exchange rate policy are the NDRC, PBC and MOF. The MOC does not have a clear currency policy preference, being a mega ministry responsible for foreign as well as domestic trade. The long-term preferences of the PBC for a flexible exchange rate regime and the MOF for a fixed exchange rate regime remain. But the immediate concern of the CCP leadership is rural poverty and social instability. Hence the NDRC is against free float of the renminbi because this will at least in the short term lead to substantial appreciation, which adversely affects agriculture. The NDRC finds support from the PBC as substantial renminbi appreciation is likely to create more NPLs and worsen the finances of AMCs. However, Chinese policymakers have learnt from history – as recent as 1988–89 – that high inflation is socially destabilizing and can seriously threaten party rule. Historically, party rule was never threatened by deflation. On the contrary, the experience of Chinese policymakers with deflation or what they termed retrenchment (*jinsuo*) was as a cure for runaway inflation. That is why party leaders, although they are alert to possible deflation *à la* Mckinnon resulting from the discontinuation of the currency peg, are more concerned with the strong likelihood of high inflation with continuation of the peg. The NDRC, while it does not support substantial renminbi revaluation in the short term, recognizes that there must be a substitute for renminbi revaluation to control inflation, lest it spirals out of control. The PBC does not favour administrative measures to control credit, but it has no choice in the short term because substantial appreciation is not an option. The NDRC, with its strong planning tradition, does not object to administrative measures because they give the NDRC influence over credit policy, which would normally be the preserve of the PBC. However, the NDRC also realizes that administrative measures in a market economy are no longer as effective as they were in China's previous highly centralized economy. Thus it sees a role for currency revaluation as well as administrative measures to control inflation, and supports a managed float exchange rate. A managed float enables monetary independence and allows gradual revaluation of the renminbi, but also permits a reverse policy of devaluation if deflation threatens.

Only the MOF among the three key ministries would be in favour of retaining the currency peg, but it is not as influential as the other two ministries. All the key institutional policymakers with views on the exchange rate are represented in the CLGFE. Of the members in the CLGFE that do not formally represent the NDRC, PBC or MOF, Wu Yi has special responsibility over China's relations with the WTO and is therefore the de facto spokesperson for the MOC. As indicated above, she was a strong advocate of ending export rebates and is one of the most internationally minded among China's leadership. She is therefore not adverse to reducing support to exports. But being mindful of the adverse impact of renminbi devaluation on the rural economy, she would have supported the managed float that allows gradual appreciation of the renminbi. Li Rongrong as head of the SASAC is responsible for state-owned enterprises (SOEs), which as a group continue to underperform and are the major source of NPLs in banks. Renminbi appreciation lowers prices, increases real interest rates and puts pressure on SOEs. He would have supported retaining the peg, but he is the most junior member in the CLGFE and likely to be the least influential.

In the end, the CLGFE decided to discontinue the peg and allow the renminbi to appreciate, but not to the extent that it impacts adversely on agriculture, while efforts are made at the same time to reconfigure the budget to shift the onus of assisting the rural sector in the long term away from the exchange rate to fiscal policy. Exporters no longer have an obvious advocate on their behalf without the MOFTEC and reducing support to exports has become part of this reconfiguration. Preliminary moves have been made to reduce support to exports – we estimated in Chapter 4 that export subsidies and renminbi rate of return from each US dollar of exports have declined significantly – and this is likely to continue as China's latest Five-Year Plan (2006–2010), the Eleventh, has signalled a shift away from export- to domestic demand-driven economic growth (NDRC 2006b, Chapter 1). This reorientation away from exports allows more official support to be given to the rural sector, but it will also slow the excess investment in export production and arrest the decline in China's terms of trade. In examining China's decision to discontinue the renminbi–US dollar peg and replace it with a managed float exchange rate it is clear that, while institutional interests and personal backgrounds were important, what was pivotal was the fear among senior party leaders of social instability from poverty and income inequality in the countryside and high inflation.

NOTES

1. They were elected as president and premier at the next National People's Congress the following March.
2. That meeting was held on 15–17 November. US–China WTO final negotiations were conducted on 10–15 November, with signing of the final agreement on 15 November. See Li et al. (1999).
3. One of the proposals in the draft regulations allows incorporated foreign banks the right to issue credit cards.
4. See for example the advertisement of the Industrial Commercial Bank of China (Asia) for NDF contracts. The advertisement informs potential customers that they 'can seize the investment opportunities by subscribing the renminbi NDF contract of buying or selling renminbi against US dollars depending on your expectation of the movement of the renminbi exchange rate' (http://www.icbcasia.com/eng/retail/invest/rmbndf.shtml) (accessed 12 May 2006).

5.   The view of the IMF was clearly stated in its 2004 World Economic Outlook and reiterated by its managing director, Rodrigo de Rato, at a meeting with journalists (Becker 2004).
6.   It is significant that the IMF did not call for a lifting of capital controls, or for an explicit appreciation of the renminbi; what it proposed was a gradual increase in flexibility for the renminbi. Against much pressure on it by the US Congress, the IMF had resisted labelling China a currency manipulator. It recognized that there was a wide range of opinion on the equilibrium renminbi exchange rate and that unpredictable capital flows are a major driver of China's balance of payments.
7.   One study (Goh and Kim 2006) indicated that the renminbi rate in 2000–2002 was close to the equilibrium rate.
8.   He is also director of the World Economics and Politics Research Institute of China's Academy of Social Sciences.
9.   The centre's renminbi project was begun in 2002. The Chinese translation is of Mckinnon and Schnabl's 2003 paper, 'China: stabilizing or deflationary influence in east Asia', which was available at http:www.stanford.edu/~mckinnon/papers/china.pdf.
10. Official data underestimate investment as much of what is often classified as government consumption is actually investment. In 2004 net exports contributed about 2 per cent to the 10.1 per cent growth in GDP or 20 per cent of GDP growth (calculation based on data in World Bank 2006, pp. 3 and 11).
11. Public expenditure on health as a share of GDP in China remained constant between 1990 and 2002 at 2 per cent. This compares with the 2002 shares of 8 per cent in Norway, 6.6 per cent in the US, 3.5 per cent in Russia and 1.5 per cent in Vietnam (UNDP 2005, pp. 285–6). Illiteracy rates – one of the sub-sets of indicators that are used to calculate the HDI – vary enormously between regions in China. Provincial rates of illiteracy and semi-illiteracy range from a low of 1.3, 1.6 and 1.7 per cent of population in Beijing, Liaoning and Tianjin to a high of 24.8, 32.2 and 61.7 per cent in Gansu, Qinghai and Tibet (Yang and Zhang 2001, pp. 227–8).
12. This is recognized in the Eleventh Five-Year Plan approved by the National People's Congress in March 2006.
13. In 2005 he published an article in the *People's Daily* lauding the contributions of Chen Yun, a deceased senior party leader, to Chinese economic thought and the development of China's economy (Wang 2005). Chen was one of Deng Xiaoping's close colleagues and was at one time in charge of China's economy and its chief economic planner. While Chen supported economic reform, he was a firm believer in the importance of maintaining balance in the economy – including the balance between industry and agriculture – and wary of over-reliance on the market.
14. This term refers to the generation of which so many never recovered their lost opportunity to an education during the Cultural Revolution and were never able to fulfil their potential.
15. One of Anhui's most famous exports is household maids in the employment of the growing number of middle- and upper-income families in the rich cities of China.
16. For the first time in the history of the PRC's five-year plans, major economic indictors in the Eleventh Five-Year Plan (put forward in 2006) are presented as 'anticipated' rather than obligatory. See NDRC (2006b, Chapter 1).
17. The spread in late 2004 when deposit and lending rates were raised to cool the economy was about 3 per cent. See http://www.pbc.gov.cn/detail.asp?col=462&ID=272 and http://www.pbc.gov.cn/detail.asp?col=462&ID=978 (both accessed 23 August 2006).
18. The PBC has less of a problem, since almost all PBC bills are short-term maturity (Bottelier 2005, p. 15).
19. As Ma Kai explained, the government's 'visible hand' had to work in conjunction with the market's 'invisible hand' to achieve 'macro-control' (Yu Jingbo 2005).
20. The banks are the 'big four' state-owned commercial banks in China.
21. With a booming economy and rising foreign reserves, the PBC, according to Xie, had to issue central bank notes and use administrative measures to achieve these twin goals (Yu Ning 2004).
22. We start with the accounting identity (denoted in renminbi units): A (assets) = L (liabilities) + P (proprietorship). Rearranging the identity, we can write: C (capital–asset ratio) = P/A =

$1-(L/A)$. For simplicity, we assume no foreign currency liabilities, since most liabilities of the banks are in renminbi. Renminbi revaluation reduces the value of A and therefore the value of C.

23. Discontinuation of the currency peg would increase China's monetary independence and signal to the rest of the world that China is a 'responsible big country', which actively seeks to fix its bilateral trade imbalances with other countries (Yu 2004, pp. 85–6). Yu recommended allowing the exchange rate in the long run to deviate up to 15 per cent from its benchmark rate.

24. It is important to emphasize here that export subsidies flow largely to the manufacturing sector.

25. The currencies are the US dollar, euro, yen, Korean won, Singaporean dollar, pound sterling, Malaysian ringgit, Russian rouble, Australian dollar, Thai baht and Canadian dollar.

26. This was confirmed at the CCP's Sixth Plenum in October 2006 when it approved the resolution on building 'a harmonious socialist society' (*hexie shehuizhuyi*) (CCP 2006).

27. These projections were derived from the authors' static computable general equilibrium model.

28. The newspapers are the *Sing Tao* (2005) and *South China Morning Post* (Wang Xiangwei 2005). See also *Anhui News* (2005).

7. Conclusion

It is clear from our analysis that China's exchange rate policies since 1949 have been determined first and foremost by assessments of, and aspirations for, China's political economy. Early in the reform period, the politics of socialism still produced a highly centralized form of economic organization and a rigid exchange rate regime. When the leadership of the Chinese Communist Party (CCP) decided to abandon the plan economy in favour of a government–market mix involving intensive engagement with the global economy, China's exchange rate policies became vitally important – to China and to the world outside.

To the Chinese authorities in 2006, exchange rate policy matters are considered in terms of their impact upon not just the national economy but also domestic social stability, which has long been among the most crucial of national priorities. To the world outside, China's exchange rate policies affect global distributions in balances of trade and payments. Nations whose economies rely ever more heavily on trade and commerce with China favour policies that will stimulate business on terms favourable to themselves. This is especially true of nations in the Asia Pacific that engage with China as an economic partner rather than as a strategic threat. While the US government and national policy are in the hands of a powerful clique of 'realist' and 'dragon slayer' leaders, their perspective shaping policy perceives China's exchange rate policy as contributing to China's ascent as a 'great power' and thus as a potential strategic competitor rather than a valuable economic partner to the US.

During the Asian financial crisis, the major concern in China over exchange rate policy was how to achieve 8 per cent growth in GDP, which was deemed necessary to soak up retrenched workers from state-owned enterprises (SOEs), without losing control over inflation. In 2005, when the renminbi–US dollar peg was discontinued, policy attention was on how to not disadvantage the countryside while reining in inflation. We see an overriding concern in both periods for the maintenance of social stability. The former period was, however, under the leadership of Jiang Zemin and Zhu Rongji, who while concerned with social stability, paid more attention than any previous Chinese government to the globalization of China's economy, believing that in the long run this was the best guarantee for preserving party rule. The shift in emphasis with the ascension of Hu Jintao and Wen Jiabao to party leadership was inspired by their view, when confronted with serious social instability, that globalization on its own is no quick panacea for poverty.

The difference in emphasis of the two sets of leaders is reflected in the relative influences of the key ministries in macroeconomic policymaking. The focus of Jiang and Zhu on the benefits of globalization propelled the People's Bank of China to be the most influential ministry in macroeconomic policymaking at the expense of the State Development and Planning Commission (SDPC) and the Ministry of Finance. But the focus of Hu and Wen on the costs of globalization led to the reconfiguration of the SDPC into the National Development and Reform Commission (NDRC) and allowed it to be a dominant player again in macroeconomic policymaking.

China's exchange rate policies were and are constrained by the rules and mechanics, as well as the vagaries, of the global economy. But China has choices within these constraints, and developments in China's exchange rate policy indicate a move towards national policy independence. As we have made clear in Chapters 5 and 6, China's exchange rate decisions were not simply answering to external (principally US) pressure but were formed on the basis of domestic assessments of domestic circumstances to serve domestic interests, whatever other nations such as the US may like to think of their own capacity to pressure China into compliance. Exchange rate decisions are made on the basis of what policymakers perceive to be in the nation's best interests and thus constitute dynamic interplay between national priorities and the interests of institutional and non-institutional actors in the policy arena.

Overall we see that China's exchange rate policy decisions mirror the confidence that China is exhibiting while ever more of the nation's people and their leaders respond to the seemingly relentless forces of globalization – not yet with alacrity, but certainly no longer with trepidation as in earlier times. If we cast globalization as a 'big bad wolf', China's exchange rate policy signals a national government that is clearly no longer afraid. Chinese authorities and many in the commercial centres today engage with globalization on their own terms, recognizing possible opportunities for personal and national benefit rather than an intruding, unstoppable and harmful force threatening both national stability and national sovereignty.

As the argument of this book details across the chapters, policymaking in China became more institutionalized as the politics of reform and the practical results that followed served to reconfigure the institutional landscape. The case-studies we have discussed demonstrate clearly how China's post-Mao economic policymaking structure is the product of specific human and institutional policy actors who are influenced not only by their relative ranks in the bureaucratic hierarchy that produce particular policies, but also by distinctive concerns and personal experiences that are often unique to China's national experience. In this general sense, then, China's exchange rate policies are doubtlessly influenced by a personal dimension that concerns the human nature of policymakers and their understanding of, and response to, the process of national policymaking. But then there is the complex web of historical, political, economic, strategic and social factors on which, through which, and for which all national policies are made. It is this labyrinthine mix that makes China's exchange rate policymaking *sui generis*. The policy process for the renminbi exchange rate is, like all national policies in China, intricate and difficult to untangle. But it is comprehensible nonetheless, as we have attempted to demonstrate in this book.

References

ACFB (Editorial Committee of *Almanac of China's Finance and Banking*) (various issues since 1986), *Almanac of China's Finance and Banking*, Beijing: Zhongguo jinrong.

ACFERT (Editorial Committee of *Almanac of China's Foreign Economic Relations and Trade*) (1991), *Almanac of China's Foreign Economic Relations and Trade*, Beijing: Zhongguo shehui kexue chubanshe.

Anderson, Jonathan (2004), 'How I learned to stop worrying and forget the yuan', *Far Eastern Economic Review*, **168** (1), 37–42.

Anderson, Kym (1990), *Changing Comparative Advantages in China: Effects on Food, Feed and Fibre Markets*, Paris: Development Centre of OECD.

Anhui News (2005), 'Zhongyang caijing lingdao xiaozu guanyuan cheng san nong wenti fei jiejue buke' (Central Leading Group in Finance and Economics official declares that the *san nong* problems must be solved), http://finance.anhuinews.com/system/2005/02/24/001141291.shtml (accessed 9 March 2007).

Anon. (1994), *Who's Who in China: Current Leaders*, Beijing: Beijing Foreign Languages Press.

Anon. (1998), 'Renminbi bu xuyao ye buhui bianzhi' (The RMB does not have to devalue and will not devalue), *Zhongguo jinrong* (China's Finance), **9**, 1.

Appleyard, Dennis R. and Alfred J. Field (1998), *International Economics*, International edition, San Francisco, CA: McGraw-Hill.

Ba Shusong (1999), *Zhongguo waihui shichang yunxing yanjiu* (A study of China's foreign exchange market), Beijing: Jingji kexue chubanshe.

Bachman, David (2001), 'The paradox of analysing elite politics under Jiang', *China Journal*, **45**, January, 95–100.

Bai Hejin (ed.) (2002), *Zhonghua renmin gongheguo jingji dashi jiyao, 1978–2001* (Major economic events of the People's Republic of China, 1978–2001), Beijing: Zhongguo jihua chubanshe.

Bai Hejin et al. (1998), *Jingji Zhongguo* (Economics-oriented China), Beijing: Caizheng jingji chubanshe.

Balassa, Bela (1964), 'The purchasing power parity doctrine: a reappraisal', *Journal of Political Economy*, **72**, 584–96.

Banister, Judith (2004), 'Manufacturing employment and compensation in China', Bureau of Labor Statistics, http://www.bls.gov/fls/#publications (accessed 5 September 2005).

Banister, Judith (2005), 'Manufacturing earnings and compensation in China', *Monthly Labor Review*, **8**, August, 22–40.

Bao Kexin (1996), 'Zhongguo xian jieduan huilü jizhi de xuanze' (The present choice of China's exchange rate regime), in Research Department of China Foreign Exchange Trading Centre (ed.), *Zhongguo waihui shichang de shijian yu tansuo* (Practices and experiments of China's foreign exchange market), Beijing: Zhongguo jinrong chubanshe.

Bartke, Wolfgang (1991), *Who's Who in the People's Republic of China*, 3rd edition, Munich: K.G. Saur.

Baum, Richard (1994), *Burying Mao*, Princeton, NJ: Princeton University Press.

Baum, Richard and Alexei Shevchenko (1999), 'The "state of the state"', in Merle Goldman and Roderick MacFarquhar (eds), *The Paradox of China's Post-Mao Reforms*, Cambridge: Harvard University Press.

Beck, Simon (1998), 'Tang gives full backing to Clinton', *South China Morning Post*, 30 September, http://www.scmp.com (accessed 30 September 1998).

Becker, Elizabeth (2004), 'IMF asks China to free its currency from dollar', *New York Times*, 30 September, http:www.nytimes.com/2004/09/30/business/worldbusiness/30trade.html (accessed 30 September 2004).

Bell, Michael W., Hoe Ee Khor and Kalpana Kochhar (1993), 'China at the threshold of market economy', Occasional Paper, No. 107, Washington, DC: International Monetary Fund.

Bernanke, Ben S. (2005), 'The global saving glut and the US current account deficit', Sandridge Lecture, Virginia Association of Economics, Richmond, Virginia, 10 March, http://www.federalreserve.gov/boarddocs/speeches/2005/200503102/de (accessed 21 March 2006).

Bloomberg (2003), 'China may end yuan's peg next year to slow inflation', *New Straits Times*, 31 December, B16.

Borensztein, Eduardo and Paul R. Masson (1993), 'Exchange arrangements of previously centrally planned economies', International Monetary Fund Occasional Paper, No. 102.

Bottelier, Pieter (2005), 'China's emerging domestic debt markets: facts and issues', *Perspectives*, 6 (2), 11–24, http://www.oycf.org/Perspectives/29_06302005/3_Bottelier_DebtMarket.pdf (accessed 31 August 2006).

Boulding, Kenneth E. (1959), 'National images and international systems', *Journal of Conflict Resolution*, **3**, 120–31.

Boulding, Kenneth E. (1969), 'National images and international systems', in James N. Rosenau (ed.), *International Politics and Foreign Policy*, New York: Free Press.

Brahm, Laurence (2003), 'A wake-up call for China's new leaders', *South China Morning Post*, 30 August, http://www.scmp.com/focusnews/ZZZOJW8RHJD.html (accessed 23 September 2003).

Broz, J. Lawrence (2002), 'Political system transparency and monetary commitment regimes', *International Organization*, **56**, 861–7.

Bureau of Economic Analysis (BEA) (2006), 'National Economic Accounts: gross domestic product', http://www.bea.gov/bea/dn/home/gdp.htm (accessed 17 March 2006).

Bureau of Labor Statistics (BLS) (2004), 'International comparisons of hourly compensation costs for production workers in manufacturing', 18 November, http://www.bls.gov/news.release/pdf/ichcc.pdf (accessed 5 September 2005).

Calvo, Guillermo A. and Manmohan S. Kumar (1993), 'Financial markets and intermediations', International Monetary Fund Occasional Paper, No. 102.

Cao Xiao (1998), 'Jiang, Zhu jinrong gaige xin gouxiang; shen, shi, qu, zhihui yinhang quan quxiao' (Jiang's and Zhu's financial reform new idea: abrogate the right of provinces, municipalities and regions to direct banks), *Jingbao yuekan* (Economic Monthly), January, 32–3.

Cao Zhenhuan (1991), 'Zhongguo wuaimao tizhi de jinyibu gaige he wuanshan' (Further reform and improvement of China's foreign trade regime), in ACFERT (1991).

Cassel, Gustav (1918), 'Abnormal deviations in international exchanges', *Economic Journal*, **28**, 413–15.

Cerra, Valerie and Anuradha Dayal-Gulati (1999), 'China's trade flows: changing price sensitivities and the reform process', Working Paper of the International Monetary Fund, No. 1.

Chan, Vivien Pik-Kwan (1998a), 'China: surprise choice to head research office', *South China Morning Post*, 14 April.

Chan, Vivien Pik-Kwan (1998b), 'Zhu limits power of reform office', *South China Morning Post*, 16 April.

Chang, Gordon G. (2001), *The Coming Collapse of China*, New York: Random House.

Chen Guidi and Wu Chuntao (2005), *Zhongguo nongmin diaocha* (Investigation into China's peasants), Taibei: Dadi.

Chen Jian (1987), 'Jianli woguo waihui shichang de shexiang jiqi kexingxing tantao' (On the feasibility of establishing China's foreign exchange market), *Guoji jingji wenti* (International Trade Journal), **6**, 41–4.

Chen Nai-ruenn and Walter Galenson (1969), *The Chinese Economy under Communism*, Chicago, IL: Aldine.

Chen Yuan (1993/94), 'Central banking reform in China', *Central Banking*, **4** (3), 64–5.

Chen Yuan (ed.) (1994), *Jianshe shehui zhuyi shichang jingji tizhi xilie tushu* (Plans for constructing a socialist market economy system), Beijing: Zhongguo caizheng jingji chubanshe.

Cheng Chu-yuan (1954), *Monetary Affairs of Communist China*, Hong Kong: Union Research Institute.

China Briefing (2002), 'Corruption', *Far Eastern Economic Review*, 29 August, 24.

China Development Research Foundation (CDRF) (2006), 'Liu He', http://www.cdrf.org.cn/2006cdf/liuhe_cn.pdf (accessed 28 July 2006).

China Security Review Commission (CSRC) (2002), *Report to the Congress of the US: The National Security Implications of the Economic Relationship between the United States and China*, July.

China Vitae (2004), 'Ma Kai', http://chinavitae.com/biography_display.php?id=720 (accessed 19 August 2005).

Chinaonline (1999), 'Wu Bangguo, Vice-premier, State Council: biographic profile', http://www.chinaonline.com/refer/biographies/secure/BB-REVWuBangguo3.asp (accessed 6 January 2005).

Chinese Communist Party (CCP) (2006), 'Zhonggong zhongyang guanyu goujian shehuizhuyi hexie shehui ruogan zhongda wenti de jueding' (Resolution of the CCP Central Committee on major issues regarding the building of a harmonious socialist society), 11 October, http://news.xinhuanet.com/politics/2006-10/18/content_5218639.htm (accessed 14 October 2006).

Chou, Shun-Hsin (1963), *The Chinese Inflation: 1937–1949*, New York: Columbia University Press.

Corden, W.M. (1979), *Inflation, Exchange Rates and the World Economy*, Oxford: Oxford University Press.

Coudert, Virginie and Cecile Couharde (2005), 'Real equilibrium exchange rate in China', CEPII Working Paper, No. 1, http://www.cepii.fr/anglaisgraph/workpap/summaries/2005/wp05-01.htm (accessed 17 July 2006).

Dai Xianglong (ed.) (1998), *Zhongguo renmin yinhang wushinian* (Fifty years of the People's Bank of China), Beijing: Zhongguo jinrong chubanshe.

Desai, Padma and Jagdish Bhagwati (1979), 'Three alternative concepts of foreign exchange difficulties in centrally planned economies', *Oxford Economic Papers*, **31** (3), 358–68.

Dunaway, Steven and Xiangming Li (2005), 'Estimating China's "equilibrium" real exchange rate', IMF Working Paper, No. 202, October.

East South West North (Dong nan xi bei) (2005), 'The Chen Xiwen interviews', http://www.zonaeuropa.com/20050705_1.htm (accessed 19 August 2005).

Eckert, Paul (2005), 'US critics see security threat in China oil bid', Reuters, http://today.reuters.com/business/newsarticle.aspx?type=tnBusinessNews&storyID=nN13639287&imageid=&cap, 13 July (accessed 22 September 2005).

Eckstein, Alexander (1977), *China's Economic Revolution*, Cambridge: Cambridge University Press.

The Economist (2004a), 'The looming revolution', 13 November, 77–9.

The Economist (2004b), 'Asian currencies: a need for flexibility', 4 December, 63–5.

The Economist (2004c), 'The passing of the buck?' 27 November, 81–2.

Edwards, John (1996), *Keating: The Inside Story*, Ringwood: Penguin Australia.

Edwards, Sebastian (2003), 'Exchange rate regimes', in Martin Feldstein (ed.), *Economic and Financial Crises in Emerging Market Economies*, National Bureau of Economic Research, Chicago, IL and London: University of Chicago Press.

Elliott, Larry (2004), 'Dollar risks a downhill skid', *Guardian Weekly*, 26 November – 2 December, 29.

Engardio, Pete, Dexter Roberts and Brian Bremner (2004), 'The China price', *Business Week*, 6 December.

Ernst & Young (2006), 'China: non-performing loan market report', Global Nonperforming Loan Report 2006.

External Relations Department (ERD) (2004), 'Transcript of a teleconference call on China with Steven Dunaway, IMF Mission Chief to China', 25 August, Washington, DC: International Monetary Fund.

Fazhi ribao (Legal Daily) (2003), 'Lianghui: renwu zhuizong' (Two meetings: tracking the personalities), 18 March, http:www.legaldaily.com.cn/gb/rwzz/2003-03/18/content_19061.htm (accessed 24 July 2006).

Federal Reserve Bank of New York (FRBNY) (2004), *Global Economic Indicators*, 14 December, http://www.ny.frb.org/research/directors_charts/global_all.pdf (accessed 15 December 2004).

Feng Zhongping (1998), 'ASEM II attracts world attention', *Beijing Review*, **41** (11–17 May), 7–9.

Ferguson, Niall (2002), *The Cash Nexus: Money and Power in the Modern World, 1700–2000*, London: Penguin Books.

Fernald, John G., Hali Edison and Prakash Loungani (1999), 'Was China the first domino? Assessing links between China and the rest of emerging Asia', *Journal of International Money and Finance*, **18** (4), 515–36.

Fewsmith, Joseph (1999), 'China and the WTO: the politics behind the agreement', *NBR Report*, National Bureau of Asian Research, November.

Financial Management Service (FMS) (2006), *MTS: Monthly Treasury Statement*, US Treasury Department, http://www.fms.treas.gov/mts/index.html, February (accessed 17 March 2006).

Fleming, J. (1962), 'Domestic financial policies under fixed and under floating exchange rates', IMF Staff Papers, No. 9 (November), 369–79.

Frank, Andre Gunder (1998), *ReOrient: Global Economy in the Asian Age*, Berkeley, CA: University of California Press.

Frenkel, Jacob A. (2003), 'Exchange rate regimes: comment', in Martin Feldstein (ed.), *Economic and Financial Crises in Emerging Market Economies*, National Bureau of Economic Research, Chicago, IL and London: University of Chicago Press.

Friedberg, Aaron (2000), 'The struggle for mastery in Asia', *Commentary*, **110** (4), 17–26.

Frieden, Jeffry A. (1991), 'Invested interests: the politics of national economic policies in a world of global finance', *International Organisation*, **45** (4), 425–51.

FT Lex (2006), 'Renminbi', *Financial Times*, 7 August, http:www.ft.com/cms/s/7a 941786-25b0-11db-a12e-0000779e2340.html (accessed 7 August 2006).

Fung, Hung-Gay, Wai K. Leung and Jiang Zhu (2004), 'Non-deliverable forward market for Chinese RMB: a first look', *China Economic Review*, **15**, 348–52.

Fung, K.C. and Lawrence J. Lau (2003), 'Adjusted estimates of United States–China bilateral trade balances: 1995–2002', *Journal of Asian Economics*, **14**, 489–96.

Gale, Fred, Bryan Lohmar and Francis Tuan (2005), 'China's new farm subsidies', United States Department of Agriculture, February, www.ers.usda.gov/publications/WRS0501 (30 August 2006).

Gao Xin (1999), *Jiang Zemin de muliao* (Jiang Zemin's counsellors), Hong Kong: Mingjing chubanshe.

Gao Xin (2004), *Wen Jiabao zhuan* (Biography of Wen Jiabao), Hong Kong: Mingjing chubanshe.

Gao Xin and He Pin (1999), *Shui lingdao Zhongguo* (Who are leading China?), Hong Kong: Mingjing chubanshe.

Garnaut, John (2006), 'Beijing heavy hitter takes aim at revaluation's backers', *Sydney Morning Herald*, 29 August, http://www.smh.com.au/news/business/beijing-heavy-hitter-takes-aim-at-revaluations-backers/2006/08/28/1156617274 539.html# (accessed 29 August 2006).

Gaulier, Guillaume, Francoise Lemoine and Deniz Unal-Kesenci (2006), 'China's emergence and the reorganisation of trade flows in Asia', CEPII Working Paper, No. 5, http://www.cepii.fr/anglaisgraph/workpap/summaries/2006/wp06-05.htm (accessed 17 July 2006).

Genberg, Hans, Robert N. McCauley, Yung Chul Park and Avinash Persaud (2005), *Official Reserves and Currency Management in Asia: Myth, Reality and the Future*, London: Centre for Economic Policy Research.

Goh, Ming He and Yoonbai Kim (2006), 'Is the Chinese renminbi undervalued?', *Contemporary Economic Policy*, **24**, 116–26.

Goldstein, Morris (2004), 'Adjusting China's exchange rate policies', revised version of paper presented at the International Monetary Fund seminar on China's foreign exchange rate system, Dalian, China, 26–27 May, Working Paper, Washington, DC: Institute for International Economics.

Goldstein, Morris and Nicholas Lardy (2004), 'Two-stage currency reform for China', *Asian Wall Street Journal*, 12 September.

Golub, Philips (2004), 'All the riches of the east restored', *Le Monde Diplomatique*, October, 8–9.

Gong Haochen and Dai Guoqiang (2000), *Zhongguo jinrong fazhan baogao* (China's financial development report), Shanghai: Shanghai caijing daxue chubanshe.

Grant Thornton (2005), 'Leading Chinese manufacturers beat U.S. counterparts in several world-class operating practices while paying far lower wages', Grant Thornton LLP Study, Grant Thornton International, http://66.102.7.104/search?q=cache:CNxEQGkKDGcJ:www.grantthornton.com/content/113996.asp++%22Manufacturing+Performance+Institute%22&hl=en (accessed 1 October 2005).

Guan Tao (1997), 'Dui woguo jiuwu qijian liyong waishang zhijie touzi qingkuang de yuce' (Projection on foreign direct investment in China's ninth five-year plan period), *Zhongguo waihui guanli* (China's foreign exchange management), No. 2.

Gunter, Frank R. (2004), 'Capital flight from China: 1984: 2001', *China Economic Review*, **15**, 63–85.

Guoji shouzhi fenxi xiaozu (GSFX) (2006), '2005 nian Zhongguo guoji shouzhi baogao' (Report on 2005 China's balance of payments), Guojia waihui guanli ju (State Administration for Foreign Exchange), 4 April.

Guojia Tongji Ju (GTJ) (1987), *Zhongguo tongji nianjian* (China Statistical Yearbook), Beijing: Zhongguo tongji chubanshe.

Hai Wen and Zhong Kaifeng (1999), 'The impacts of the Asian economic crisis on China's foreign trade', unpublished manuscript, China Centre for Economic Research, Peking University.

Hamrin, Carol Lee and Suisheng Zhao (eds) (1995), *Decision Making in Deng's China*, Armonk, NY: M.E. Sharpe.

Han Jiyun (1991), 'Dui renminbi huilü "shuangguizhi" de sikao' (On the 'double-track system' of the renminbi exchange rate), *Guoji maoyi wenti* (International Trade Journal), **6**, 35–7.

He Baogang (1997), *The Democratic Implications of Civil Society in China*, New York: St Martin's Press Inc.

He Liping (2000), 'The future of the exchange rate regime in China', *World Economy and China*, **8** (3), 6–25.

He Meirong (2003), *Who's Who: Current Chinese Leaders*, Hong Kong: Wen Wei Publishing Co. Ltd.

Heilmann, Sebastian (2005), 'Regulatory innovation by Leninist means: Communist Party supervision in China's financial industry', *China Quarterly*, **187**, 1–14.

Hermann, Richard K., James F. Voss, Tonya Y.E. Schooler and Joseph Ciarrochi (1997), 'Images in international relations: an experimental test of cognitive schemata', *International Studies Quarterly*, **41**, 403–33.

Higgins, Matthew and Thomas Klitgaard (2004), 'Reserve accumulation: implications for global capital flows and financial markets', *Current Issues in Economics and Finance*, September/October, **10** (10), 1–8.

Higgins, Patrick and Owen Humpage (2005), 'The Chinese *renminbi*: what's real, what's not', *Economic Commentary*, 15 August, Research Department, Federal Reserve Bank of Cleveland, http://www.clevelandfed.org/Research/Com2005/0815.pdf (accessed 29 August 2006).

Ho, Horace M.K. and Yvonne Fong (2004), 'Asia Offshore Report 2004', Manivest Asia Ltd, http://www.manivestasia.com/library/articles/MISP-AsiaOffshoreReport2004W.pdf (accessed 18 October 2005).

Hoge, Jr, James F. (2004), 'A global power shift in the making', *Foreign Affairs*, July/August, http://www.foreignaffairs.org/20040701facomment83401/james-f-ho ge-jr/a-global-power-shift-in-the-making.html (accessed 29 August 2006).

Hong Kong Trade Development Council (HKTDC) (1998), 'Market profile on Mainland China', http://www.tdctrade.com/main/china.htm (accessed 9 October 1998).

Hong Kong Trade Development Council (HKTDC) (2003), 'Rate of export rebate to be lowered by 3–4 per cent', *Business Alert – China*, Issue 10, 1 October, http://www.tdctrade.com/alert/cba-e0310.htm (accessed 30 June 2006).

Hong Kong Trade Development Council (HKTDC) (2004), 'Market profile on Chinese mainland', http://www.tdctrade.com/main/china.htm (accessed 4 December 2004).

Hope, Nicholas and Fred Hu (2006), 'Reforming China's banking system: how much can foreign strategic investment help?' Working Paper, No. 276, Stanford Center for International Development.

Howe, Christopher (1978), *China's Economy*, New York: Basic Books.

Hsiao, Katharine Huang (1971), *Money and Monetary Policy in Communist China*, New York: Columbia University Press.

http://www.gpoaccess.gov/usbudget/fy07/browse.html.

Hu Haiou and Wu Guoxiang (2000), *Zhongguo jinrong gaige de lilun yu shijian* (China's financial reform: theory and practice), Shanghai: Fudan daxue chubanshe.

Huang Jing (2000), *Factionalism in Chinese Communist Politics*, Cambridge: Cambridge University Press.

Huang Suquan (1998), 'Renminbi huilu zoushi fenxi' (Trend analysis of RMB rate), *Yinhang yu qiye* (Banking and Industry), 10–11.

Huang Yiping and Yang Yongzheng (1998), 'China's financial fragility and policy responses', *Asian-Pacific Economic Literature*, **12** (2), 1–9.

Hulse, Carl (2006), 'Senate approves budget, breaking spending limits', *New York Times*, 17 March, http://www.nytimes.com/2006/03/17/politics/17spend.html?th& emc=th (accessed 17 March 2006).

Huntington, Samuel P. (2005), *Who Are We? America's Great Debate*, London: Free Press.

IMF (International Monetary Fund) (1990), *The Economy of the USSR*, Washington, DC: World Bank.

IMF (International Monetary Fund) (2004a), *International Financial Statistics* (Electronic Database) (accessed 3 December 2004).

IMF (International Monetary Fund) (2004b), *Annual Report*, 30 April.

IMF (International Monetary Fund) (2004c), *World Economic Outlook*, September.

IMF (International Monetary Fund) (2005a), *World Economic Outlook*, September.

IMF (International Monetary Fund) (2005b), *IMF Country Report*, No. 05/411, November.

IMF (International Monetary Fund) (2006), *World Economic Outlook*, April.

Jia Baohua (1998), 'Renminbi: shidang bianzhi keneng li da yu bi' (Renminbi: appropriate devaluation may benefit more than hurt), *Gaige neican* (Inside Information on Economic Reform), **17**, 14.

Jia Baohua (1999), 'Huilu yu chukou buke fenkai taolun' (The exchange rate and exports cannot be discussed separately), *Gaige neican* (Inside Information on Economic Reform), **2**, 29.

Jing Xuecheng (1996), 'Huobi keduihuanxing yu wuaihui shichang' (Currency convertibility and foreign exchange market), in Research Department of China

Foreign Exchange Trading Centre (ed.), *Zhongguo waihui shichang de shijian yu tansuo* (Practices and experiments of China's foreign exchange market), Beijing: Zhongguo jinrong chubanshe.

Johnson, Chalmers (1982), *MITI and the Japanese Economic Miracle: The Growth of Industrial Policy, 1925–1975*, Stanford, CA: Stanford University Press.

Johnston, Alastair Iain (2003), 'Is China a status quo power?' *International Security*, **27** (4), 5–56.

Jordan, Mary (2003), 'Mexico now feels pinch of cheap labour: an economy built on low wages finds itself undercut by influx of Chinese imports', *Washington Post Foreign Service*, 3 December, A19.

Junzheng (2005), 'Zhongyang lingdao xiaozu bangongshe' (Central leadership group administrative office), 13 September, http://www.chinajunzheng.com/bbs/htm_data/58/05081/17990.html (accessed 13 August 2006).

Karmin, Craig (2003), 'Currency trading: China's currency peg may drag on the dollar', *Wall Street Journal*, 26 February, C1.

Kelly, Paul (1998), 'Great stumble forward', *Weekend Australian*, 25–26 April, 28.

Kennedy, Paul M. (1987), *The Rise and Fall of the Great Powers: Economic Change and Military Conflict from 1500 to 2000*, New York: Random House.

Kessler, Glenn (2005), 'US says China must address its intentions: how its power will be used is of concern', *Washington Post*, 22 September, A16.

Kissinger, Henry A. (2004), 'America's assignment', *Newsweek*, 9 November, 26–31.

Krugman, Paul (1998), 'Japan: still trapped', http://www.wws.princeton.edu/~pkrugman/japtrap2.html

Lai Rongwen (1999), 'Zhongguo dalu xiagang wenti zhi yanjiu' (Research on mainland China's unemployment problem), *Gongdang Wenti Yanjiu* (Communist Party Research), **25** (July), 54–66.

Lam, Willy Wo-Lap (1998), 'Rising star in politburo to vet policy papers', *South China Morning Post*, 22 July.

Lam, Willy Wo-Lap (1999), *The Era of Jiang Zemin*, Singapore: Prentice Hall.

Lam, Willy (2007), 'China strongman Hu Jintao is manufacturing his own power base out of allies from Tibet, Xinjiang and Gansu', *Asia Sentinel*, http://www.asiasentinel.com/index.php?option=com_content&task=view&id=341.

Lampton, David M. (2005), 'Paradigm lost: the demise of "weak China"', *National Interest*, Fall, 67–74.

Lardy, Nicholas R. (1983), *Agriculture in China's Modern Economic Development*, Cambridge: Cambridge University Press.

Lardy, Nicholas R. (1992), *Foreign Trade and Economic Reform in China 1978–1990*, Cambridge: Cambridge University Press.

Lardy, Nicholas (2002), *Integrating China into the Global Economy*, Washington, DC: Brookings Institution Press.

Lau, Lawrence J. (2003), 'Is China playing by the rules? Free trade, fair trade, and WTO compliance', Testimony at a hearing of the Congressional-Executive Commission on China, 24 September.

Lawrence, Susan V. and Lorien Holland (1999), 'Deal of the century', *Far Eastern Economic Review*, 25 November, 81.

Li Anding, Liu Zhenying and He Jiazheng (1999), 'Renqing xingshi, mingque renwu, zhuazhu jiyu, kaituo jinqu, jianding xinxin, tuanjie fendou: Zhongyang jingji gongzuo huiyi zai Beijing zhaokai' (Have a clear understanding of the situation, clarify the tasks, grasp the opportunity, open up and forge ahead, strengthen one's confidence, unite to struggle: Central Economic Work Conference opens in Beijing), *Renimin ribao* (People's Daily), 18 November, 1.

Li Baijing (1998), 'Li Guixian tanhe Dai Xianglong' (Li Guixian impeached Dai Xianglong), *Cheng ming* (Contention), December.

Li Baijing (1999), 'Zhongyang jingji gongzuo huiyi neiqing' (Inside information on the Central Economic Work Conference), *Cheng ming* (Contention), January, 29–31.

Li Fuyang (1998), 'Renminbi huilu de zhengce mubiao yu qushi fenxi' (Analysis of RMB exchange rate trends and objective of RMB exchange rate policy), *Zhongguo jinrong* (China's Finance), **4**, 6–7, 17.

Li Shantong, Zhai Fan and Xu Lin (2000), 'Jiaru shijie maoyi zuzhi dui Zhongguo de yingxiang' (Impact on China from entry into the WTO), in Yu Yongding, Zheng Bingwen and Song Hong (eds), *Zhongguo 'rushi' yanjiu baogao: jinru WTO de Zhongguo chanye* (Research report on China's entry into the WTO: impact on China's industries), Beijing: Shehui kexue wenjian chubanshe.

Li Shaomin, He Shaofeng and You Hanming (1998), *Zhongguo de gaige yu gongshang jingying* (China's economic reform and industrial and commercial management), Hong Kong: City University of Hong Kong Press.

Li Xiaozhuang (1998), *Zhu Rongji renma* (Zhu Rongji's people), Hong Kong: Xiafeier guoji chuban gongsi.

Li Yang (1998), 'Zhongguo jingji duiwai kaifang guocheng zhong de zijin liudong' (Capital flows in an increasingly open Chinese economy), *Jingji yanjiu* (Economic Research), **2** (February), 14–24.

Lieberthal, Kenneth and David Lampton (eds) (1992), *Bureaucracy, Politics, and Decision Making in Post-Mao China*, Berkeley, CA: University of California Press.

Lieberthal, Kenneth and Michel Oksenberg (1988), *Policymaking in China: Leaders, Structures, and Processes*, Princeton, NJ: Princeton University Press.

Liew, Leong H. (1994), 'The economics of regional property rights in China', *Papers in Regional Science: The Journal of the RSAI*, **73** (2), 169–88.

Liew, Leong H. (1997), *The Chinese Economy in Transition: From Plan to Market*, Cheltenham, UK and Lyme, USA: Edward Elgar.

Liew, Leong H. (1998), 'A political economy analysis of the Asian financial crisis', *Journal of the Asia Pacific Economy*, **3** (3), 321–3.

Liew, Leong H. (1999), 'The impact of the Asian financial crisis on China: the macroeconomy and state-owned enterprise reform', *Management International Review*, **39** (4), 85–104.

Liew, Leong H. (2001), 'What is to be done? WTO, globalisation and state–labour relations in China', *Australian Journal of Politics and History*, **47** (1), 39–60.

Liew, Leong H. (2004), 'Policy elites in the political economy of China's exchange rate policymaking', *Journal of Contemporary China*, **13**, 21–51.

Liew, Leong H. and Akira Kawaguchi (1995), 'Inflation or monetary overhang? Planners' preferences in China', *Applied Economics*, **27**, 469–75.

Lin Guijun (1996), 'Dui woguo yinhang jian waihui shichang yunxing de fenxi' (On the operation of China's interbank foreign exchange market), *Guoji maoyi wenti* (International Trade Journal), **3**, 43–50.

Lin Guijun (1990), 'Dui renminbi huilü xiatiao de fenxi' (On the devaluation of the renminbi), *Guoji maoyi wenti* (International Trade Journal), **3**, 16–20.

Lin Yifu (2000), 'Wo dui renminbi bianzhi de kanfa' (My views on devaluing the renminbi), *Yazhou zhoukan* (Asia Week), **3**, 16 January, http://www.yzzk.com/200003af.htm (accessed 23 January 2000).

Liu Guangcan, Sun Lujun and Guan Tao (1997), *Zhongguo waihui tizhi yu renminbi ziyou duihuan* (China's exchange rate regime and RMB's convertibility), Beijing: Zhongguo caizheng jingji chubanshe.

Liu Guangdi (1984), *Zhongguo de yinhang* (China's banks), Beijing: Beijing chubanshe.

Liu Xinyi (2001), *Zhongguo shuiwu shouce* (*Handbook of China's taxation*), Beijing: Jingji Guanli Chubanshe.

Lohr, Steve (2004), 'IBM sought a China partnership, not just a sale', *New York Times*, 13 December, http://www.nytimes.com/2004/12/13/technology/13ibm.html (accessed 14 December 2004).

Long Guoqiang (1999), 'Tiaozheng chukou tuishui zhengce de xiaoying fengxi' (Analysis of the effect of adjusting the tax reimbursement policy on exports), in Ma Hong and Wang Mengkui (eds), *Zhongguo fazhan yanjiu* (China development studies research), Beijing: Zhongguo fazhan chubanshe.

Long Weiying (ed.) (1997), *Zhongguo waihui shichang nianjian* (Almanac of China's foreign exchange market), Beijing: Zhongguo jinrong chubanshe.

Lu Jianren (1998), 'Dongya jinrong weiji de yingxiang' (Impact of the East Asian financial crisis), *Dangdai yatai* (Contemporary Asia Pacific), **10**, 12–16.

Lu Lian (2000), 'Qianxinian Zhongguo jingji zhongda juece yu Jiang Zhu jianghua' (China's major economic policies in the new millennium and Jiang's and Zhu's speeches), *Jingbao yuekan* (Economic Monthly), January, 31.

Lü, Shiyun (1996), 'Huilü yu huobi zhengce' (Exchange rate and monetary policy), in Research Department of China Foreign Exchange Trading Centre (ed.), *Zhongguo waihui shichang de shijian yu tansuo* (Practices and experiments of China's foreign exchange market), Beijing: Zhongguo jinrong chubanshe.

Lu Yi (1998), 'Dongnanya huobi weiji de jinrong fenxi' (Financial analysis of Southeast Asia's monetary crisis), *Jinrong cankao* (Finance Reference), **1**, 56–8.

Luo Bing (1998), 'Zhu Rongji lin jingji shenyuan' (Zhu Rongji's temporary economic abyss), *Cheng ming* (Contention), **8**, August, 6–7.

Luo Bing (1999), 'Zouxiang ducai zhi lu' (Heading for the road of a dictator), *Cheng ming* (Contention), December, 11.

Ma Hong and Sun Shangqing (1988), *Studies on China's Price Structure*, Shanxi: Shanxi People's Publishing House and China Social Science Publishing House.

MacFarquhar, Roderick (1974, 1983, 1997), *The Origins of the Cultural Revolution*, 3 vols, New York: Columbia University Press.

MacFarquhar, Roderick (1983), *The Origins of the Cultural Revolution 2: The Great Leap Forward 1958–1960*, Oxford: Oxford University Press.

Maddison, Angus (2005), 'Measuring and interpreting world economic performance 1500–2001', *Review of Income and Wealth*, **51** (1), 1–35.

Mah Feng-hwa (1971), *The Foreign Trade of Mainland China*, Chicago, IL: Aldine Atherton.

Mao Chunming (1995), *Zhonghua Renmin Gongheguo Zhongguo Renmin Yinhang fa shiyi* (Explanation of PRC People's Bank of China ACT), Beijing: Zhongguo jinrong chubanshe.

Martin, Will (1991), *China's Foreign Exchange System*, paper presented at the Conference on China's Reform and Economic Growth, Research School of Pacific and Asian Studies, Australian National University.

McGregor, Richard (2005), 'Rice tells Beijing to take action on trade imbalance', *Financial Times*, 22 March, 1.

Mckinnon, Ronald (2005a), 'Exchange rate or wage changes in international adjustment? Japan and China versus the United States', Economics Department Working Paper, May, www.stanford.edu/~mckinnon/papers/ swpo5007.pdf (accessed 13 August 2006).

Mckinnon, Ronald (2005b), 'China's new exchange rate policy: will China follow Japan into a liquidity trap?, www.stanford.edu/~mckinnon/papers/WeeklyEconom ist_Oct_2005.pdf (accessed 13 August 2006).

Mckinnon, Ronald and Gunther Schnabl (2004a), 'Zhongguo shi dongya diqu de wending liliang haishi tongsuo yali zhi yuan?' (China: a stabilizing or deflationary influence in East Asia?), in Yu Yongding and He Fan (eds), *Renminbi xuannian: renminbi huilü de dangqian chujing he weilai gaige* (Whither RMB? Current problems and future adjustments), Beijing: Zhongguo qingnian chubanshe.

Mckinnon, Ronald and Gunther Schnabl (2004b), 'The East Asian dollar standard, fear of floating, and original sin', *Review of Development Economics*, **8**, 331–60.

Mei Xinyu (2004), 'Zhongguo yu haian jinrong zhongxin kuajing ziben liudong yanjiu' (China and offshore financial centres and cross-border capital flows), *Jingji huoyewenxuan* (Economics loose-leaf selections), Beijing: Zhongguo caizheng jingji chubanshe.

Miyashita, Tadao (1976), *The Currency and Financial System of Mainland China* (Translation of *Chugoku no tsuka kin'yu seido*), New York: Da Capo Press.

MOC (Ministry of Commerce) (2006), 'Main mandate of the Ministry of Commerce', http://english1.mofcom.gov.cn/mission/mission.html (accessed 11 July 2006).

MOF (Ministry of Finance) and SAT (State Administration of Taxation) (1999a), Circular No. 17: Guanyu tigao bufen huowu chukou tuishuilü de tongzhi (On the upward adjustment of the export tax rebate rate of some commodities).

MOF (Ministry of Finance) and SAT (State Administration of Taxation) (1999b), Circular No. 225: Guanyu jinyibu tigao bufen huowu chukou tuishuilü de tongzhi (On the further upward adjustment of the export tax rebate rate of some commodities).

MOF (Ministry of Finance) and SAT (State Administration of Taxation) (2003), Circular No. 222: Guanyu tizheng chukou huowu tuishuilü de tongzhi (On the adjustment of export tax rebate rate).

MOFERT (Ministry of Foreign Economic Relations and Trade) (1991), *Almanac of China's Foreign Economic Relations and Trade 1991*, Beijing: Zhongguo shehui kexue chubanshe.

Moore, Thomas G. and Dixia Yang (2001), 'Empowered and restrained: Chinese foreign policy in the age of economic interdependence', in David M. Lampton (ed.), *The Making of Chinese Foreign and Security Policy in the Era of Reform*, Stanford, CA: Stanford University Press.

Morrison, Wayne and Marc Labonte (2005), 'China's exchange rate peg: economic issues and options for US trade policy', *CRS Report for Congress RL32165*, Congressional Research Service, Library of Congress, 10 May.

Mundell, Robert (1963), 'Capital mobility and stabilisation policy under fixed and flexible exchange rates', *Canadian Journal of Economics and Political Science*, **29** (4), 475–85.

National Bureau of Statistics (NBS) (1981–2006), *Zhongguo tongji nianjian* (China Statistical Yearbook), Beijing: Zhongguo tongji chubanshe.

National Bureau of Statistics (NBS) (1999), *Comprehensive Statistical Data and Materials of 50 Years of New China*, Beijing: China Statistics Press.

National Bureau of Statistics (NBS) (2006), National Bureau of Statistics of China website, http://www.stats.gov.cn (accessed 6 April 2006).

National Development and Reform Commission (NDRC) (2005), 'Chukou tuishui zhengce xiang difang qingxie, wuwang zenqiang yi zhi qusheng shili' (Export rebates policy slants towards localities, do not forget to increase the focus on strengthening through quality), http://www.sdpc.gov.cn/zwjjbd/zhxw/t20050812_3 929.htm (accessed 18 August 2005).

National Development and Reform Commission (NDRC) (2006a), 'Main functions of the NDRC', http://en.ndrc.gov.cn/mfndrc/default.htm (accessed 18 July).

National Development and Reform Commission (NDRC) (2006b), 'Major economic indicators of economic and social development in the 11th Five-Year Plan period', http://en.ndrc.gov.cn/hot/t20060529_71334.htm (accessed 30 August 2006).

Naughton, Barry (1999), 'China: domestic restructuring and a new role in Asia', in T.J. Pempel (ed.), *The Politics of the Asian Economic Crisis*, Ithaca, NY: Cornell University Press.

Naughton, Barry (2003), 'The emergence of Wen Jiabao', *China Leadership Monitor*, **6**, 36–47.

Ni Hongri (2005), 'Quxiao nonye san shui xuyao jiejue de wu da wenti ji zhengce jianyi' (Policy recommendation on resolving the five major problems as a result of eliminating the three agricultural taxes), in Ma Hong and Wang Mengkui (eds), *Zhongguo fazhan yanjiu* (China development studies), Beijing: Zhongguo fazhan chubanshe.

Office of Management and Budget (OMB) (2006), 'Historical tables', in 'Budget of the United States Government', http://www.gpoaccess.gov/usbudget/fy07/browse.html (accessed 17 March 2006).

Office of Public Affairs (OPA) (2004a), 'Debt limit', US Treasury Department, 3 November, JS-2073, http://www.treasury.gov/press/releases/js2073.htm (accessed 15 December 2004).

Office of Public Affairs (OPA) (2004b), 'Report to the Congress on international economic and exchange rate policies', US Treasury Department, 3 December, JS-2127, http://www.treasury.gov/press/releases/js2127.htm (accessed 15 December 2004).

Office of Public Affairs (OPA) (2005a), 'Testimony of Treasury Secretary John W. Snow before the Senate Committee on Banking, Housing and Urban Affairs on the Treasury Department's "Report to Congress on International Economic and Exchange Rate Policies"', US Treasury Department, 26 May, JS-2473, http://www.treasury.gov/press/releases/js2473.htm (accessed 12 June 2005).

Office of Public Affairs (OPA) (2005b), 'Statement of Treasury Secretary John W. Snow on the "Report to Congress on International Economic and Exchange Rate Policies"', US Treasury Department, 28 November, JS-3024, http://www.treasury.gov/press/releases/js3024.htm (accessed 17 March 2006).

Onishi, Yasuo (ed.) (2003), *China's New Leadership* (IDE Spot Survey), Chiba: Institute of Developing Economies.

Organization for Economic Co-operation and Development (OECD) (2005), *OECD Economic Surveys: China*, Paris: OECD Publishing.

Ou Jiawa (1995), 'Policy choices of the Central Bank', in On Kit Tam (ed.), *Financial Reform in China*, London: Routledge.

Panagariya, Arvind (1993), 'Unravelling the mysteries of China's foreign trade regime', *World Economy*, **16** (1), 51–68.

Pang Jiying (1996), 'Zhuanggui shiqi de zhongguo waihui shichang' (China's foreign exchange market in the economic transition), in Research Department of China Foreign Exchange Trading Centre (ed.), *Zhongguo waihui shichang de shijian yu tansuo* (Practices and experiments of China's foreign exchange market), Beijing: Zhongguo jinrong chubanshe.

Pearson, Margaret M. (1999), 'China's integration into the international trade and investment regime', in Elizabeth Economy and Michel Oksenberg (eds), *China Joins the World: Progress and Prospects*, New York: Council on Foreign Relations Press.

Pearson, Margaret M. (2001), 'The case of China's accession to GATT/WTO', in David M. Lampton (ed.), *The Making of Chinese Foreign and Security Policy in the Era of Reform, 1978–2000*, Stanford, CA: Stanford University Press.

Pei, Minxin (2006a), 'The dark side of China's rise', *Foreign Policy*, March/April, http://www.foreignpolicy.com/story/cms.php?story_id=3373 &print=1 (accessed 1 March 2006).

Pei, Minxin (2006b), *China's Trapped Transition: The Limits of Developmental Autocracy*, Cambridge, MA: Harvard University Press.

People's Bank of China (PBC) (1993), 'Guanyu jinyibu gaige waihui guanli tizhi de gonggao' (Circular on further reform of foreign exchange administration system), 12 December.

People's Bank of China (PBC) (1994–2005), *The People's Bank of China Quarterly Statistical Bulletin*, Beijing: People's Bank of China.

People's Bank of China (PBC) (2005), 'Public announcement of the People's Bank of China on reforming the RMB exchange rate regime', Xinhuanet, htttp://news.xinhuanet.com/English/2005-07/21/content_3250123.htm (accessed 22 December 2005).

People's Bank of China (PBC) (2006a), 'Lilü shichanghua jieshao' (Introduction to the marketization of interest rates), http://www.pbc.gov.cn/huobizhengce/huobizhengcegongju/lilvzhengce/lilvzhengcejieshao/lilvshichangjieshao.asp (accessed 17 June 2006).

People's Bank of China (PBC) (2006b), 'Hang lingdao' (Leaders of the People's Bank of China), http://www.pbc.gov.cn/renhangjianjie/hanglingdao.asp (accessed 20 August 2006).

People's Bank of China (PBC) (2006c), 'Jigou shezhi' (Organization set up), http://www.pbc.gov.cn/index_fenzhi.asp (accessed 20 August 2006).

Pesek Jr, William (2004), 'Sexy China casts shadows on a not-rising sun', Bloomberg.com, http://www.bloomberg.com/apps/news?pid=71000001&refer=columnist_pesek&sid=aAqMl.yy (accessed 16 December 2004).

Plowiec, Urszula (1988), 'Economic reform and foreign trade in Poland', in Josef C. Brada, Ed A. Hewett and Thomas A. Wolf (eds), *Economic Adjustment and Reform in Eastern Europe and the Soviet Union*, Durham, NC: Duke University Press.

Prasad, Eswar and Thomas Rumbaugh (2004), 'Overview', in Eswar Prasad (ed.), 'China's growth and integration into the world economy: prospects and challenges', Occasional Paper, No. 232, Washington, DC: International Monetary Fund.

Prasad, Eswar, Thomas Rumbaugh and Qing Wei (2005), 'Putting the cart before the horse? Capital account liberalization and exchange rate flexibility in China', IMF Policy Discussion Paper, No. 1, Washington, DC: International Monetary Fund.

Prasad, Eswar and Shang-Jin Wei (2005), 'The Chinese approach to capital inflows: patterns and possible explanations', IMF Working Paper, No. 79, Washington, DC: International Monetary Fund.

Preeg, Ernest H. (2005), 'The rapid development of China's advanced technology industry and its impact on military modernization', in Charles Horner, Mary C. FitzGerald and Ernest Pregg (eds), *China's New Great Leap Forward: High Technology and Military Power in the Next Half-Century*, Cicero, IN: Hudson Institute.

Prestowitz, Clyde (2003), 'Snowed under: why the treasury secretary didn't get very far with China and Japan last week', *American Prospect*, 8 September, http://www.prospect.org/web/page.ww?section=root&name=ViewWeb&articleId=1298 (accessed 28 December 2004).

Price Waterhouse Coopers (PWC) (2004–6), *NPL Asia*, http://www.pwchk.com/home/eng/nplasia_newsletter.html (accessed 23 August 2006).

PYC (1995), *Price Yearbook of China*, Beijing: Zhongguo wujia bianjibu.

Qiao, Wei (1996), 'Lun woguo waihui shichang de lishi yange he fazhan qianjing' (The evolution and prospect of China's foreign exchange market), in Research Department of China Foreign Exchange Trading Centre (ed.), *Zhongguo waihui shichang de shijian yu tansuo* (Practices and experiments of China's foreign exchange market), Beijing: Zhongguo jinrong chubanshe.

Ramo, Joshua Cooper (2004), *The Beijing Consensus*, London: Foreign Policy Centre.

Ravallion, Martin (2004), 'Looking beyond averages in the trade and poverty debate', Policy Research Working Paper, No. 3461, Washington, DC: World Bank, November.

Ravallion, Martin and Shaohua Chen (2004), 'China's (uneven) progress against poverty', Policy Research Working Paper, No. 3408, Washington, DC: World Bank, November.

Ren Hui (2001), 'Zhongguo ziben waidao de guimo cesuan he duice fenxi' (Estimation of capital flight in China and countermeasures), *Jingji yanjiu* (Economic Research), **11**, 69–75.

Reuters (2002a), 'Taiwan chip moves to help China's tech plans', *South China Morning Post*, 3 April, http://technology.scmp.com (accessed 9 April 2002).

Reuters (2002b), 'Toshiba plans new plant in China', *South China Morning Post*, 12 April, http://technology.scmp.com (accessed 24 April 2002).

Reuters (2002c), 'NEC in talks on China LCD venture', *South China Morning Post*, 18 April, http://technology.scmp.com (accessed 18 April 2002).

Riskin, Carl (1987), *China's Political Economy: The Quest for Development Since 1949*, Oxford: Oxford University Press.

Roach, Stephen S. (2003), 'Getting China right', Statement before the Commission on US–China Economic and Security Review: Hearing on China's industrial, investment and exchange rate policies: Impact on the US, http://www.caijing.com.cn/english/1005getting.htm (accessed 1 October 2004).

Roach, Stephen S. (2004), 'US imbalances and global rebalancing: implications for the Chinese economy', Beijing: China Development Research Foundation, http://report.drc.gov.cn/cdrf/enforum.nsf/0/7e3e5485885546a248256eb3003236d7?OpenDocument (accessed 22 December 2004).

Rosen, Daniel H. (2003), 'How China is eating Mexico's lunch: the *Maquiladora* system's comparative advantage is being challenged head on', *International Economy*, Spring, 22–5.

Roubini, Nouriel and Brad Setser (2004), 'The US as a net debtor: the sustainability of the US external imbalances', draft paper, http://www.stern.nyu.edu/global macro/ (accessed 17 December 2004).

Roy, Denny (1998), *China's Foreign Relations*, Lanham: Rowan & Littlefield.

Ruan Ming (1995), 'The evolution of the Central Secretariat and its authority', in Carol Lee Hamrin and Suisheng Zhao (eds), *Decision Making in Deng's China*, Armonk, NY: M.E. Sharpe.

Rumbaugh, Thomas and Nicolas Blancher (2004), 'International trade and the challenges of WTO accession', in Eswar Prasad (ed.), 'China's growth and integration into the world economy: prospects and challenges', Occasional Paper, No. 232, Washington, DC: International Monetary Fund.

Ryan, Colleen (2006), 'Beijing opens doors for banks', *Australian Financial Review*, 22 August, 11.

SAFE (State Administration of Foreign Exchange) (1998), *Zhongguo waihui guanli nianbao* (Annual Bulletin of China Foreign Exchange Administration) (internal).

SAFE (2001), Circular No. 304: Guanyu tiaozheng ziben zhang xiaobufen gouhui guanli cuoshi de tongzhi (On the adjustment of the administration of limited foreign exchange purchase in the capital account).

SAFE (2003a), Circular No. 43: Guanyu jianhua jingwai touzi waihui zijin laiyuan shencha youguan wenti de tongzhi'(On simplification of verifying the source of capita for overseas investment).

SAFE (2003b), Circular No. 120: Guanyu jinyibu shenhua jingwai touzi waihui guanli gaige youguan wenti de tongzhi (On further reform of the foreign exchange administration for overseas investment).

SAFE (2004), Circular No. 113: Guanyu jiajiang dui waihui zijin liuru he jiehui guanli youguan wenti de tongzhi (On enforcement of the administration of foreign exchange inflows and settlement for renminbi).

SAFE (State Administration of Foreign Exchange) (2003a), Circular No. 43: Guanyu jianhua jingwai touzi waihui zijin laiyuan shencha youguan wenti de tongzhi (On simplification of verifying the source of capita for overseas investment).

SAFE (State Administration of Foreign Exchange) (2003b), Circular No. 120: Guanyu jinyibu shenhua jingwai touzi waihui guanli gaige youguan wenti de tongzhi (On further reform of the foreign exchange administration for overseas investment).

SAFE (State Administration of Foreign Exchange) (2004), Circular No. 113: Guanyu jiajiang dui waihui zijin liuru he jiehui guanli youguan wenti de tongzhi (On enforcement of the administration of foreign exchange inflows and settlement for renminbi).

Sah, Raaj and Joseph E. Stiglitz (1987), 'Price scissors and the structure of the economy', *Quarterly Journal of Economics*, **102**, 109–34.

Sah, Raaj and Joseph E. Stiglitz (1992), *Peasants versus City-Dwellers*, Oxford: Clarendon Press.

Samuelson, Paul A. (1964), 'Theoretical notes on trade problems', *Review of Economics and Statistics*, **46**, 145–54.

SAT (State Administration of Taxation) (2001), 'Circular No. 74: Guanyu tigao bufen mianfang zhipin chukou tuishuilü de tongzhi' (On the upward adjustment of the export tax rebate rate for some textile commodities).

Setser, Brad (2006), 'Testimony before the US–China Economic and Security Review Commission', 22 August.

Shambaugh, David (2001), 'The dynamics of elite politics during the Jiang era', *China Journal*, **45**, January, 101–11.

Shang Ming (1999), *Xin Zhongguo jinrong wushi nian* (Fifty years of finance in new China), Beijing: Zhongguo caizheng jingji chubanshe.

Shanghai caijing daxue jinrong xueyuan (SCD) (2004), *Zhongguo jinrong fazhan baogao* (China finance development report), Shanghai: Shanghai caijing daxue chubanshe.

Shea, Esther Yi Ping (2003), *The Political Economy of China's Grain Policy Reform*, PhD Thesis, School of Economics, University of Adelaide, Australia.

Shen Xueming (ed.) (1999), *Zhonggong di shiwujie zhongyang weiyuanhui zhongyang jilu jiancha weiyuanhui weiyuan minglu* (Who's Who of members of the Fifteenth Central Committee of the Chinese Communist Party and Fifteenth Central Commission for Discipline Inspection), Beijing: Zhonggong wenxian chubanshe.

Shi Jianhuai (1995), 'Waihui guanzhi de jingji yingxiang' (Economic impact of foreign exchange control), *Guoji maoyi wenti* (International Trade Journal), **2**, 32–5.

Shi Yonghai (1998), 'Yazhou jinrong weiji dui shijie jingmao he woguo de yingxiang' (Asian financial crisis and its impact on the world economy and trade and China), *Guoji maoyi* (International Trade), **1**, 33–5.

Shirk, Susan (1993), *The Political Logic of Economic Reform in China*, Berkeley, CA: University of California Press.

Sicular, Terry, Ximing Yue, Bjorn Gustafsson and Shi Li (2007), 'The urban–rural income gap and inequality in China', *Review of Income and Wealth*, **53**, 93–126.

Sina (2005), 'Zhongyang caijing lingdao xiaozu bangongshi fuzhuren Chen Xiwen jianjie' (Brief introduction to Chen Xiwen, deputy director of the administrative office of the Central Leading Group in Finance and Economics), *Xinlang caijing* (New Wave Economics and Finance), http://finance.sina.com.cn/roll/20050815/15151887803.shtml (accessed 8 September 2005).

Sing Tao (2005), 'Nongye shui quanbu quxiao' (All agricultural taxes to be eliminated), 5 July.

Sito, Peggy (2001), 'Beijing to loosen exchange rate', *South China Morning Post*, 30 March.

Solinger, Dorothy (1999), *Contesting Citizenship in Urban China*, Berkeley, CA: University of California Press.

Song Ligang (1998), 'China', in Ross McLeod and Ross Garnaut (eds), *East Asia in Crisis: From Being a Miracle to Needing One*, London: Routledge.

Song Wenbing (1999), 'Zhongguo de ziben waitao wenti yanjiu: 1987–1997' (Issues on capital flight in China: 1987–1997), *Jingji yanjiu* (Economic Research), **5**, 39–48.

State Council (1982), 'Interim regulations on foreign exchange control of the People's Republic of China (1980)', in *China's Foreign Economic Legislation*, Beijing: Foreign Languages Press.

State Council (1986), 'Decision on strengthening foreign exchange management (1985)', in State Economic Commission Economic System Reform Bureau (ed.), *A Selection of Policies and Laws on China's Economic Management, July 1984–June 1985*, Beijing: Economic Science Publishing House.

State Council (1989), 'Regulation on various issues on accelerating and deepening reform of the foreign trade system (1988)', in *An Overview of Ten Years of Reform of the Planning System*, State Planning Commission System Reform and Laws and Regulations Departments, Beijing: Chinese Planning Publishing House.

State Council (1995a), Circular No. 29: Guanyu tiaodi chukou tuishuilü de tongzhi (On downward adjustment of export tax rebate rate).

State Council (1995b), Circular No. 3: Guanyu tiaodi chukou tuishuilü, jiaqiang chukou tuishui guanli de tongzhi (On the downward adjustment of export tax rebate rate and strengthening the administration of the rebate).

Sui Zhen (2004), 'Chukou qianshui chengyin fenxi ji jiejue wenti de silu' (Determinants of unpaid export rebates and solution), *Waimao diaoyan* (Trade Inquiry), no. 23, MOC Research Institute.

Sun Lujun (1997), '1997 nian woguo guoji shouzhi ji xiangguan zhengce yanjiu' (China's international income and payments in 1997 and related policies), *Waihui cankao* (Foreign Exchange Reference), **3**.

Sun Ming (2003a), 'Xie Ping, Yi Gang lüxin: liang xuezhe zhizhang zhonghang guanjian siju' (Xie Ping, Yi Gang take up new posts: two scholars to control key departments in central bank), *21 Shiji jingji baodao* (21st Century Economic Herald), 27 October.

Sun Ming (2003b), 'Daikuan lilü zai fudong, suibu qüjin shichanghua' (Enlarging the band within which the loan interest rate can float as a small step toward promoting marketization), *21 Shiji jingji baodao* (21st Century Economic Herald), 15 December.

Sun Mingchun (1995), 'Guanyu renminbi huilü heli shuiping de tantao' (Towards a rational level of renminbi exchange rate), *Guoji maoyi wenti* (International Trade Journal), **1**, 31–4.

Tanner, Murray Scot (1999), 'The National People's Congress', in Merle Goldman and Roderick MacFarquhar (eds), *The Paradox of China's Post-Mao Reforms*, Cambridge: Harvard University Press.

Tao Shigui (1995), 'Yinhang jieshou hui zhong de wenti ji duice jianyi' (Issues in the settlement of foreign exchange account), *Guoji maoyi wenti* (International Trade Journal), **1**, pp. 41–3.

Tao Shigui (1998), 'Waihui chongxiao zhengce de xiaoying fenxi yu duice sikao' (The efficacy of foreign exchange sterilisation and policy implications), *Guoji maoyi wenti* (International Trade Journal), **2**, 26–32.

Tomlinson, Heather and David Adam (2005), 'China takes lead on stem cells', *Guardian Weekly*, 28 January–3 February, 5.

Tsang Shu-Ki (1994), 'Towards full convertibility? China's foreign exchange reforms', *China Information*, **9** (1), 1–41.

Tyson, Laura D'Andrea (1992), *Who's Bashing Whom? Trade Conflict in High-Technology Industries*, Washington, DC: Institute for International Economics.

UNCTAD (2003), *World Investment Report*, Geneva: United Nations.

UNCTAD (2004), *World Investment Report*, Geneva: United Nations.

UNCTAD (2005a), *World Investment Report*, Geneva: United Nations.

UNCTAD (2005b), *Trade and Development Report*, Geneva: United Nations.

UNDP (2002), 'Human Development Report', http://hdr.undp.org/reports/global/2002/en (accessed 4 August 2006).

UNDP (2005), 'Human Development Report', http://hdr.undp.org/reports/global/2005 (accessed 4 August 2006).

UNIDO (2005), 'Capability building for catching-up', *Industrial Development Report*, Vienna: United Nations Industrial Development Organization, http://www.unido.org/file-storage/download/?file_id=44688 (accessed 4 August 2006).

US Census Bureau (USCB) (2006), 'Foreign trade statistics', http://www.census.gov/foreign-trade/statistics (accessed 17 March 2006).

US–China Economic and Security Review Commission (USCC) (2004), *Report to Congress*, One hundred eighth Congress, Second Session, Washington, DC: US Government Printing Office.

US–China Economic and Security Review Commission (USCC) (2005), *Report to Congress*, One hundred ninth Congress, First Session, Washington, DC: US Government Printing Office.

US Department of Defense (USDOD) (2004), 'FY04 Report to Congress on PRC Military Power: Pursuant to the FY2000 National Defense Authorization Act', http://www.defenselink.mil/pubs/d20040528PRC.pdf (accessed 29 August 2006).

US Department of the Treasury (USDT) (2006), 'Treasury International Capital System', http://www.treas.gov/tic/mfhhis01.txt, http://www.treas.gov/tic/mfh.txt, 15 March (accessed 22 March 2006).

US Government (2006), *Historical Tables, Budget of the United States Government, Fiscal Year 2007*, Washington, DC: US Government Printing Office.

Waley-Cohen, Joanna (1999), *The Sextants of Beijing*, New York: W.W. Norton & Company.

Wang Baogang (1993), 'Waihui liucheng zhidu de tantao' (On the foreign exchange retention system), *Guoji maoyi wenti* (International Trade Journal), **3**, 55–6.

Wang Chunzheng (2005), 'Jingshi jimin, ruizhi duxing' (A great economic manager for the people: wise, farsighted and sincere), *Renmin ribao* (People's Daily), 17 June, 9.

Wang Dongmin (1985), 'The reform of the renminbi exchange rate and the reform of the price system', *Liaoning University Bulletin*, **2**, 21–4.

Wang Lixin and Joseph Fewsmith (1995), 'Bulwark of the planned economy: the structure and role of the State Planning Commission', in Carol Lee Hamrin and Suisheng Zhao (eds), *Decision Making in Deng's China*, Armonk, NY: M.E. Sharpe, pp. 51–65.

Wang Weixu and Zeng Qiugen (2003), *Jingti Meiguo de dierci de yinmou* (Be vigilant against America's second plot), Beijing: Guangming ribao chubanshe.

Wang Weixu and Zeng Qiugen (2004), *Renminbi huilü: tiaozhan yu biange xuanze* (Renminbi exchange rate: challenge and choice of transformation), Beijing: Guangming ribao chubanshe.

Wang Xiangwei (2005), 'Mainland official hails bloody riots as a sign of democracy', *South China Morning Post*, 4 July.

Wen Jiabao (2005), Zhengfu gongzuo baogao (Government Work Report), *Renmin ribao* (haiwaiban) (People's Daily Overseas Edition), 6 March, 2.

Wikipedia (2004), http://en.wikipedia.org/wiki/Nasdaq (accessed 14 December 2004).

Wolf Jr, Charles, K.C. Yeh, Benjamin Zycher, Nicholas Eberstadt and Sung-Ho Lee (2003), *Fault Lines in China's Economic Terrain*, Santa Monica, CA: Rand.

Wong, Christine (1987), 'Between plan and market: the role of the local sector in post-Mao China', *Journal of Comparative Economics*, **11**, 385–98.

Wong, Linda (2004), 'Market reforms, globalization and social justice in China', *Journal of Contemporary China*, **13** (38), 151–72.

Woo Wing Thye (1994), 'The art of reforming centrally planned economies: comparing China, Poland, and Russia', *Journal of Comparative Economics*, **18** (2), 276–308.

World Bank (1994), *China: Foreign Trade Reform*, Washington, DC: World Bank.

World Bank (1996), *The Chinese Economy: Fighting Inflation, Deepening Reforms*, Washington, DC: World Bank.

World Bank (1997a), *China 2020*, Washington, DC: World Bank.

World Bank (1997b), *China 2020: Sharing Rising Incomes*, Washington, DC: World Bank.

WTO (2003), *International Trade Statistics*, Geneva: WTO.

WTO (2005a), *World Trade Report*, Geneva: WTO.

WTO (2005b), 'Protocols of accession for new members since 1995, including commitments in goods and services', Accession Documents, December, http://www.wto.org/english/thewto_e/acc_e/completeacc_e.htm#chn (accessed 6 February 2006).

WTO yu fazhi luntan (WTO and Law Forum) (WL) (2002), 'Xianggang meiti: Zhongyang jinrong anquan xiaozu jinri shili' (From Hong Kong's media: Central Finance Safety Small Group established today), http://www.wtolaw.gov.cn/display/displayInfo.asp?IID=200212011108428586 (accessed 21 July 2006).

Wu Guogang (1995), 'Documentary politics: hypotheses, process, and case studies', in Carol Lee Hamrin and Suisheng Zhao (eds), *Decision Making in Deng's China: Perspectives from Insiders*, Armonk, NY: M.E. Sharpe.

Wu, Harry X. (1994), 'The reform of China's foreign exchange regime: behind the unification', CERU Working Paper, No. 15, Adelaide: University of Adelaide.

Wu, Harry X. (1997), 'Reform in China's agriculture and trade implications', Briefing Paper Series, No. 9, Canberra: East Asia Analytical Unit, Australian Department of Foreign Affairs and Trade.

Wu, Harry X. (1998), 'Reform of China's foreign exchange regime and its implications in the light of the Asian financial crisis', *MOCT–MOST Economic Policy in Transitional Economies*, **8** (3), 81–105.

Wu, Harry X. and Esther Y.P. Shea (2006), 'Domestic financial architecture, macro volatility and institutions: the case of China', paper presented at CEDE–IDRC Conference on International Financial Architecture, Macro Volatility and Institutions: The Developing World Experiences, United Nations, New York, April.

Wu Nianlu and Chen Quangeng (1992), *Renminbi huilu yanjiu* (Renminbi exchange rate research), Beijing: Zhongguo jinrong chubanshe.

Wu Wei and Song Gongping (1991), *Zhongguo waihui guanli* (China's foreign exchange administration), Beijing: Zhongguo jinrong chubanshe.

Xiao Chong (ed.) (1998), *Zhonggong disidai mengren* (CCP's fourth generation powerful personalities), Hong Kong: Xiafeier guoji chuban gongsi.

Xiao Ren (1998), 'Zhu Rongji tan jinrong gaige he fangfan jinrong fengxian' (Zhu Rongji discusses financial reform and prevention against financial risks), *Jingbao yuekan* (Economic Monthly), June.

Xiao Zhengqin (1999a), 'Zhu Rongji zhinangtuan de tese' (Characteristics of Zhu Rongji's think tanks), *Xinbao*, 6 January.

Xiao Zhengqin (1999b), 'Zhu Rongji yunyong zhinangtuan zhihui de jiqiao' (Zhu Rongji makes use of the acrobatic wisdom of his think tanks), *Xinbao*, 25 January.

Xiao Zhengqin (1999c), 'Guowuyuan yanjiushi: Zhu zhinang zhongzhen' (State Council Research Office: strategic post for Zhu's think tanks), *Xinbao*, 26 January.

Xie Ping (2003), 'Financial challenges in China', in Jan Joost Teunissen (ed.), *China's Role in Asia and the World Economy: Fostering Stability and Growth*, The Hague: FONDAD.

Xinhua (2003), 'Hua Jianmin, State Councillor', *Xinhuanet*, http://news.xinhuanet. com/English/2003-03/17/content_783554.htm (accessed 4 January 2005).

Xinhua (2006a), 'Hui Liangyu jianli' (Hui Liangyu's brief history), *Xinhuanet*, http://news.xinhuanet.com/ziliao/2002-02/22/content_285979. htm (accessed 26 July 2006).

Xinhua (2006b), 'Li Rongrong jianli' (Li Rongrong's brief history), *Xinhuanet*, http://news.xinhuanet.com/ziliao/2002-02/22/content_295696. htm (accessed 20 July 2006).

Xinhuashe (1998), 'Jiang Zemin zhuxi jieshou Meiguo jizhe caifang' (American journalists interviewed President Jiang Zemin), *Renmin ribao* (People's Daily), 23 June, 1.

Xu Jiong (2005), 'Yuanqi jieshou hui dingjia qu baoshou, Zhou Xiaochuan liting yansheng jiaoyi' (Conservatism in pricing forward contracts, Zhou Xiaochuan pushes for trades in derivatives), *21 shiji jingji baodao* (21st Century Economics News), 3 August.

Xu Quanhong and Lin Hao (2004), 'Chukou tuishui zhence: fei zhongxing yuanze quxiang' (Export tax rebate: the non-neutral principle), *Zhongguo jingmao* (*Chinese Economy and Trade*), no. 7.

Yang Fan (1993), 'Renminbi huilü zoushi yanjiu' (Research on trends in the renminbi exchange rate), *Zhongguo wujia* (China Prices), **3**, 20–21.

Yang Fan (2000), *Renminbi huilü yanjiu: Jianlun guoji jinrong weiji yu zhongguo shewai jingji* (On the renminbi exchange rate: international financial crisis and China's external economy), Beijing: Shoudu jingji maoyi daxue chubanshe.

Yang Fangjiang and Zhang Zumin (2001), *Zhejiang nongcun jumin shenghuo jingji fenxi* (Economic analysis of the livelihood of Zhejiang's village residents), Hangzhou: Zhejiang renmin chubanshe.

Yang Lian (2006), 'Dark side of the Chinese moon', *New Left Review*, **32**, March–April, http://newleftreview.org/?page=article&view=2556, (accessed 28 August 2006).

Yang Yongzheng (2003), 'China's integration into the world economy: implications for developing countries', IMF Working Paper, No. 245, Washington, DC: IMF.

Ye Weiqiang (2003), 'China's economy in 2004: between inflation and deflation', *Caijing Magazine*, http://www.caijing.com.cn/english/2003/1 (accessed 7 January 2005).

Yee, Herbert and Ian Storey (eds) (2002), *The China Threat: Perceptions, Myths and Reality*, London: RoutledgeCurzon.

Yi Gang (1996), *Zhongguo de huobi, yinhang he jinrong shichang*: 1984–1993 (China's currency, banks and financial market: 1984–1993), Shanghai: Renmin chubanshe.

Yi Gang and Fan Min (1997), 'Renminbi huilü de jueding yinsu ji zoushi fenxi' (The determinants of RMB exchange rate and its trend), *Jinji yanjiu* (Economic Research), **10**, 26–35.

Yi Gang and Song Ligang (1998), 'East Asia in crisis: from being a miracle to needing one?' *Australian Financial Review*, 7 May, http://www.afr.com.au/content/980507/verbatim (accessed 8 May 1998).

Yomiuri Shimbun (2005), 'China gorging and Japan–China resource and energy conflicts', *Japan Focus*, 29 June, http://www.japanfocus.org/ article.asp?id=318 (accessed 13 October 2005).

Yu Jingbo (2005), 'Ma Kai: China's economy and macro-control policy', *China News*, 17 February, http://www.chinanews.cn/news/2004/2005-02-17/1716.shtml (accessed 10 July 2006).

Yu Ni (2005), 'Central Bank loans free-for-all', Caijing, No. 138, http://caijing.hexun.com/english/detail.aspx?issue=138&sl=2488&id=1253128 (accessed 27 July 2006).

Yu Ning (2004), 'CCB and BOC receive their last bonus', Caijing, No. 109, http://caijing.hexun.com/english/detail.aspx?issue=109&sl=2484&id=1359055 (accessed 21 May 2006).

Yu Yongding (2004), 'Xiaochu renminbi shenzhi kongju zheng' (Dispel the fear of renminbi revaluation), in Yu Yongding and He Fan (eds), *Renminbi xuannian: renminbi huilü de dangqian chujing he weilai gaige* (Whither RMB? Current problems and future adjustments), Beijing: Zhongguo qingnian chubanshe.

Zhang Chenghui (1999), 'Dangqian huobi zhengce de zuzhi yu tiaozheng' (Obstacles to current monetary policy and adjustment), in Ma Hong and Wang Mengkui (eds), *Zhongguo fazhan yanjiu* (China development studies research), Beijing: Zhongguo fazhan chubanshe.

Zhang Genming (1997), '1997 nian zhongguo guoji shouzhi yu huilu biandong qushi' (China's international income and payments and the trend of the RMB exchange rate), *Jingji yu xinxi* (Economics and information), 6.

Zhang Jilin (2001), *Renminbi fei guanfang huilü dingjia yanjiu* (Pricing of RMB unofficial exchange rate), PhD thesis, Nankai University.

Zhang Zhixiang and Xu Jiananming (1998), 'Dui yazhou jinrong weiji de jidian renshi' (Recognizing several characteristics of the Asian financial crisis), *Zhongguo jinrong* (China's Finance), 3, 24–6.

Zhao Lingbin (1998), 'Renminbi shengbian dui Gangyuan huilu de yingxiang' (Effect of revaluation or devaluation of the *renminbi* on the HK dollar exchange rate), *Ming Pao*, July, 29–31.

Zheng Shiping (1997), *Party vs. State in Post-1949 China: The Institutional Dilemma*, Cambridge: Cambridge University Press.

Zhong Jing (2004), 'Offshore financial centers affect cross-border capital flow in China', *China Economic Net*, June 10, http://en.ce.cn/Insight/t20040607_1016937.shtml (accessed 10 June 2004).

Zhong Yan (1997), 'Xin sanji xueren' (New grade-3 scholars), *Huaxia wenzhai* (China news digest), http:www.cnd.org/HXWZ/CM97/cm9712d.hz8.html (accessed 13 August 2006).

Zhongguo baipishu (ZB) (1998), (China's White Paper), Beijing: Gaige chubanshe.

Zhongguo dangzheng xinxiwang (ZDX) (2005), (China's Party and State News Network), http://www.1921.cn/new/zggc/2005020/101.htm (accessed 13 August 2006).

Zhongguo jinrong xuehui (ZJX) (1999), *Zhongguo jinrong nianjian* (Almanac of China's finance and banking), Beijing: Zhongguo jinrong nianjian bianjibu.

Zhongguo jinrong xuehui (ZJX) (2000, 2004), *Zhongguo jinrong nianjian* (Almanac of China's finance and banking), Beijing: Zhongguo jinrong nianjian bianjibu.

Zhongguo renmin yinhang yanjiuju (ZRYY) (1999), *Zhongguo xiandai zhongyang yinhang tizhi* (China's contemporary central bank system), Beijing: Zhongguo jinrong chubanshe.

Zhonghua Renmin Gongheguo Guowuyuan Gongbao (ZGG) (Gazette of the State Council of the People's Republic of China) (1998), Beijing.

Zhonghua Renmin Gongheguo nianjian (ZN) (Yearbook of the People's Republic of China) (1999), Beijing: Nianshe.

Zhou Hanmin (1998), 'Lun Yazhou jinrong weiji xingshi xia tuijin Zhongguo rushi nuli de zhongyao yiyi' (Important significance of working hard to advance China's entry into the WTO during Asia's financial crisis), *Shanghai duiwai maoyi xueyuan xuebao* (Shanghai Foreign Trade Institute journal), June, 1–8.

Zhou Xiaochuan and Xie Ping (1993), *Zouxiang renminbi keduihuan* (Towards the convertibility of renminbi), Beijing: Jingji guanli chubanshe.

Zhou Yingruo (1994), 'Waihui guanli tizhi de zhongda gaige' (The significant reform of the foreign exchange system), *Jinrong yanjiu* (Journal of Financial Research), **3**, 17–19.

Zhu Baoliang (1998), 'Yazhou jinrong weiji hou de renminbi huilü zoushi' (The movement of the renminbi after the Asian financial crisis), *Guoji maoyi* (International Trade), **2**, 41–3.

Index

China People's Political Consultative Conference (*Zhongguo renmin xieshang huiyi*) 35

China Poverty Fund (*Zhongguo fupin jijinhui*) 199

China Securities Regulatory Commission (CSRC) 110

Chinese Academy of International Trade and Economic Cooperation (CAITEC) 99

Chinese Communist Party (CCP) 4, 6, 29, 146, 174, 206

chronicle of reform 105–11

chuanghui chengben (the cost of foreign exchange earnings) 114

CITIC Industrial Bank 103, 137

civil society 23–4

'class struggle' 42

Clinton, Bill 5, 142, 182, 190

Coming Collapse of China, The (Chang) 18

Committee on Financial and Economic Affairs (CFEA) (*Caizheng jingji weiyyuanhui*) 32–3, 37–8

commodities 33, 45, 50–57, 71

companies *see* trading enterprises

competition 188

computer equipment 14–16

consumer goods 53

consumer price index (CPI) 72, 125–7

consumption, under central economic planning 50–54

Coordinating Committee for Multilateral Export controls (Cocom) 45

correlation of international interest rates 135, 136

Coudert, Virginie 123

Couharde, Cecile 123

credit cards 111

credit controls 172, 203–4

Cultural Revolution 198

currencies 30–34

currency speculation 186–7

current account 2, 6, 10–11, 19, 90–92

current account convertibility 86–8, 109, 163–4

Dai Gengyou 148, 151, 152, 197

Dai Xianglong 109, 148, 151, 164, 165, 171, 172, 197, 205

data availability 113

defence technology 14–16

deflation 169, 170, 208

deindustrialization 10

demand, effect on exports 124

Deng Xiaoping 7, 82, 122, 126, 135, 143, 147, 148, 158, 170

deregulation of foreign exchange trading 137

devaluation
1989 and 1998–9 compared 164–74
domestic cost as argument for 114
elites, policymaking influence 146–57
and expectations 82
and inflation 78–81, 165
under initial reforms 42, 69–72, 75
institutional actors, influence on policy 157–64
international concerns 1, 21, 142–3
newspaper commentary 24
under plan-market system 76–8
policymaking process 143–6
'price wars' 79

'disguised fiscal expenditure' 94

dollar (Hong Kong) 35, 39–40, 127, 129–32, 135, 136, 170–171

dollar (US) 1–2, 11–12, 127, 129–32, 135, 136, 137, 138–9, 140
see also renminbi-US dollar peg

domestic economic concerns 156, 157–9, 161–4, 168–70, 188–9, 206–9, 212–14

domestic enterprises 85, 87, 90, 100, 101, 108, 206

'dragon slayers' 6, 212

dual exchange rates 73

dual-track foreign exchange system 75–82, 83–4, 115, 119, 124

Duan Yingbi 148, 198, 199

Dunaway, Steven 19, 138, 187

Eckstein, Alexander 45

economic growth 1–2, 4–6, 17–20, 168–70, 171, 173

economic plan 49–57

economic policy 148, 195–6
see also policymaking

education 192–3, 198–9

Edwards, Sebastian 184

Eichengreen, Barry 184

net international investment position
(NIIP) 10
Netherlands 142
newspaper commentary 9, 17, 24, 142,
174, 182, 188
nickel 7
non-deliverable forwards (NDFs)
138–40, 185, 186, 187
non-performing loans (NPLs) 203–4
Northwestern Faction 207

official renminbi rates
and swap market rates 74–81, 116–18,
120–121, 124, 160
two-tiered system 105
unification with swap market rates
83–8, 108, 115, 156, 161
Oksenberg, Michel 144
Omnibus Trade and Competitiveness Act
(US) 19–20, 21
OPEC (Organization of Petroleum
Exporting Countries) 12–13
Ou Jiawa 162
Overseas Chinese Banking Corporation
38
overseas investments 111
overvaluation of renminbi 55, 61, 64,
114

'panda huggers' 6
passive money flows 54
PBC Act (*Zhongguo renmin yinhang fa*)
(1995) 163
Pei, Minxin 18
People's Bank of China (PBC)
criticisms 173
elites, influence on policy 148, 156,
189, 196, 197
establishment of 30
exchange rates 39, 162–4, 166,
170–172, 202–5, 208
foreign exchange management 35–6,
57–61, 62
independence of 184
and inflation 163, 170
inter-bank foreign exchange market
85
interest rate reform 133
Monetary Policy Committee 109,
151–2, 189, 197

Monetary Policy Department (*Huobi
zhengce si*) 151–2, 197
money supply control 95–101
PBC Act (*Zhongguo renmin yinhang
fa*) (1995) 163
policymaking role 26, 63, 146–7, 154,
175, 213
People's Republic of China (PRC) 3–4,
39
see also China
'permanent normal trade relations'
(PNTR) 182
personal foreign exchange holdings 106,
110
personal savings 133
Pesek, William, Jr. 4
petroleum 71
plan-market system 75–82, 160
planned economy 49–57
planning framework reforms (1979–87)
66–75
policy decision making 145–6
policymaking
devaluation considerations 164–74
elites 146–57, 194–200, 213–14
influences 212–14
institutional actors, influence on
policy 157–64, 200–205, 213–14
and policy decision making 145–6
process of 143–6
structure 146–8, 195–6
US concern with China 3–6, 8–17,
20–21
Politburo 146, 147, 148, 149, 150, 163,
174, 196, 199
post-Mao reforms
central economic planning (1954–78)
64–5
and foreign exchange management 25
macroeconomic problems (1997–)
89–102, 109–11
reforms in plan-market system
(1988–93) 75–82, 106–8
reforms within planning framework
(1979–1987) 66–75, 105–6
unification and current account
convertibility (1994–2002) 83–8,
108–10
pound (UK) 39–40, 127, 129–32, 135,
136